BATTLES
OF THE
CRUSADES
1097 ~ 1444

BATTLES
OF THE
CRUSADES
1097 ~ 1444

FROM DORYLAEUM TO VARNA

KELLY DEVRIES   IAIN DICKIE   MARTIN J. DOUGHERTY   PHYLLIS G. JESTICE   CHRISTER JÖRGENSEN   MICHAEL F. PAVKOVIC

BARNES & NOBLE

NEW YORK

Editorial and design by
Amber Books Ltd

Project Editor: Michael Spilling
Picture Research: Terry Forshaw
Design: Joe Conneally

ISBN-13: 978-0-7607-9334-3
ISBN-10: 0-7607-9334-4

Printed and bound in Dubai

1 3 5 7 9 10 8 6 4 2

CONTENTS

INTRODUCTION

'GOD WILLS IT! GOD WILLS IT!' SO, ACCORDING TO CHRONICLER ROBERT OF RHEIMS, RESPONDED THE CONGREGATION AT CLERMONT IN 1095 AS POPE URBAN II JUSTIFIED LAUNCHING A CHRISTIAN MILITARY CAMPAIGN TO RECOVER THE SO-CALLED HOLY LAND – THE LAND WHERE JESUS CHRIST HAD LIVED MORE THAN A MILLENNIUM EARLIER.

The First Crusade did not just attract soldiers but also non-military people whose faith directed them to the Holy Land. Led by popular preachers such as Peter the Hermit – depicted meeting with Byzantine Emperor Alexius I Comnenus in this nineteenth-century painting by Gillot Saint-Evre – these pilgrims arrived in Constantinople first, where they met little welcome, were shuttled across the Bosporus Strait and almost all killed in their first encounter with the Seljuk Turks.

Robert reported Urban's oratory thus: 'From the confines of Jerusalem... a horrible tale has gone forth and very frequently has been brought to our ears; namely, that a race from the kingdom of the Persians, an accursed race, a race utterly alienated from God, a generation, forsooth, which has neither directed its heart nor entrusted its spirit to God, has invaded the lands of those Christians and has depopulated them by the sword, pillage, and fire... On whom, therefore, is the task of avenging these wrongs and of recovering this territory incumbent, if not upon you? You, upon whom above other nations God has conferred remarkable glory in arms, great courage, bodily energy, and the strength to humble... those who resist you.'

Not all of Urban's facts were correct, of course – in fact, very few of them were. For one, the potential opponents of these Christians, who would be called 'Crusaders' because they 'took up the cross'. were not from a race of the Persians. They were Seljuk Turks, a Muslim dynasty of Oghuz Turkic origin who had moved from Central Asia to Persia in the tenth century and then further into the Middle East in the middle of the eleventh century.

By 1055 the Seljuks had captured Baghdad, the richest city of the Middle East, and by 1064 Georgia and Armenia. Four years later, in 1068, under the able command of Sultan Ap Arslan, they began an invasion of the Byzantine Empire.

Byzantium was far from the great power it once had been. For more than two centuries wars with the Bulgars, Russians and Sicilian Normans had drawn Byzantine armies to the northern frontier and the Mediterranean Sea, while civil wars and inheritance squabbles had weakened the political and military leadership. As the Turks threatened their eastern frontiers, the Byzantines mobilized their forces and met them at the battle of Manzikert on 26 August 1071, where they were soundly defeated and their Emperor, Romanos IV Diogenes, captured. As the Byzantines retreated across Asia Minor, the Seljuk Turks followed, conquering almost the

entire peninsula during the next seven years. The new Byzantine Emperor, Alexius I Comnenus, could do nothing. In desperation he requested aid from Pope Urban II in recovering his lost lands, in the form of an army to fight against the Seljuk Turks in the Middle East. This request excited the Pope for two reasons. First, he could direct a conquest of the Holy Land. Second, by recruiting soldiers to fight in the Middle East, Urban would be removing them from Europe.

Warfare within Europe had been endemic for more than a century and a half, almost since the end of the Viking invasions, and had devastated Christian society. Attempts to quell this activity with the Peace and Truce of God, meant to curtail violence against the clergy, monks, women and the poor, had been largely inadequate. Sending those who perpetuated this warfare elsewhere might prove to be more effective, especially if they could also do something beneficial to Christianity while they were at it. So, on 27 November 1095, Pope Urban II convened the Council of Clermont, attended by a large number of ecclesiastical and political leaders, and called for a Crusade to the Holy Land, perhaps using the words of Robert of Rheims written above, and perhaps answered by the people: 'God wills it! God wills it!'

THE CRUSADERS GATHER

How many soldiers did the Pope anticipate might answer his call to Crusade? He had directed it at all arms-bearers, but could he really have expected the call to religious warfare to appeal to as many fighting men as did 'take up the cross'? In fact, Urban's call turned out to be extremely successful. Almost immediately, bishops and priests began carrying the Crusade throughout Europe, appealing to all military professionals to fight in the Holy Land. No kings answered the call, but several famous lords and knights did: Raymond of Saint-Gilles, Count of Toulouse; Hugh of Vermandois, brother to Philip I, the French King; Robert, Count of Flanders; Stephen, Count of Blois and son-in-law of William the Conqueror; Robert, Duke of Normandy and son of William the Conqueror; Godfrey de Bouillon, Duke of Lower-Lorraine, and

his brother, Baldwin; Bohemond Guiscard, the son of Robert Guiscard, and his nephew, Tancred. Accompanying them were also a very large number of lesser nobles, knights, squires and sergeants, all with their retinues. Travelling with the soldiers was Adhemar, the Bishop of Le Puy, titular leader of the Crusade, and hundreds of priests and monks, several of whom left accounts of the campaign. This army started for the Middle East on Assumption Day, 15 August 1096.

However, itinerant preachers, such as Peter the Hermit and Walter the Penniless, interpreted the Pope's call to Crusade more broadly than was intended. They preached to the poor whom they served that they too could and should participate in the wars to take place in the Holy Land. A large number of them, including women and children, also began the Crusading march, full of faith, but unarmed, unarmoured, with no military leadership and completely unprepared for what they were to encounter.

Unfortunately, it was this second army,

Pope Urban II initiated the Crusades at the Council of Clermont in November 1095, calling all Catholic soldiers to free the Holy Land from the 'Saracens'. The response was remarkable as troops from throughout all of Western Europe answered the call. They decorated themselves with crosses applied to their surcoats, shields and banners as a symbol of their devotion to God and the Church.

the peasant army, that reached the Byzantine Empire first. They had been generally welcomed by Christians across Central and Eastern Europe, although this may have been more out of fear than support. But they were certainly not what Emperor Alexius Comnenus wanted when he had asked for assistance against the Seljuk Turks. Once they arrived at Constantinople their very presence burdened the Empire's sparse resources. So, he quickly transported them to the Asian side of the Bosporus, where on 6 August 1096 they resumed their march. They did not get far, only reaching Nicaea before meeting the Turks in battle. Many died, while those who were captured were either forced to convert to Islam or killed. Only a few survivors returned to Constantinople. Their Crusade had not even lasted to the end of October.

THE FIRST CRUSADE

By this time the military Crusaders were also arriving in the capital of the Byzantine Empire. Of course, this force was closer to what Alexius had requested, at least initially. Every day it seemed new Crusaders arrived. Soon they had become too numerous to simply join the Byzantine army, nor were they likely to allow Byzantine leaders to command them. According to Alexius's daughter, Anna Comnena, whose account of the Crusaders in Constantinople is unique in presenting a royal viewpoint of interaction between the western Europeans and their Byzantine hosts, the Crusaders were haughty and vulgar. One ecclesiastical leader even sat himself on the Emperor's throne. All the same, if this army was successful in capturing any Muslim territory, the Emperor wanted it for his empire. After all, whatever land was taken had previously been Byzantine. For food, supplies, and transportation across the Bosporus, Alexius was able to elicit an oath of fealty from the Crusader leaders, and a promise that anything won would be his.

The march was not a simple exercise, and the Crusaders had completely misunderstood the size, terrain and climate of Asia Minor. There were significant problems feeding such a sizeable army,

although many Greek Christians along the way were willing to help out as much as they could. Even with such help the Crusading armies – they were actually regional armies loosely aligned with each other – had difficulty finding water and living off the land. Some, including many of the highest nobles, gave up and returned home, but most kept on marching toward the Holy Land. Those who continued on the First Crusade were buoyed by their

Right: This map shows the route taken by the various Crusader forces to reach the Holy Land. Although France provided the bulk of the troops for the First Crusade, the Crusaders were a truly multinational force, with elements from England, Catalonia, Italy and the Rhineland.

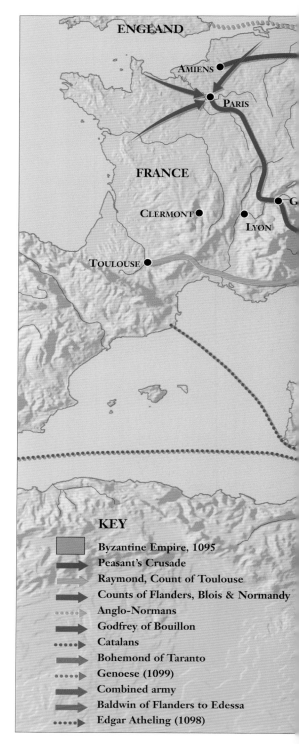

KEY

	Byzantine Empire, 1095
	Peasant's Crusade
	Raymond, Count of Toulouse
	Counts of Flanders, Blois & Normandy
	Anglo-Normans
	Godfrey of Bouillon
	Catalans
	Bohemond of Taranto
	Genoese (1099)
	Combined army
	Baldwin of Flanders to Edessa
	Edgar Atheling (1098)

military encounters with the Turks, infrequent as they were. On 14 May 1097, the Crusaders laid siege to Nicaea, and two days later the army of Sultan Kilij Arslan I, who had been alerted to their presence, tried to raze it. Skirmishes were followed on 21 May by a battle in which the Crusaders easily triumphed. Six weeks later, on 1 July, the two armies met again, at Dorylaeum. It was here that the Crusaders first encountered the primary Seljuk tactical force: their mounted archers. And it was here that the Turks met the primary Crusader tactical force: their heavy cavalry – the same soldiers who had so impressed Anna Comnena that they were 'irresistible; [they] would bore [their] way through the walls of Babylon'. Ultimately, it was the latter who triumphed over the former at Dorylaeum.

The Crusaders continued their march through the rest of Asia Minor, without

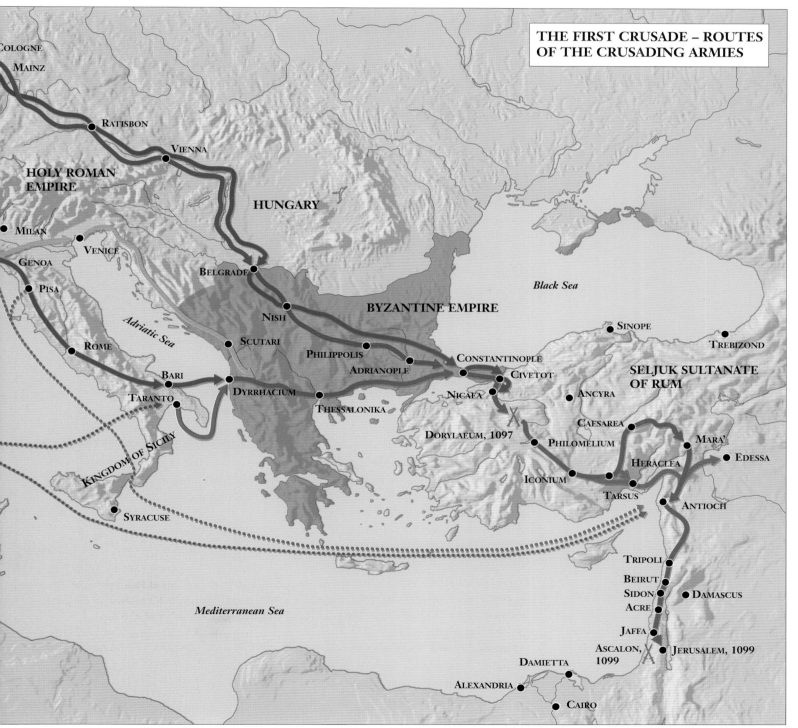

THE FIRST CRUSADE – ROUTES OF THE CRUSADING ARMIES

COLOGNE
MAINZ
RATISBON
VIENNA
HOLY ROMAN EMPIRE
HUNGARY
MILAN
VENICE
GENOA
PISA
BELGRADE
ROME
Adriatic Sea
NISH
SCUTARI
BYZANTINE EMPIRE
Black Sea
SINOPE
TREBIZOND
PHILIPPOLIS
BARI
DYRRHACIUM
ADRIANOPLE
CONSTANTINOPLE
TARANTO
THESSALONIKA
CIVETOT
NICAEA
ANCYRA
SELJUK SULTANATE OF RUM
KINGDOM OF SICILY
DORYLAEUM, 1097
CAESAREA
PHILOMELIUM
MARA'
HERACLEA
EDESSA
ICONIUM
SYRACUSE
TARSUS
ANTIOCH
TRIPOLI
BEIRUT
SIDON
DAMASCUS
ACRE
Mediterranean Sea
JAFFA
ASCALON, 1099
JERUSALEM, 1099
DAMIETTA
ALEXANDRIA
CAIRO

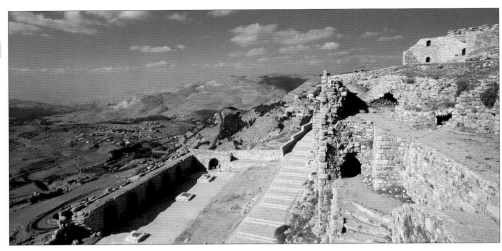

Due to a lack of large hardwood trees in the Holy Land, the Crusaders followed the Middle Eastern custom of building their fortifications in stone. The ruins of Kerak Castle in Jordan, built on a precipitous mountainside c. 1142, serve as a good example of the size and strength of these Crusader fortifications.

further opposition from the Seljuks, who were attempting to regroup after their losses. They reached Antioch in October 1097 and began a siege of this large and well-fortified ancient city. By now the Crusaders were wracked by starvation; some had died and all were weakened by their deprivation. Most of the cavalry had lost their horses, with only the most noble – at least those who had not abandoned the Crusade – still mounted. But the soldiers who remained believed that their quest was a religious pilgrimage, that their violence was performed for and sanctioned by God. They were going to succeed or die – either would ensure their eternal salvation.

After several months of siege, on 3 June 1098, the Crusaders were able to 'convince' a commander of one of the towers, a man named Firouz, to allow them entrance. The besiegers rushed into Antioch, quickly capturing the city. It could not have happened at a more fortuitous time, as on 5 June a large Seljuk army, led by Kerbogha, the Atabeg of Mosul, arrived and began its own siege. The situation looked dire until, on 28 June 1098, one of the Crusader priests, Peter Bartholomew, claimed that a dream had directed him where to find the lance of Longinus (the lance that pierced Christ's side on the cross). The Crusaders saw this as a sign of God's continued support of their endeavour and charged out of the city, defeating a very surprised Muslim force.

ON TO JERUSALEM

In determining the causes of the Seljuk Turkish defeat at Dorylaeum, Antioch and

elsewhere during the First Crusade most historians look to the war between the Seljuks and Fatamid Egyptians that had been fought during the last half of the eleventh century. Because of their size and religious significance, both Antioch and Jerusalem had been fought over. The Turks captured Antioch in 1085 and had held onto it until lost to the Crusaders.

But Jerusalem had been more difficult to retain. Despite losing the city in 1070, the Fatamids had retaken it early in 1099 as the Crusaders were marching south from Antioch. Therefore, when the Crusaders – now likely numbering no more than 20,000 – reached Jerusalem, they faced a weakened city and fatigued population, but a city where the walls remained strong. On 15 July 1099 these gave way, and the First Crusaders entered the city. Sadly, there followed a massacre of the inhabitants, perpetrated by ardent religious enthusiasts who saw nothing wrong in killing anyone who disagreed with their Christian beliefs. Raymond d'Aguiliers, a chaplain in the army and eyewitness to the massacre writes:

> … wonderful sights were to be seen. Some of our men (and this was more merciful) cut off the heads of their enemies; others shot them with arrows, so that they fell from the towers; others tortured them longer by casting them into the flames. Piles of heads, hands, and feet were to be seen in the streets of the city. It was necessary to pick one's way over the bodies of men and horses… Indeed, it was a just and splendid judgment of God that this place should be filled with the blood of the unbelievers, since it had suffered so long from their blasphemies.

CONSOLIDATION

The First Crusaders fought one further battle in 1099, on 12 August, at the battle of Ascalon, defeating a Fatamid Egyptian relief army that was attempting to recapture Jerusalem.

During the half-century that followed the fall of Jerusalem, the Crusaders enlarged their holdings in the Holy Land. These they refused to restore to the Byzantine Empire or to establish as Papal fiefs after Bishop Adhemar of Le Puy died on 1 August 1098 outside of Antioch. Instead, the Crusader leaders established their own realms: Bohemond Guiscard became Prince of Antioch and the area around it; Baldwin of Bouillon, who had taken an army northeast of Antioch to Edessa and captured it, established a county there; Raymond of Toulouse became Count of Tripoli after the city was captured in 1109; and Godfrey de Bouillon, who by the fall of Jerusalem had become the leader of the Crusaders, became the King of Jerusalem. But a large number, if not most, of the soldiers returned home, their quest successfully completed. Only a few wished to stay in the Holy Land. Before too long, the kingdom of Jerusalem had only 300 soldiers to defend it, while other Crusader principalities had even smaller numbers.

As the soldiers who remained could not alone defend all that they had gained, the Crusaders also began building stone castles of unprecedented size, some large enough to sustain their garrisons for five years or, it was hoped, as long as it would take to receive relief from Europe. In addition, to increasing their numbers, the Crusaders founded military monastic orders: the Knights Hospitallers, the Knights Templars and the Teutonic Knights being the most prominent.

For a while the Crusaders continued to be successful. Caesarea fell to them in 1101, Tartous in 1102, Jubail in 1104, Tripoli in 1109, Beirut and Sidon in 1110, and Tyre in 1124. However, on the battlefield they were not always victorious. At Harran in 1104, for example, a small army of Seljuk Turks defeated an even smaller army of Crusaders primarily drawn from the principalities of Edessa and Antioch. The battle of Sarmada in 1119 (also known as the Field of Blood) was another defeat, where the Seljuks destroyed a force of Antiochenes, led by

Always small in numbers, the Crusaders were forced to build many strongholds to maintain their position in the Holy Land. This map shows the major Crusader castles of Outremer in the mid-thirteenth century. Knights Hospitaller castles are marked in blue, while those of the Templar Knights and Teutonic Knights are marked in red and green respectively. Other Crusader strongholds are marked in purple.

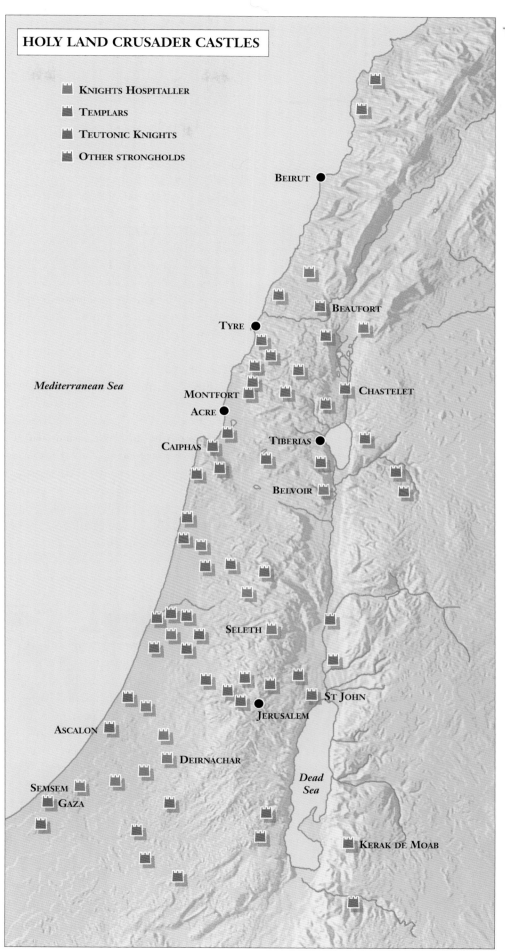

HOLY LAND CRUSADER CASTLES

- KNIGHTS HOSPITALLER
- TEMPLARS
- TEUTONIC KNIGHTS
- OTHER STRONGHOLDS

BEIRUT

BEAUFORT

TYRE

Mediterranean Sea

MONTFORT   CHASTELET

ACRE

CAIPHAS   TIBERIAS

BELVOIR

SELETH

St JOHN

JERUSALEM

ASCALON

DEIRNACHAR

Dead Sea

SEMSEM
GAZA

KERAK DE MOAB

their regent, Roger of Salerno, with more than 3500 from 3700 Crusaders killed in the battle or massacred shortly after it.

THE SECOND CRUSADE

A second Crusade was initiated in 1144 when the city and county of Edessa, located some distance northeast of Antioch and the other Crusader realms, was attacked and captured by Seljuk Turks led by Zengi, the Governor of Mosul. Edessa was poorly manned and had no natural defences, so its fall was perhaps foreseeable, but its loss was seen by most in Europe and the Holy Land as a significant defeat for the causes of Christianity. Immediately, a new Crusade was called, and preachers again travelled throughout Europe. A large number of soldiers once more 'took up the cross', including two kings, Conrad III of Germany and Louis VII of France.

Yet, no matter who or how many participants there were, they could not keep this Crusade from becoming one of the most disastrous military campaigns in history. The Second Crusaders began to quarrel with the resident Crusaders almost as soon as they arrived in Jerusalem, blaming them for the fall of Edessa because they had dealt too mercifully with the Muslims. The resident Crusaders, including Templar and Hospitaller leaders, in turn resented this presumption by the new

arrivals. They also resented the new arrivals' rejection of their plan.

The local Crusaders proposed to take an army north to Aleppo, the capital city of Nur-ad-Din (Zengi's son and heir after he died in 1146). Kings Conrad and Louis instead preferred to march on Damascus, a city led by a Muslim ally of the resident Crusaders who was an enemy of Nur-ad-Din, and a closer target. On 24 June 1148 the Second Crusaders marched on Damascus. But their siege was very short-lived, lasting for less than a week. Even before reaching the city, the two kings argued over who was to be credited for their victory. They need not have bothered. Their attack failed miserably, so miserably in fact that the citizens of the town turned against their leader, the former ally of the Crusaders, replacing him with Nur-ad-Din. Not only had the Second Crusaders made no headway in regaining Edessa, they had actually lost all the lands surrounding the Holy Lands' Christian principalities and, in doing so, greatly empowered the Seljuk Turks. Conrad III immediately set out for home, followed the next year by Louis VII. Both blamed the resident Crusaders for the military debacle.

Interestingly, the only success of the Crusade involved neither of these kings and nor was it in the Holy Land. A fleet of Northern European Crusaders on their way to the Middle East stopped in Lisbon in 1147 and assisted the Portuguese King Afonso I Henriques in his successful *Reconquista* (reconquest) of the city.

Nur-ad-Din's defeat of the Second Crusaders, and his bloodless capture of Damascus that followed, gave him confidence to extend his realm further. The Crusader principalities certainly worried about their fate, but for they moment they were spared as the Turkish leader decided to bypass his recent enemies and attack Fatamid Egypt instead, which fell to him in 1168. This was important to the Crusaders for two reasons. First, they were now surrounded on three sides by Nur-ad-Din's forces. They could still be reinforced by Europe from the Mediterranean Sea, but had no chance of making alliances with other Muslim leaders who also opposed Nur-ad-Din. Second, the conquest of Egypt

Saladin's rise to leadership and subsequent defeat of the Crusaders at Hattin and Jerusalem initiated the Third Crusade. Three European kings answered the call to respond to Saladin's military successes, but although they captured Acre and defeated the Sultan at the Battle of Arsuf, they could not regain the lands lost to him.

led directly to the rise of the man who was to become the greatest Muslim general to face the Crusaders: Saladin.

SALADIN

Saladin was a Kurd, born in Tikrit in what is now Iraq. He rose to prominence as the nephew of Shirkuh, one of Nur-ad-Din's military leaders responsible for the campaign in Egypt. When Shirkuh died, Saladin succeeded him, becoming the governor of the captured lands there. Nur-ad-Din opposed Saladin's leadership, and conflict between the two seemed inevitable until Nur-ad-Din died in 1174, leaving Saladin as the leader of all Muslims in the Middle East. Some did try to oppose him, including Nur-ad-Din's son, As-Salih Ismail al-Malik, and at least two attempts were made on his life by members of the Assassins cult, paid for by opponents. By 1185, after marrying Nur-ad-Din's widow and pacifying all other claimants to his absolute leadership, Saladin became the first Sultan of a new dynasty, the Ayyubids.

Saladin's most important military skill may have been his ability to lead Muslims of different ethnic and religious groups who had for much of their history fought each other. He did this by creating a common enemy for all of them in shape of the Christian Crusaders. Since the end of the Second Crusade, though relations between Christians and Muslims had always been strained, they had rarely turned violent. Nur-ad-Din had carried out two small campaigns, in 1171 and 1173, but neither grew into larger conflicts. However, Saladin felt the Crusader principalities were vulnerable, especially as their leadership seemed so disunited.

The King of Jerusalem at the time was Baldwin IV the Leper, whose terrible affliction caused an early death with no heir. When young, Baldwin had been an effective political and military leader. In fact, in 1177, while only 16, Baldwin faced and defeated a Muslim force led by Saladin himself at the battle of Montgisard. But as the effects of his illness began to debilitate him over the next eight years – he died in 1185 – disagreements over military strategy occurred frequently among other Crusader leaders, especially between the cautious

regent, Raymond III, Count of Tripoli, and the bellicose Guy of Lusignan, Baldwin's brother-in-law. Guy's war-mongering was fuelled by the Grand Master of the Templars, Gerard of Ridfort, and one of the more fascinating characters of the entire Crusades, Reynald of Chatillon, then Lord of Oultrejourdain and Castellan of Kerak and Montreale Castles.

Reynald had been causing problems in the Middle East for many years by this time. While married to Constance, Countess of Antioch, he had already offended the Byzantine Emperor, Manuel I Comnenus, by attempting the conquest of Cyprus. He spent more than 15 years in an Aleppo jail after being captured during one of his many raids into Syria and Armenia from Antioch. He also planned an attack on Mecca and Medina as one of his many pirating activities on the Red Sea; although not going on the

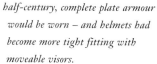

As the Crusades drew on, arms and armour technology progressed. In the First Crusade European knights wore a nasal helmet and mail armour that covered the torso, groin and shoulders. By the end of the thirteenth century, the mail armour covered the body and a helmet enclosed the head. Shields had gone from being long and kite shaped to being small and triangular. By the end of the fourteenth century plates had begun to be attached to the mail – in another half-century, complete plate armour would be worn – and helmets had become more tight fitting with moveable visors.

While most Europeans fought in the Holy Land, Southern France and northeastern Europe, Spanish Christian soldiers fought a 'reconquest' (reconquista) of the Muslim-controlled parts of the Iberian peninsula. Some Spanish kings were more ardent in their waging of the reconquista *than others. One of these, Pedro II, King of Aragon from 1196 to 1213, was given the cognomen 'the Catholic', because of his participation at the Crusade battles of Las Navas de Tolosa in 1212 and Muret in 1213.*

expedition himself, a number of his soldiers were captured and subsequently beheaded in Cairo. Finally, he made it a practice to attack and plunder the caravans that passed anywhere near Kerak Castle, one of which contained Saladin's sister.

THE THIRD CRUSADE

Saladin may have been trying to trick Reynald into this rash action by putting his sister in a caravan that was likely to be an obvious target for him. He may also have been waiting for the squabbling over inheritance that he knew would occur at the death of Baldwin the Leper. Raymond of Tripoli, who had acted as Baldwin's regent since 1174, and Guy of Lusignan, his closest male relative – although by marriage only – fought over who was to reign as king of Jerusalem. Raymond wanted to make peace

with Saladin, while Guy – joined by Reynald of Chatillon and the Templars – wanted war. The latter became king and in 1187 he set out on a campaign against Saladin. The result was the disastrous battle of Hattin, where almost the entire Crusader army was killed or captured (Reynald being personally beheaded by Saladin), the subsequent capture of Jerusalem and the launching of the Third Crusade.

The loss of Jerusalem had stunned Europe, with a new Crusade immediately called for by Pope Gregory VIII. It attracted three kings: Frederick I Barbarossa of Germany, Philip II Augustus of France and Henry II of England (who was replaced by his son, Richard the Lionheart at his death in 1189). Frederick Barbarossa travelled overland to the Holy Land, but after the 67-year-old king drowned in the River Göksu in Asia Minor, very little of his force, already decimated by disease, fatigue and apathy, carried on to their destination.

Philip and Richard travelled with their armies by ship and arrived safely – with Richard attacking Christian Cyprus on the way – but began to quarrel over military leadership. Together, they were able to capture Acre in 1191, but soon afterwards Philip returned to France.

Richard the Lionheart stayed a year longer, but with few positive results. Trying to provoke Saladin to battle, Richard executed more than 3000 prisoners taken at Acre, sparing neither the women nor the children. He then marched down the coast towards Jerusalem, capturing unfortified towns and villages along the way. And when Saladin finally did give him a battle, at Arsuf on 11 September 1191, Richard was victorious. However, Richard could never muster numbers or strength enough to recapture Jerusalem. The closest he came was a truce with Saladin that allowed his soldiers to visit the city unarmed, and only a few at a time. The Third Crusade had also failed.

THE FOURTH CRUSADE

By now the Crusader principalities had been reduced to Antioch, Tripoli and Acre. The resident Crusaders there still hung on, with their numbers increased by soldiers who did not return to Europe from the Third Crusade. But they were not strong enough to regain any lost lands or to face Saladin in anything larger than a skirmish. The new Pope, Innocent III, tried to help out by calling another, fourth, Crusade, but although a large force of soldiers gathered in Venice in 1201 – this time without any royal participation – they never reached the Holy Land. The Venetians, led by their aged and blind Doge, Enrico Dandolo, instead used them as their own army, first directing them to attack a Catholic Hungarian city, Zara, which threatened Adriatic trading monopolies of Venice. Then the Venetians took the Fourth Crusaders to Constantinople, where the capital of Byzantium was besieged from June 1203 to April 1204. The city was sacked and from then, until 1261, the Latin Empire of Constantinople took the place of the Byzantine Empire in the Eastern Mediterranean.

Although the Venetians profited greatly from their trade monopoly with the city, the Latin Empire was never a truly successful realm, as was demonstrated at the battle of Adrianople on 14 April 1205 when the first Emperor, Baldwin I (Count Baldwin IX of Flanders), and his army were defeated by a small force of Bulgarians. Ultimately, in 1261, an attack from the exiled Byzantine Emperor, Michael VIII Palaeologus, acting in concert with the Genoese, returned the Byzantine Empire to power. However, relations between Byzantium and Europe, along with those between the Christians of Constantinople and Rome, would never be the same.

CRUSADES IN EUROPE

More than anything the Fourth Crusade distracted those who might otherwise have been inclined to join the Crusaders in the Holy Land. Innocent III berated those who participated in the attack on Constantinople, insisting that they proceed on their journey, but no one did, further embarrassing a papacy that had not delivered a substantial victory in the Middle East for more than a hundred years. An anti-Crusade sentiment had also begun to grow. Many suggested that God no longer favoured them because they were targeting

the wrong enemy: that Islam in the Holy Land could not be defeated until heresy at home was faced. Thus Innocent III's call to Crusade against the Albigensians in Southern France was widely welcomed and supported. From 1209 to 1229 one of the most savage conflicts in European history was waged against those heretics, and against anyone thought to be aiding them. Mercy disappeared and inhumanity reigned. No better example of this exists than the assault on Béziers that took place on 21 July 1209. Despite there being only a small minority of Albigensians in the town, the Crusaders slaughtered the entire population, with the Papal legate attending the soldiers, Arnaud-Amaury, uttering one of the most horrifying statements of any military leader when asked how to discern who was a heretic and who was not: 'Kill them all; God will know his own.'

A similar Crusade was also fought in northeastern Europe against people who had never accepted (or even heard of) Jesus Christ. This Crusade was actually not a new endeavour, as northern Europeans and Scandinavians had been trying to spread Christianity into the region for much of the second half of the twelfth century. Their action was officially approved and encouraged by Pope Celestine III in 1193 but it was not until the thirteenth century, after

Teutonic knight, c. 1400. One can see in this illustration that the roots of the Teutonic Order were military–monastic in the simple white garb with its equally simple cross as the only decoration upon shield, uniform and horse. The main strength of the Order's military might was its mounted knights, who acted as the foremost offensive arm in any battle.

INTRODUCTION

The reputation of French King Louis IX, St Louis, was built on piety, not on military leadership. His Crusades to Egypt and North Africa both ended in failure: in Egypt in 1247–48, he – and almost his entire army – was captured. In 1270, he died at the futile siege of Tunis.

the failure of the Fourth Crusade, that a large number of Crusaders arrived to participate in the campaign. Chief among them were members of the Teutonic Knights, a monastic military order that had been founded in the Holy Land at the end of the twelfth century but had gradually moved north, assisting the Hungarians in their war against the non-Christian Cumans in 1211. They then protected the borders of Transylvania for more than a decade, and finally joined the Northern Crusade in 1226. From then until the sixteenth century this order directed the Crusade, bringing it many successes and large amounts of lands for most of that time, but also suffering several memorable defeats, including that at Lake Peipus (sometimes called the 'Battle on the Ice') on 5 April 1242, when a large number of Teutonic Knights and other Crusaders were defeated by a diverse force of non-professional soldiers drawn primarily from Novgorod and Livonia and led by the Grand Prince of Novgorod, Alexander Nevskii.

Their cause also suffered at the battle of Grunwald (or Tannenberg) on 15 July 1410, when troops from the Grand Duchy of Lithuania and the Kingdom of Poland –

now Christian, but resentful of the Teutonic Knights' oppression of them – demolished the Teutonic Knight army that faced them, pushing the Order from their lands back into Prussia.

RECONQUISTA

Various Spanish kingdoms were also fighting Crusades in their own peninsula and had done so since even before the First Crusade to the Holy Land was called. However, they saw it as a *Reconquista* (reconquest), a struggle to retake the Iberian lands that had been conquered by Muslim armies from 711 to 720. Although freed from service on other Crusades, it was only when Spanish Christians had dedicated and determined leaders that they made any gains at all. Undoubtedly, two of the greatest of these were kings of Castile, Alfonso VIII and his grandson, Fernando III. Alfonso led a Spanish army, raised from all the kingdoms, to perhaps the greatest *Reconquista* victory at the battle of Las Navas de Tolosa in 1212, while Fernando captured Cordoba, Jaen, Seville, Arcos, Medina-Sidonia, Jerez and Cadiz between 1217 and 1252. These Crusading feats would not be equalled until the reigns of Ferdinand of Aragon and Isabella of Castile, when in 1492 they completed the *Reconquista* with the surrender of the final Muslim state in Spain, the kingdom of Granada.

LATER CRUSADES

There were few Crusades in the Holy Land during the thirteenth century and they were almost always unsuccessful. The Children's Crusade of 1212, in which a large number of adolescent and adult peasants thought that they could simply defeat the Muslims with their 'child-like' faith, was so embarrassing to Pope Innocent III and other ecclesiastical leaders that they stopped it before the Crusaders could get too far. Others were poorly planned and executed, including that of Andrew II, King of Hungary, and Leopold VI, Duke of Austria, in 1217–19; those of Emperor Frederick II in 1227 and 1228; and those of King Louis IX in 1248–50 and 1254. Of course, there were some victories, such as the capture of the Egyptian city of Damietta by Leopold VI in 1219 and its recapture by Louis IX in 1248 or the conquest of an unpopulated and derelict Jerusalem by Frederick II in 1228 (it was lost again in 1244). But these did not outweigh the large number of defeats that were suffered, such as at the battle of La Forbie, fought on 17–18 October 1244, where a Muslim force defeated a large army that was drawn mostly from the Crusade principalities, or at Mansura, fought on 8 February 1250, where Louis IX lost nearly his entire army – he himself being taken prisoner a few days later – to the Egyptian Mamluk general Baibars.

The Crusaders could not even benefit from the Mongol invasion of the Muslim Middle East in the middle of the thirteenth century. Although the Mongols conquered all of Turkey, Persia and Syria, and destroyed Aleppo, Damascus, and Baghdad, and even considered the Crusader principalities as their allies, the Crusaders gained nothing. Indeed, Muslim military and political power had been shifting from Syria to Egypt since Saladin's death in 1193, and Mongol destruction of those former strong cities of Seljuk rule solidified power there. It also strengthened the confidence of the Mamluk Egyptians who, led again by Baibars, had defeated the Mongols at the battle of Ain Jalut in 1260. They quickly turned their attention to the remaining Crusader principalities, and there was nothing that the inhabitants there could do. With no sign of reinforcements from an apathetic Europe, the remaining Crusader holdings began to fall: Caesarea, Haifa and Arsuf in 1265; Antioch in 1268; and Tripoli in 1289. Finally, in 1291, the last of the Crusaders in the Holy Land left when Acre fell to the Mamluks.

RISE OF THE OTTOMANS

Calls for a new Crusade began again after the fall of Acre and continued throughout the fourteenth, fifteenth and sixteenth centuries. It actually became customary for a European king to 'take up the cross' during that period only subsequently to break their promise. By the middle of the fourteenth century, however, the Muslim enemy of those making these calls had changed.

A new force, the Ottoman Turks, had by now risen in Anatolia and the eastern Mediterranean to threaten the borders of lands much closer to the European Christian kingdoms than before. Before too long, the Ottomans had changed the whole balance of political and military power throughout southeastern Europe, the eastern Mediterranean and the Middle East. Even before the middle of the fifteenth century, not only had they occupied most of these lands, but they had also soundly defeated a large Anglo-Franco-Burgundian-Hungarian Crusading force at the battle of Nicopolis in 1396 and another at Varna in 1444. Nor did their military successes end there – they captured Constantinople in 1453, Rhodes in 1521, Hungary in 1526, and Egypt, the Saudi peninsula, and much of Northern Africa in the early to mid-sixteenth century. Even when they were defeated, for example at the siege of Vienna in 1529, Malta in 1565 and at the naval battle of Lepanto in 1571, they were a potent and dangerous foe, and would remain so into the twentieth century.

While this late fifteenth-century illumination depicts the First Crusaders' capture of Nicaea in 1097, it shows the soldiers wearing contemporary plate armour. War had changed dramatically in the five Crusading centuries, as had the Crusaders' enemy, from the Seljuk to the Ottoman Turks.

DORYLAEUM
1097

IN NOVEMBER 1095, POPE URBAN II (1042–1099) ADDRESSED A LARGE NUMBER OF THE NOBILITY AND CLERGY OF FRANCE AT CLERMONT. IN WHAT MUST HAVE BEEN A POWERFUL SERMON, HE CALLED FOR AN EXPEDITION TO AID THE CHRISTIANS OF THE EAST, NOTABLY THE BYZANTINES, AGAINST THE TURKS, AND TO LIBERATE JERUSALEM AND THE HOLY PLACES.

WHY DID IT HAPPEN?

WHO Some 50,000 Crusaders, including 7000 knights and a small Byzantine allied contingent under Tatikios, faced a force of 10,000 Seljuk Turks and their Danishmund Turk allies under the Sultan of Rhum, Kilij Arslan.

WHAT The Turks ambushed the Crusaders as they entered the Anatolian Plateau, while the latter were divided on the march from Nicaea.

WHERE Along the Byzantine military road, in a valley northwest of Dorylaeum, some 160km (100 miles) southwest of Constantinople.

WHEN 1 July 1097.

WHY The Crusaders had taken Nicaea, the capital of the Sultanate of Rhum and were now marching through central Anatolia. Kilij Arslan now sought to defeat the Crusaders on the march.

OUTCOME The Turks had some initial success against the Crusaders' vanguard, but ultimately the Crusader army inflicted heavy losses on the Turks, opening the way for a Byzantine conquest of Anatolia.

The Crusade was to be treated as a pilgrimage, and in return for their participation the Crusaders would receive remission of their sins. There would also, of course, be the usual profit expected from warfare at the time. The impact of Urban's message was profound – many of the great nobles of western Christendom 'took up the cross' and began raising forces for the campaign. Included among these were the brothers of the kings of England and France, as well as many other powerful leaders.

Urban planned for the Crusade to begin on 15 August of the following year, the date of the Feast of the Assumption. In the meantime, the kings and princes began to raise money and men for the upcoming expedition. Four major contingents began to emerge. The northern French counted among their leaders: Robert II, Count of Flanders; Robert of Normandy, brother to the King of England; Stephen of Blois; and Hugh of Vermandois, the brother to the King of France. The Provencal knights

While the religious motivations of the crusaders are sometimes doubted, it is clear that religion did play a role in motivating both the nobles and the commoners who 'took the cross' and set out to liberate Jerusalem. The nobility were also encouraged by the possibility of booty won through righteous combat and feudal bonds.

were led by Raymond, Count of Toulouse, the nominal leader of the entire Crusade, and Bishop Adhemar de Puy, the Papal legate to the Crusade. Crusaders from Lorraine included Godfrey de Bouillon and his brothers Eustace III of Boulogne and Baldwin of Boulogne. Finally, there were the Norman nobility from Italy led by Bohemond of Taranto and his nephew Tancred. These groupings were to take various routes to the east, with the intention of mustering the whole force at Constantinople.

THE 'PEOPLES' CRUSADE'

In addition to the armies of the princes, there were other spontaneous if less well-organized and supported movements. One of the better known was the so-called 'Peoples' Crusade' led by Peter the Hermit. While often described as an ill-equipped and poorly disciplined rabble, this army of 20,000 included a core of 700 knights and other fighting men. Although the People's Crusade thus possessed a solid fighting force, it lacked two important elements – leadership and resources. These Crusaders arrived at Constantinople in August 1096, before the better-organized forces had even departed Europe, and despite Byzantine advice, pressed forward against the Seljuks. This haste was no doubt due partially to the lack of a unified command structure and to pressing supply problems. Unfortunately, the members of the People's Crusade were met by the Seljuks under Kilij Arslan on 21 October. The Crusaders fought well until the knights, who had been lured out by the

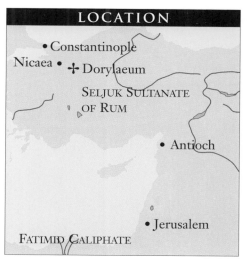

After the capture of Nicaea, the crusaders decided to march on Antioch. They chose to advance through Anatolia by following the Byzantine military road rather than moving along the coast.

TURKOMAN HORSE ARCHER

The armies of the Seljuk Turks of the Sultanate of Rhüm were still composed primarily of nomadic steppe cavalry like this Turkoman mounted archer. A small number of the Seljuks would have worn some armour by this time, but most were unarmoured save for a light shield. The tactics of the Seljuks centred on shooting massive valleys of arrows against their enemies in order to goad them into launching a charge. The Turks would then scatter rather than meet the charge and then wheel back upon isolated groups of the enemy as the charge lost its cohesion. It was these tactics that the Turks used against the People's Crusade, destroying it as a fighting force.

This painting depicts the Crusader leader Godfrey of Bouillon making an oath of allegiance to the Byzantine emperor Alexius I in the latter's palace in Constantinople, 1097.

lightly armed Turkish cavalry, were cut off and routed. With this destruction of their best fighting men and most important leaders, the remaining fighting men and non-combatants were put to flight and most were killed. Perhaps 3000 survived the slaughter and these would later join the ranks of First Crusade.

AT CONSTANTINOPLE

Meanwhile, the other contingents of Crusaders had begun marching towards the mustering point at Constantinople. They arrived over the course of several months, with Godfrey de Bouillon and the Crusaders from Lorraine arriving first, shortly before Christmas 1096. The last to arrive were Bohemond and his Normans and Raymond of Toulouse with his Provencal contingent at the end of April. While at Constantinople, there was a certain amount of friction between the

Byzantine Emperor, Alexius I, and the Crusader leadership. There were, for example, traditional conflicts between the Italian Normans and the Byzantines as well as a certain amount of suspicion given the activities, and lack of success, of the People's Crusade. In the end, these difficulties were resolved when Alexius was able to exact oaths of fealty from the Crusader princes and conclude a treaty with them that settled issues relating to the division of conquered territories. The arrangement with the Byzantines was not a formal alliance; clearly Alexius was concerned about the complex political situation among the various Islamic and Turkish states of the region should the Crusaders fail, something that seemed all too likely given the fate of the People's Crusade. As a result, direct military support by Imperial troops was to be limited. Nonetheless, the arrangement did give serious and concrete benefits to the

Crusaders. The Byzantines did provide some military aid, including supplies and a small contingent of troops under general Tatikios, who was also the Emperor's representative on the campaign. The Byzantines also supplied a number of small ships that were used in the siege of Nicaea. Other, less direct, support included information on the local political situation, geographic and topographical details, and, most significantly, intelligence on the arms, armour and tactics of their enemies.

THE CAMPAIGN

By the beginning of May, the Crusaders were ready to launch their campaign against the Seljuk Turks. They had amassed a considerable force, perhaps as many as 70,000, including a considerable number of non-combatants. Many of these latter were provided with arms and could support the fighting men when necessary. The army was huge, clearly the largest western army in centuries. It was at least three or four times as large as that with which William the Conqueror had invaded England a scant 31 years before.

On 6 May, this formidable force arrived at its first objective, the city of Nicaea and the capital of the Sultan of Rhum, Kilij Arslan. The Sultan was in the east, hoping to capitalize on political unrest in Baghdad that might have allowed him to capture the old Roman fortress town of Melitene. But, upon learning of the Crusaders' arrival at his capital, he was forced to return and defend it, especially as his family was still there.

SIEGE OF NICAEA

The Crusader army arrived over a matter of weeks and began laying siege to the city. Their piecemeal deployment gave Kilij

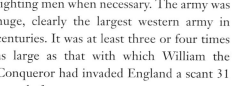

THE OPPOSED FORCES

CRUSADERS (estimated)	
Knights:	7000
Infantry:	43,000+
Total:	**50,000+**

SELJUK TURKS (estimated)	
Cavalry:	10,000
Total:	**10,000**

The Leaders of the First Crusade – Godfrey of Bouillon, Raymond of Toulouse and Bohemond of Taranto. The First Crusade was led by a number of princes whose retinues and resources were the core of the army's combat power. When the princes worked in unison, the army was very successful; but when they quarreled, the Crusaders faced serious problems.

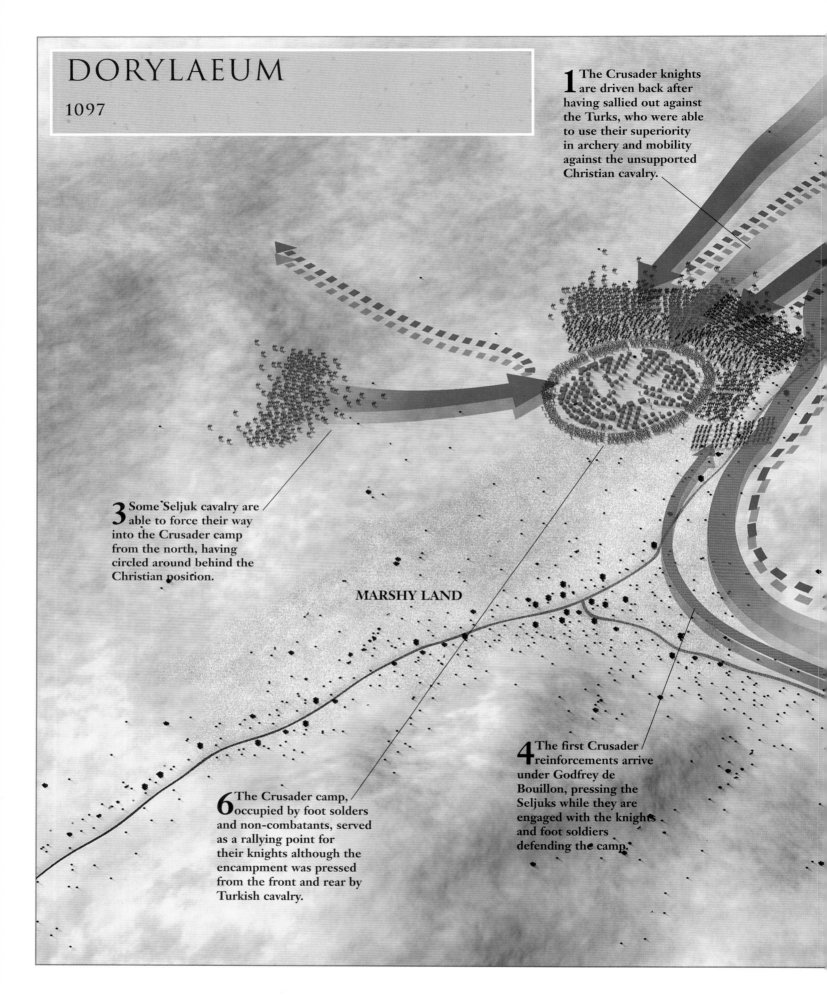

DORYLAEUM

1097

1 The Crusader knights are driven back after having sallied out against the Turks, who were able to use their superiority in archery and mobility against the unsupported Christian cavalry.

3 Some Seljuk cavalry are able to force their way into the Crusader camp from the north, having circled around behind the Christian position.

MARSHY LAND

6 The Crusader camp, occupied by foot solders and non-combatants, served as a rallying point for their knights although the encampment was pressed from the front and rear by Turkish cavalry.

4 The first Crusader reinforcements arrive under Godfrey de Bouillon, pressing the Seljuks while they are engaged with the knights and foot soldiers defending the camp.

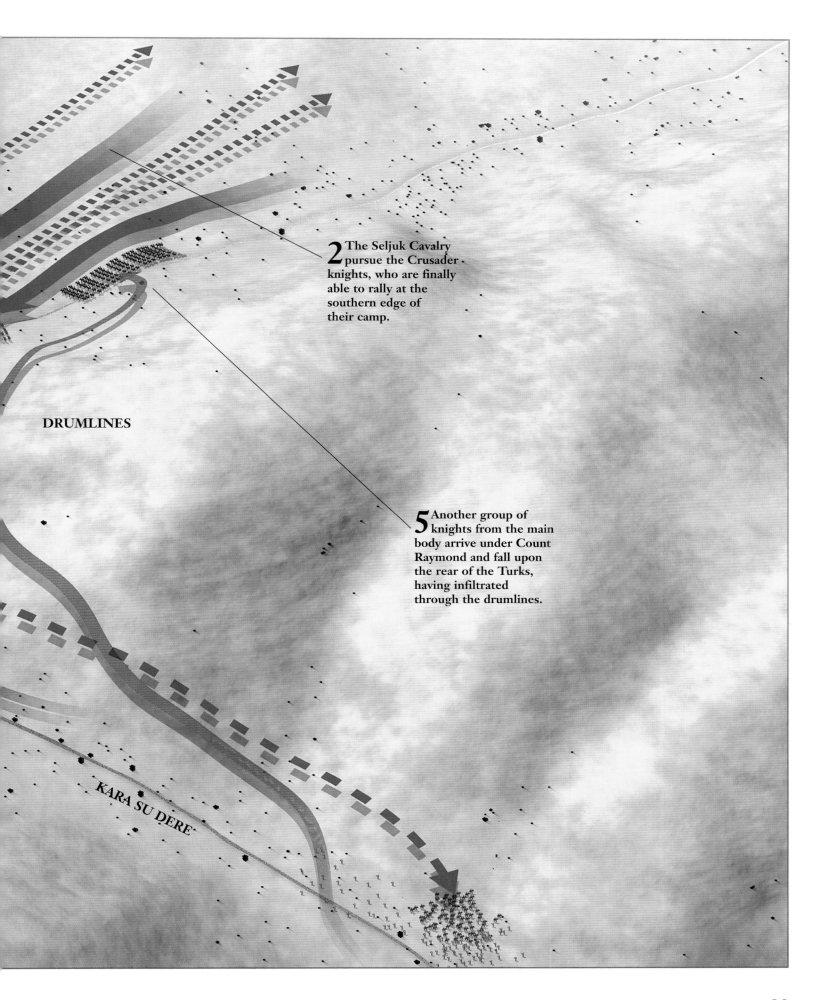

2 The Seljuk Cavalry pursue the Crusader knights, who are finally able to rally at the southern edge of their camp.

DRUMLINES

5 Another group of knights from the main body arrive under Count Raymond and fall upon the rear of the Turks, having infiltrated through the drumlines.

KARA SU DERE

This 1839 painting by Henry Auguste Calixte Serrur (1794–1865) shows the Crusaders besieging the Seljuk city of Nicaea in 1097.

Arslan the opportunity either to reinforce the city or even inflict a defeat on the Christians that might compel them to lift the siege. The Sultan attacked the Provencal contingent on 16 May as they were encamping to invest the city's south gate. Despite an initial lack of coordination between the Crusader contingents, the Provencals put up a good fight until they were reinforced by other troops. Moreover, the Turks seem to have been hampered by the terrain. Attacking the Crusaders between the city walls and a range of wooded hills near the city did not give the Turkish horse archers room to manoeuvre, and in close quarters the heavy armour of the Crusaders gave them a decided advantage.

As a result of this defeat, Kilij Arslan was forced to withdraw his forces, leaving the Crusaders to begin their siege. The Byzantines provided plans for siege engines and the material to construct them, and eventually ships to blockade the lake so that

DORYLAEUM

the city could no longer be supplied over water. As well as constructing these siege engines the Crusaders began digging to undermine the walls.

As the siege progressed, Kilij Arslan's wife tried to flee the city but was intercepted by a Byzantine ship. The defenders realized that their situation was hopeless and so came to a secret arrangement with the Byzantines. Their final surrender and the Byzantine occupation of the city took place on 19 June.

ON THE MARCH AGAIN

The Crusaders now planned to continue towards Syria, Palestine and their ultimate objective, Jerusalem. They decided to follow the Byzantine military road to the southwest towards Dorylaeum and then across the Anatolian Plateau towards Syria. This route provided them with access to potential allies in the form of the various Christian principalities of Armenia, who might have been helpful not only against the Turks, but also against the Byzantines with whom they had longstanding hostility. The Crusaders wasted little time in continuing the campaign. Within a week, the first contingents were on the move. Given the size of the army, and the lack of a truly unified command structure, the Crusader army was divided into two groups. The first was a vanguard, numbering fewer than 20,000 men, with Bohemond, Tancred, Stephen de Blois and Robert of Normandy, and including the small Byzantine force under Tatikios. The main body consisted of more than 30,000 men and was accompanied by Robert, Count of Flanders, Godfrey de Bouillon, Raymond of Toulouse and Hugh of Vermandois.

Meanwhile, Kilij Arslan had regrouped his forces and was joined by a force of Danishmund Turks with whom he had forged an alliance, for a total of 10,000 cavalrymen. His plan was to ambush the Crusaders while their forces were divided.

His chosen spot was at the juncture of two valleys, one leading from the north and the other from the west, which then opened into a larger plain. The space would allow him to draw out the Crusader knights and then surround them as they moved out of range of their infantry support. It would also give him local superiority of numbers at a key point on the battlefield and allow his mounted archers room to manoeuvre. The Sultan of Rhum was not going to repeat the mistake he had made at Nicaea.

DEPLOYMENT OF FORCES

The Crusaders discovered the presence of the Turks on the evening of 30 June, although their numbers do not seem to have been known. The next morning, the

Adhémar of Le Puy was the official Papal representative on the campaign. He helped to forge a climate of cooperation among the leaders that helped contribute to the army's early successes. He died of disease after the victory at Antioch.

Crusader vanguard continued their advance into the plain, where it became obvious that the Turks had mustered a very large force that was advancing across the plain from the south. This discovery compelled the Crusaders to pitch camp to provide them with a defendable base. The camp was constructed by the foot troops in the vanguard, positioned where the two valleys opened on to the plain, with marshy ground protecting its western approach. Bohemond deployed his mounted knights in front of the camp to intercept the main body of Turkish horsemen advancing from the south. The main body of the Christian force was advancing from the west and was a mere 5–6km (3–4 miles) behind the vanguard.

THE BATTLE

The battle began in earnest as soon as the Crusaders had established their camp and were prepared to defend it. Bohemond then advanced against the Turks with his main body of mounted knights. In doing so, he played to the strength of the enemy. As the knights moved forwards, they found themselves assailed by volleys of arrows from the mounted archers. Separated from the support of their foot soldiers defending the camp, the knights were shot at without being able to come to grips with the nomadic horse archers. At the same time, some of the Turkish cavalry, literally riding circles around the knights, attacked the Christian camp and apparently forced their way into it in the course of fierce hand-to-hand fighting.

The Christian knights were ultimately driven back to the southern edge of their camp, where they were rallied by Robert of Normandy. Once order and formation were restored, the knights were able to hold the southern edge of the camp since the Turks were no longer able to manoeuvre as freely as before. Indeed, the Turkish cavalry seem to have been forced into close-quarters

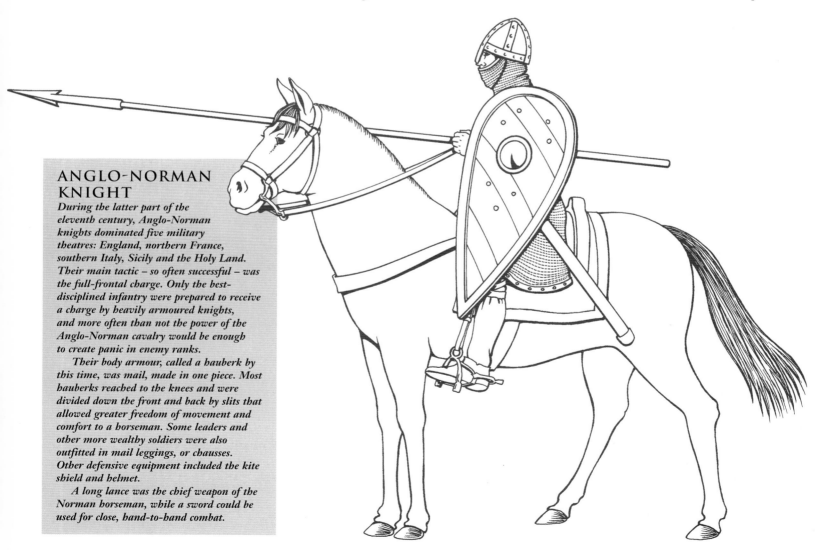

ANGLO-NORMAN KNIGHT

During the latter part of the eleventh century, Anglo-Norman knights dominated five military theatres: England, northern France, southern Italy, Sicily and the Holy Land. Their main tactic – so often successful – was the full-frontal charge. Only the best-disciplined infantry were prepared to receive a charge by heavily armoured knights, and more often than not the power of the Anglo-Norman cavalry would be enough to create panic in enemy ranks.

Their body armour, called a hauberk by this time, was mail, made in one piece. Most hauberks reached to the knees and were divided down the front and back by slits that allowed greater freedom of movement and comfort to a horseman. Some leaders and other more wealthy soldiers were also outfitted in mail leggings, or chausses. Other defensive equipment included the kite shield and helmet.

A long lance was the chief weapon of the Norman horseman, while a sword could be used for close, hand-to-hand combat.

combat with the Christian knights and definitely got the worse of the encounter, since this was where the larger horses and heavier armour of the Crusaders gave them a distinct advantage. But even so, the battle was slowly but inexorably wearing the Crusaders down.

Fortunately for Bohemond and the rest of the vanguard, help arrived around noon in the form of reinforcements from the Crusaders' main body. It had taken several hours for the knights of the main body to arm themselves and to cover the 5–6km (3–4 miles) that separated the two contingents, no doubt in part due to the fact that the intervening stretch of road was occupied by stragglers. The first troops to arrive seem to have been a group led by Godfrey de Bouillon. These knights attacked out of the valley from the west, which brought them into contact with the Turkish left flank. At this point the Turks were still occupied in fighting the knights of the vanguard on the southern edge of the Crusader camp.

Their lightly armoured Seljuk cavalry was now caught between two forces of heavily armoured Crusader knights.

Additional reinforcements from the Crusader main body under Count Raymond filtered through a line of drumlins (elongated hills formed from glacial drift) scattered along the western edge of the plain. Using this cover allowed the Crusaders to advance unobserved and to fall upon the rear of the Turkish army.

This new assault proved too much for the Turks who, having suffered heavy casualties, broke off the combat and retreated to the south. The battle ended with the Crusaders pursuing the Turks off the field, sacking their camp in the process. Both sides had suffered significant losses, with the Crusaders losing perhaps 4000 men and the Turks about 3000.

AFTERMATH

Dorylaeum was an important victory for the Crusaders. Certainly they had suffered from a lack of unity of command and had allowed themselves to be caught in separate groups while on the march.

Yet the Crusader army showed enough unit cohesion to win their first major pitched battle against the enemy.

A cohesion that came from the leadership qualities of the Crusader princes, who demonstrated their ability to react to new and unusual circumstances and inspire confidence in their men.

The battle of Dorylaeum opened the way for the Byzantine reconquest of Anatolia and the Crusaders' continuing advance to Syria.

When the knights were initially driven back to their camp, Robert of Normandy was one of the leaders who rallied them. In such a situation it was important for the crusaders to recognize their leaders, hence Robert has removed his helmet.

ANTIOCH
1098

HAILED AS MIRACULOUS BY CONTEMPORARIES, THE CHRISTIAN VICTORY AT ANTIOCH CAME AT A TIME THE CRUSADERS WERE STARVING AND HEAVILY OUTNUMBERED BY THEIR ENEMIES. THE BATTLE OF ANTIOCH WAS A GREAT TACTICAL TRIUMPH THAT SAVED THE FIRST CRUSADERS FROM ANNIHILATION.

WHY DID IT HAPPEN?

WHO The army of the First Crusade fought a much larger mixed force of Turkish cavalry and Syrian infantry, led by Kerbogah, Atabeg of Mosul.

WHAT The Crusaders exited the recently captured city of Antioch to engage the Turkish besieging forces on the plain outside the city.

WHERE Along the west bank of the Orontes River, just outside the walls of Antioch (modern Antakya, Turkey).

WHEN 28 June 1098.

WHY The Turkish force wanted to drive out the invading Crusaders; the Crusaders had to engage with the Turks or face starvation if they remained in Antioch.

OUTCOME The Crusader force won a major tactical victory. Although the majority of Kerbogah's force never engaged the enemy, it withdrew, leaving the Crusaders in possession of the region.

The army of the First Crusade arrived before the walls of Antioch on 21 October 1097. The key to Syria, Antioch was a major city with massive Byzantine walls and a large garrison, probably a mixed force of Turks and Syrians. The Crusaders had to take the city to secure their supply lines. Antioch was so large and strong, however, that an assault was clearly out of the question. Therefore the Crusaders settled down to a long siege.

The Crusader army suffered through a wet and sickly winter, aggravated by Turkish ambushes and skirmishes that hindered the flow of supplies from the Crusader port of St Symeon. By June 1098, the Crusaders were in desperate straits. Many had died or deserted during the long winter; even more importantly from a military point of view, the winter's skirmishes and supply problems had taken an extremely heavy toll of their horses. What's more, word reached the Crusaders that a large Turkish relief force, led by Kerbogah, the Atabeg (governor) of Mosul, was drawing near.

Fortunately for the Christians, one of the Crusader leaders, the southern Norman Prince Bohemond, had opened secret negotiations with a traitor inside Antioch. On the night of 2–3 June 1098, Bohemond's ally helped a small force climb to an unguarded tower. Once inside Antioch, this advance force opened a small postern gate. The Crusaders flowed in, massacring perhaps as many as 10,000 of the city's civilian population – Christians and Jews as well as Muslims. They failed, however, to take Antioch's citadel, to which the surviving members of the Turkish garrison had retreated.

This nineteenth-century illustration of the Battle of Antioch conveys well the crusaders' desperation. The dominant figure in this scene is Adhémar, bishop of Le Puy, wielding the Holy Lance.

BYZANTINE PELTAST CAVALRYMAN

The Crusaders besieged in Antioch expected Byzantine reinforcements. Emperor Alexius's force was largely mercenary, including large numbers of cavalrymen. Recruited from many regions, there was no typical Byzantine cavalry by 1098. Many, however, would have been peltast cavalrymen as in this illustration, more lightly armoured than western knights and equipped with lighter spears that were used to stab downwards.

The very next day, 4 June, Kerbogah of Mosul's army began to arrive outside the walls. This was a very large force, drawn from many of the Turkish-held cities of Syria. Contemporary chroniclers number it in the hundreds of thousands; although there is no good estimate for the actual size of the force, it is likely that they outnumbered the Crusaders by at least two to one, and possibly considerably more. The Crusaders now had the protection of the walls that had defied them for so long, but they had entered a city already on the brink of starvation after a long siege. Thus the westerners, cut off from their supply port, almost completely out of horses and starving, were in a truly desperate situation. They had some hope of relief from the Byzantine Emperor Alexius Comnenos, who was in fact marching towards Antioch

with a large army. Alexius, however, gave up his advance when the Crusader leader Count Stephen of Blois deserted the beleaguered Christians – and told the emperor that the Crusader army had already been destroyed. It is small wonder that desertion became so endemic that the papal legate, Bishop Adhemar of Le Puy, forced the Crusade's remaining leaders to swear publicly that they would fight to the bitter end.

Kerbogah's effort to dislodge the Crusaders began with attacks on their outposts, driving the Crusaders into the city in vicious fighting that further reduced their small number of remaining horses. Kerbogah then attempted an attack coordinated with the Turkish garrison in the citadel. The result was a confused struggle in which the main Turkish force

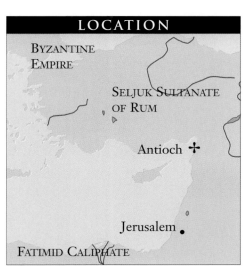

LOCATION

BYZANTINE
EMPIRE

SELJUK SULTANATE
OF RUM

Antioch ✝

Jerusalem •

FATIMID CALIPHATE

Antioch (the modern Antakya, Turkey) guarded the coastal road from Asia Minor to Palestine. The crusaders had to take and hold the city to protect their route to Jerusalem.

ANTIOCH

fortunes that Crusader morale took a turn for the better. On 11 June, the priest Stephen of Valence reported a vision in which he saw Christ promising aid to the Christian force. More spectacular by far were the stories of a poor man in the Provencal army, Peter Bartholomew. This man experienced a series of visions, culminating in the disclosure that the Holy Lance, the spear used to pierce Jesus' side during the Crucifixion, lay hidden in St Peter's Church in the city. Conveniently forgetting that they had already seen the relic of the Holy Lance in Constantinople, a party of Crusaders dug where Peter Bartholomew indicated, and eventually uncovered a spearhead on 14 June. The event was celebrated with processions and prayers of thanksgiving, but did not lead to an immediate military engagement.

It was clear, however, that the Crusaders had to break out or die, as hope faded that a Byzantine relief force would arrive. On 20 June, the Crusade leaders chose Prince Bohemond as commander of the entire army, suggesting that they now try to break out of the siege. Bohemond made his plans, and by 28 June the hungry Crusader force was ready for the attempt.

THE BATTLE

The breakout could not be kept secret; the Turks in the citadel could see all the preparations, and raised a black flag on 28 June to alert their coreligionists to the Crusaders' imminent attack. Kerbogah did little to prepare for this, however. One contemporary account tells that he sat in his camp playing chess and arguing about the proper steps to take.

There were indeed tensions between Kerbogah and his allies, the majority of whom disagreed with his strategy. At all events, as the Crusaders left the city, the various Turkish divisions were still posted at their respective gates, while a large majority of the Turkish army was still in its camp to the north.

THE OPPOSED FORCES

TURKS
No good estimate exists.
A mixed cavalry/infantry force that outnumbered the Crusader army two or three to one.

CRUSADERS
Heavy cavalry: c. 200
Infantry (mix of dismounted knights and more lightly armed troops):   c. 20,000
Total: c. 20,200

nearly broke into the city. When that attempt failed, Kerbogah began a full blockade on 14 June. He posted large contingents of his army, apparently mostly infantry, outside Antioch's main gates. Kerbogah himself remained at a main camp about 3km (2 miles) north of the city, along with most of his cavalry.

BREAKOUT

By the time the full Turkish siege began, many of the poorer Crusaders were starving to death, and even many of the knights only survived by siphoning blood from their horses' veins for nourishment – further weakening the Crusaders' pitifully small cavalry force. It is at this nadir in their

It is possible to reconstruct the battle, thanks especially to the detailed account by the chronicler Raymond of Aguilers, a participant in the First Crusade. All sources make it plain that the Crusaders had to adapt their tactics because they only had about 200 horses left that were strong enough to carry a knight into battle. In their favour, though, the Crusaders were now a highly experienced fighting force, unlike Kerbogah's troops. By this time, it is likely that all able-bodied male pilgrims had some training in combat, and would have equipped themselves from the spoils of Antioch.

Count Raymond of Toulouse was ill, so instead of leading the army from Provence he remained in the city with a small force to guard the citadel. In his place, Bishop Adhemar of Le Puy, the papal legate, commanded the Provencal division. A second force, of men from northern France, was under the joint command of Duke Hugh of Vermandois, Count Robert of Flanders and Duke Robert of Normandy, while Duke Godfrey of Lorraine led a third. Prince Bohemond remained behind, in command of the reserve.

The Crusaders were allowed to leave the city unopposed, exiting from the Bridge

This fifteenth-century illustration presents late medieval stereotypes about Muslim–Christian engagements. In reality, the Crusaders had very few cavalry at Antioch – and the Turks did not collect their enemies' heads.

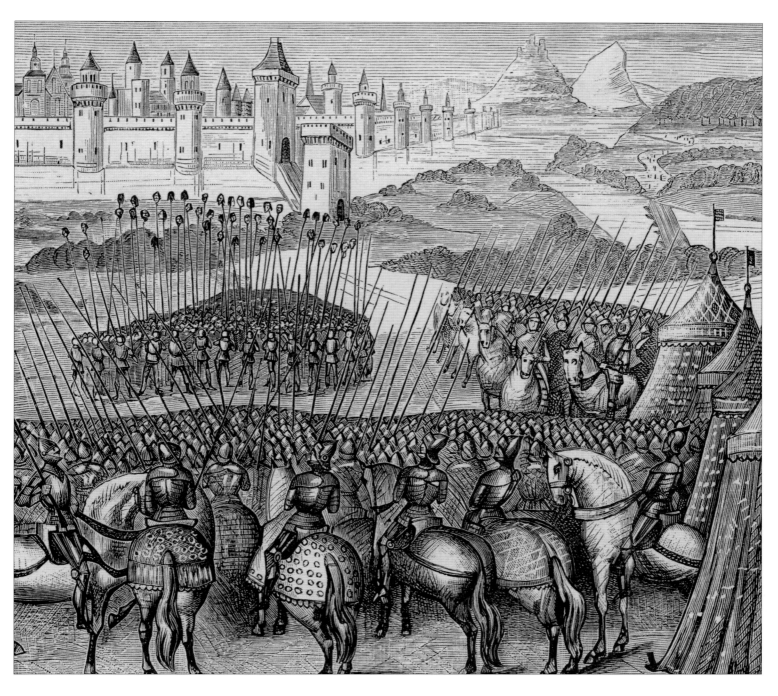

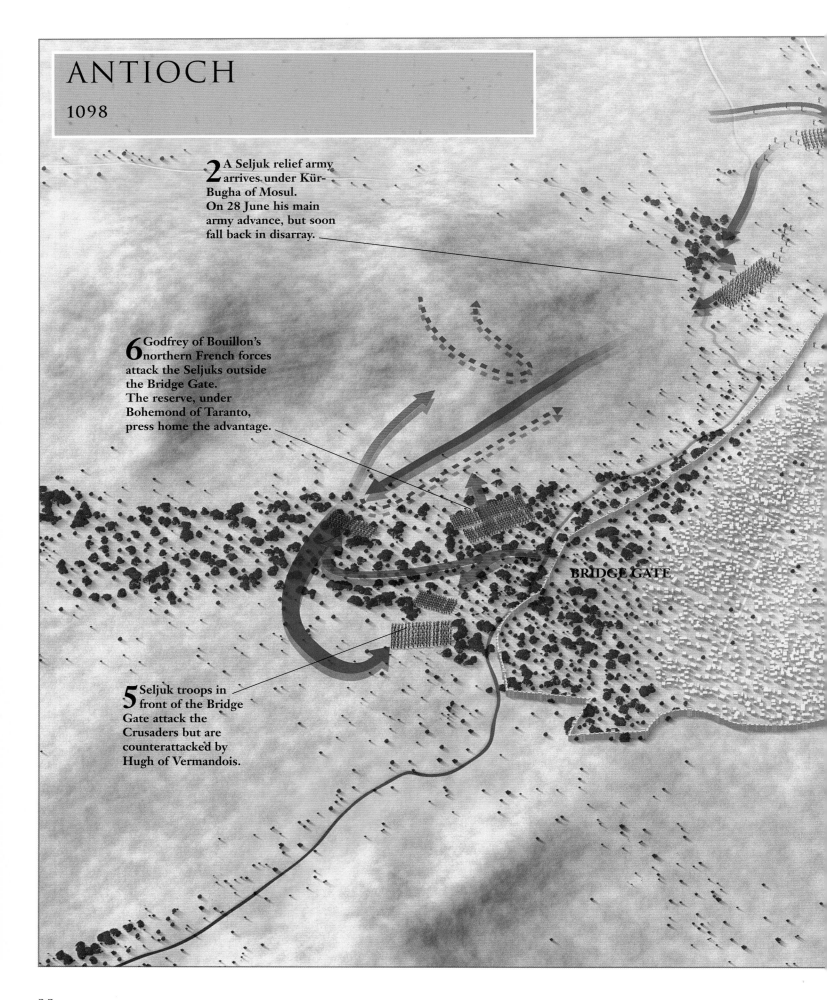

ANTIOCH
1098

2 A Seljuk relief army arrives under Kür-Bugha of Mosul. On 28 June his main army advance, but soon fall back in disarray.

6 Godfrey of Bouillon's northern French forces attack the Seljuks outside the Bridge Gate. The reserve, under Bohemond of Taranto, press home the advantage.

5 Seljuk troops in front of the Bridge Gate attack the Crusaders but are counterattacked by Hugh of Vermandois.

BRIDGE GATE

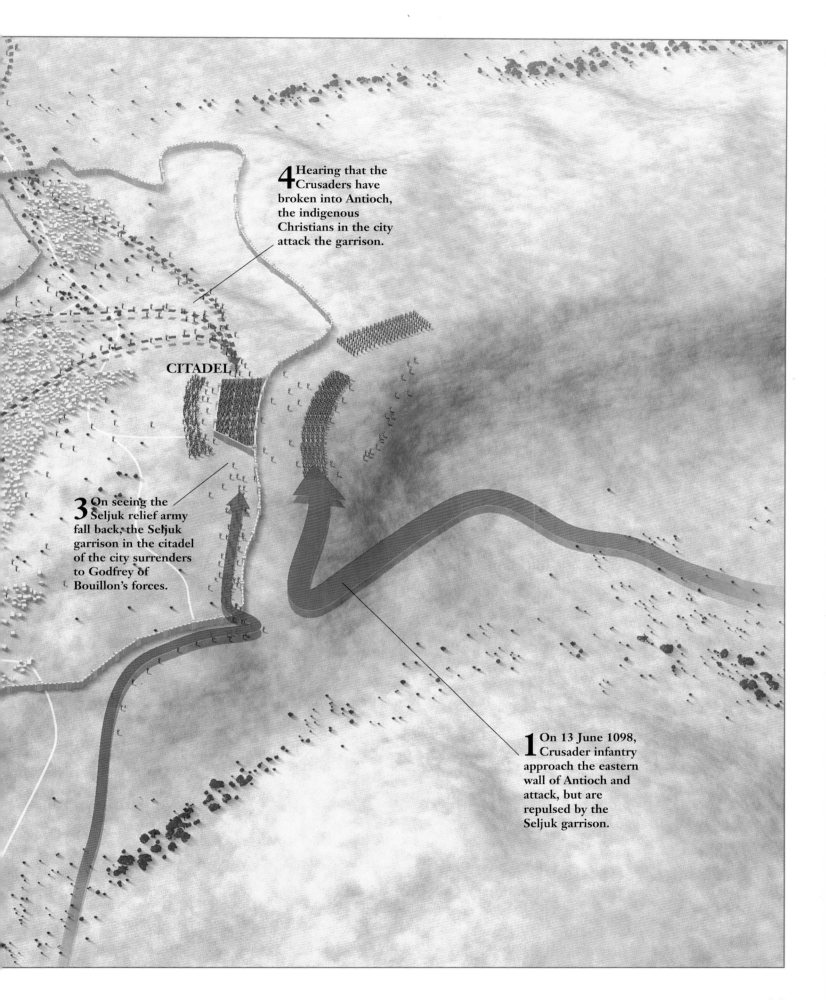

4 Hearing that the Crusaders have broken into Antioch, the indigenous Christians in the city attack the garrison.

CITADEL

3 On seeing the Seljuk relief army fall back, the Seljuk garrison in the citadel of the city surrenders to Godfrey of Bouillon's forces.

1 On 13 June 1098, Crusader infantry approach the eastern wall of Antioch and attack, but are repulsed by the Seljuk garrison.

Gate to the southwest, well away from Kerbogah's main camp. Two thousand Turcoman mounted bowmen did, in fact, approach the Bridge Gate as it opened, apparently to stop the Crusader breakout, but the Crusaders had placed a force of bowmen at the head of their column. The Crusader archers began to shoot at the Turcoman horses and the enemy quickly withdrew.

Except for Adhemar's Provencal force, each Crusader contingent turned right after crossing the bridge just outside of the city, marching quickly along the bank of the Orontes River, which thus protected their right flank. The Turkish infantry force posted outside of the Bridge Gate quickly engaged the Crusaders, but in a piecemeal fashion. Thus the northern French force was able to hold its position until Godfrey's Lotharingians joined the column to their left.

Meanwhile, the Provencal army, as it left the city, marched directly towards the mountains about 3km (2 miles) away. As with the main Crusader force, infantry were thrown out in front to screen the precious cavalry. Adhemar's troops had the riskiest position, since they had to pass through open terrain. Indeed, many of the small Turkish bands hurrying towards the battle were lured aside to attack the Provencals. Whether intentional or not, this meant that the Turkish cavalry units that made it to the battlefield threw away their attacks on the smaller Crusader force, instead of supporting their infantry along the river. The Provencals were placed in extreme danger, encircled by a much larger enemy force. But the Crusaders under Bohemond's overall leadership had the experience and dedication to face the threat. The northern French contingent, although heavily engaged at the river, improvised an infantry force, which was despatched to fight off the Turks attacking Adhemar's rear. This force was apparently completely annihilated, but Bohemond seems at this stage to have added his support, and Adhemar's contingent was able to reach the safety of the mountain ridge. His men then turned and charged their attackers, driving them off.

By reaching their assigned position, the Provencal force had succeeded in creating a tactical nightmare for Kerbogah's army.

Kerbogah had already committed serious errors by placing his main force so far from the city, by posting few cavalrymen among the forces assigned to guard the various gates, and by allowing units of his army to enter the battle one by one, without any coherent plan. The position of Adhemar's force, however, was key to the Crusader

The Christian forces of the First Crusade and their enemies used a wide array of stone-throwing devices, such as this simple petraria, a torsion catapult that depended on tightly coiled ropes for thrust.

victory. Kerbogah's main force finally reached the battlefield on the left of the northern French army along the river. They could not engage in support of the retreating Turks, though, because of Adhemar's presence nearby. If Kerbogah advanced, the Provencals were now in perfect position to threaten the unprotected Turkish right wing.

Kerbogah appears to have hesitated, perhaps not trusting his allies to cooperate under these adverse battlefield conditions. As he delayed, he received word that the Crusaders had taken possession of the Turkish camp above the Bridge Gate. At that point, Kerbogah decided to withdraw, both from Antioch and from the whole

In this fourteenth-century illustration of the Battle of Antioch, the European artist has imagined Turks fighting much like western knights, distinguishable only by their turbans and outlandish shields.

ANTIOCH

If they failed to defeat the Turks, the crusaders could expect to be massacred, as they had massacred the populace of Antioch. This 1875 engraving by Gustav Doré captures the plight of the Antiochenes.

Battering rams, as in this illustration, were not very effective against cities as strong as Antioch, and neither the crusaders nor the Muslims tried to take the city by assault.

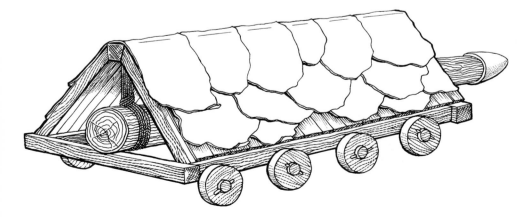

region. His retreat allowed the Crusaders to slaughter the Turkish camp followers, and they also annihilated the one Muslim division that had fully engaged them; the force set to guard the Gate Bridge. Some horsemen escaped, since the Crusaders had no cavalry capable of a pursuit, but Turkish infantry casualties were very heavy. The main Turkish force never even reached the Crusaders, and the force that withdrew at Kerbogah's command still massively outnumbered them.

LESSONS OF THE BATTLE

The battle of Antioch was a major Crusader victory, without which the armies of the First Crusade would not have survived, much less have reached Jerusalem. Thanks to their triumph, the Crusaders were able to re-open the route to their supply port, and to rest and recover from the gruelling siege and its aftermath. Since Kerbogah's force withdrew completely, they were also able to consolidate their position in Antioch and the surrounding countryside.

The battle also teaches us important lessons about the nature of the Muslim forces, in this case Turkish and Syrian, that faced the Crusader forces in the late eleventh century. Kerbogah's men were in no way inferior to the Crusaders in fighting ability or armament. Part of his cavalry force consisted of lightly armed mounted archers, but others were armoured spearmen who were comparable to the Crusader knights.

Similarly, the infantry of the two opposing forces were not radically different from each other. It was far easier for the Muslims than the Christians to supply themselves, and the Muslim armies far outnumbered the forces of their Christian enemies. Why, then, did Kerbogah suffer this embarrassing defeat outside the walls of Antioch?

From the Muslim perspective, attacking the Crusaders was not necessarily a high priority. Kerbogah had the support of a number of temporary allies, some of them traditional enemies and all of them looking towards future advantages in Muslim internal politics. They did not trust each other, and they were not comfortable under Kerbogah's leadership,

a situation that had a profound impact on what Kerbogah could do with the force putatively under his command. For many Muslims, the Crusade was simply a peripheral issue, and although the military ability was there, it seems fair to assert that the political will was not.

From the Crusader perspective, the battle of Antioch is also very revealing. To be sure, the Crusaders were trapped in a desperate situation, one in which they had two choices: they must win or die. Such situations can often evoke either miracles of courage or a catastrophic, panicked shambles. The Crusaders' ability to transform their plight into victory attests to their courage and dedication to their cause, but it also shows clearly how deeply professional the First Crusade army had become by 1098.

The leaders worked extremely well together to carry out a complex plan to perfection. At critical moments, subordinate leaders held their contingents together, and even inspired the necessary men to undertake a suicide mission to protect Adhemar's flank movement. By the time they fought the battle of Antioch, the Crusaders had already survived a major battle and countless lesser skirmishes. They were a well-led, experienced and highly professional fighting force.

Following the battle of Antioch, the Crusader army moved south and captured Jerusalem the following year. Tripoli, which had been bypassed in the Crusaders' desire to capture the Holy City, now became a target for Raymond of Toulouse. The siege of Tripoli lasted from 1102 until 1109, and led to the establishment of the Fourth Crusader state, the County of Tripoli.

JERUSALEM
1099

ON 15 JULY 1099, THE FIRST CRUSADE REACHED ITS ULTIMATE GOAL – THE CHURCH OF THE HOLY SEPULCHRE – BUT ONLY AFTER A BLOODY ASSAULT THAT SHOWED YET AGAIN THE VERSATILITY, MILITARY SKILL, AND PERSEVERANCE OF THE CRUSADER FORCES.

WHY DID IT HAPPEN?

WHO The remnants of the Christian armies of the First Crusade fought the Fatimid Egyptian garrison of Jerusalem, under the command of the governor Iftikhar-ad-Daulah.

WHAT In an extended and hard-fought assault, the Crusaders broke into Jerusalem and claimed it as Christian territory.

WHERE Jerusalem.

WHEN 13–15 July 1099.

WHY By 1099 the whole focus of the First Crusade had been the conquest of the city of Jerusalem, to regain the city of Christ's death and resurrection as the natural and God-given possession of Christendom.

OUTCOME The Crusaders took the city and established a Christian state with Jerusalem as its capital, electing Duke Godfrey of Lorraine as 'advocate' of the Holy Sepulchre.

It took a very long time for the Christian forces of the First Crusade to reach Jerusalem, their ultimate goal. While the Crusaders were still at Antioch, far to the north, another army had conquered Jerusalem – that of the Egyptian Fatimid Caliphate, a Shi'ite state that had long fought the Turks for control of Palestine. The Fatimid vizier of Egypt almost immediately opened negotiations with the leaders of the Christian army, apparently believing that the Crusaders were mostly concerned with halting Turkish aggression and territorial gain. Some of the Crusade leaders were indeed content to secure territories such as Antioch and Edessa, and lent the Fatimids a willing ear. It took a near revolt by the Crusader rank and file to force

the army back onto the road towards Jerusalem. The renewal of the march apparently took the Fatimids by surprise. Their recently gained territory was unprepared for war, with small garrisons that could not hope to keep out the Crusaders.

Thus the Crusaders' march south was largely peaceful. Some Fatimid cities on the coast negotiated free passage for the Crusaders; others, resenting Fatimid encroachment, even promised to accept Crusader overlordship – if the Crusaders succeeded in conquering Egypt. The major port of Jaffa was completely abandoned before the Crusaders got there, its walls slighted so the Crusaders could not use them for defence.

The Citadel of Jerusalem that can be seen today was built in the sixteenth century. A citadel has stood on this site, however, since the period of the ancient Israelite monarchy.

Jerusalem itself was only moderately ready to withstand a siege. The Fatimids had apparently repaired the walls after their seizure of the city in August 1098. The garrison, however, does not appear to have been large, although extant sources give us little clue of its size. We know it was a mixed force; Crusader accounts mention especially the presence of Ethiopian troops. At the last minute, the Fatimid vizier sent 400 elite cavalry to reinforce the defenders. It is unlikely that the garrison numbered more than 2000–3000. The Fatimid governor, Iftikhar-ad-Daulah, made no effort to weaken the Crusader army with sallies before the assault. After the assault, he retreated to the citadel but surrendered almost immediately, suggesting that at least by that point in the battle he did not have sufficient manpower to put up an effective fight. The fear of internal treachery also led the governor to expel most of the Christian population from the city, lest one of them open the city to their co-religionists, as had happened at Antioch.

PREPARING TO ATTACK

The Crusader army reached Jerusalem on 7 June 1099, walking barefoot as penitents and overcome with joy at the sight of the holy city. Almost immediately, the council of Crusade leaders planned an assault. They had good reason to hurry. Not only were the Crusaders eager to reach the city, which most of them had spent three years of their lives to gain, but once again the Crusaders were in a desperate situation. They were far from any Christian assistance. Food supplies were adequate, but the only reliable water source was over 2km (1.3 miles) away from the Crusader camps.

Worst of all, the Crusaders intercepted messengers who revealed (under torture) that a large Egyptian relief force was on its way to Jerusalem. A siege was simply not an option. The Crusaders did not have time for such a measure, and could not even fully invest the city for fear of sudden surprise assaults from the defenders if they split up their forces into small groups. Instead, the Christians concentrated their forces near Jerusalem's western walls, the northern French forces to the north and Raymond of Toulouse's Provencals further south.

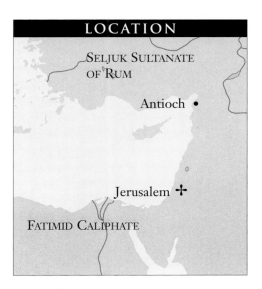

CRUSADER KNIGHT
(11TH CENTURY)
By the time of the Battle of Jerusalem, few Crusader knights had horses. Unlike later medieval knights, though, their equipment was also well suited to dismounted fighting. The chain mail hauberk weighed about 18kg (40lb), while the open helmet allowed for clear vision. The kite-shaped shield could provide good protection for infantry as well as cavalry fighting, and the average sword, 80cm (32in) in length, was not long enough to trip the dismounted knight. This knight is armed with a two-handed battle axe, which became popular amongst the Anglo-Normans and Northern French knights after the Norman conquest of England in 1066.

Raymond soon decided that the section of defences he faced was too strong to penetrate, and moved to the southwest corner of the city, despite the objections of many of his own men.

The Crusaders attempted an escalade on 13 June. Apparently, the Crusade leaders, who had quarrelled seriously ever since Antioch, disagreed on this approach, and Count Raymond of Toulouse and his Provencal army did not take part in the assault at all. The attack was pitiful. The Crusader assault was spirited but, unable to find much wood for siege equipment, they had only a single scaling ladder. Despite their best efforts, the attacking Christians were soon driven off.

Clearly, the city would not fall without proper siege equipment, but finding the heavy timber and necessary expertise was a serious problem – until a fleet of six Italian

LOCATION

SELJUK SULTANATE OF RUM

Antioch •

Jerusalem ✝

FATIMID CALIPHATE

To reach Jerusalem, the first Crusaders had to pass through the Sultanate of Rum in Asia Minor, then march down the coastal road via Antioch. Jerusalem itself is well inland.

JERUSALEM

The crusaders used siege engines like this traction trebuchet in their attack on Jerusalem. A team of men would heave the ropes together on command, making the bowl with its ammunition shoot upwards.

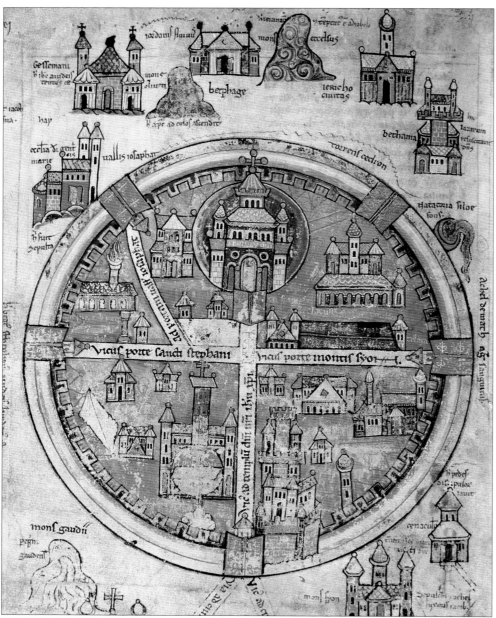

In this medieval map of Jerusalem, from Robert the Monk's chronicle of the First Crusade, Jerusalem is a microcosm of the world as medieval geographers perceived it.

ships arrived at Jaffa on 17 June, carrying supplies and the vital timber. The Crusaders sent a large force to protect the sailors in the devastated port, only to be ambushed while on their way to the coast. The fleet itself was trapped in the harbour by an Egyptian fleet. So the sailors burned five of their ships (one escaped to the open sea), then marched to the Crusader camp outside Jerusalem with their large supply train.

The sailors included expert woodworkers; Count Raymond hired a Genoese craftsman to build him a siege tower. With wood and workers now available, the Crusaders began to prepare for a fresh assault. They built two siege towers, one in the northern French camp to the north of the city, and one in the Provencal camp to the south; the northern French also constructed a very large ram, suspended in a framework that was moved on rollers or wheels. The Crusaders also constructed many more assault ladders and a number of mangonels and other stone- and bolt-throwing devices. They also made smaller siege equipment such as mantlets to protect the men dragging the towers and ram up to the walls. To complete their preparations, on 8 July the Crusaders conducted a penitential procession around the walls of Jerusalem, culminating in sermons on the Mount of Olives. Their leaders managed at least a superficial reconciliation on this occasion.

THE BATTLE

The Crusaders made two largely independent assaults on Jerusalem, one by the northern French army (commanded by Duke Godfrey of Lorraine, Tancred, Duke Robert of Normandy and Hugh of Vermandois) and one by the Provencals under Count Raymond. While this may have been a purposeful tactic to weaken the garrison by forcing them to fight at two widely separated points, Crusade chronicles suggest that the immediate reason was Count Raymond's ongoing quarrel with the northern French leaders.

The first stages of the assault began on 9 July with the long, dangerous process of levelling ground and filling in the ditch before the walls so that the siege equipment could be moved in close enough. The process was straightforward for the southern army, but in the north, however,

the Crusade leaders made a move that caught the defenders by surprise. On the night of 9–10 July they partially disassembled the siege tower that had been built in Duke Godfrey's camp, and moved it about 1km (0.6 miles) further north, positioning it to assault the wall about 100m (300 feet) from Herod's Gate. The defenders had been strengthening the defences closest to the site where the siege tower was being built, but had no time to do the same at the new position. After moving the tower, the northern Crusaders proceeded to fill in the ditch and level the ground, then set up their siege tower, ram and three mangonels.

The assault proper commenced on Wednesday 13 July at the north of the city. Jerusalem's defences here consisted of a forewall and a wider, higher inner wall; the battle on 13 and 14 July was for control of the forewall. The French Crusaders brought their ram up to the wall, with the defenders trying to stop them with a barrage of missiles. By aiming their mangonels at the troops on the walls, the Crusaders were also able to inflict serious

This fourteenth-century illustration shows Godfrey of Lorraine, after he has become ruler of Jerusalem, commanding a siege. In reality, bowmen at ground level would have been at a serious disadvantage against a city's defenders.

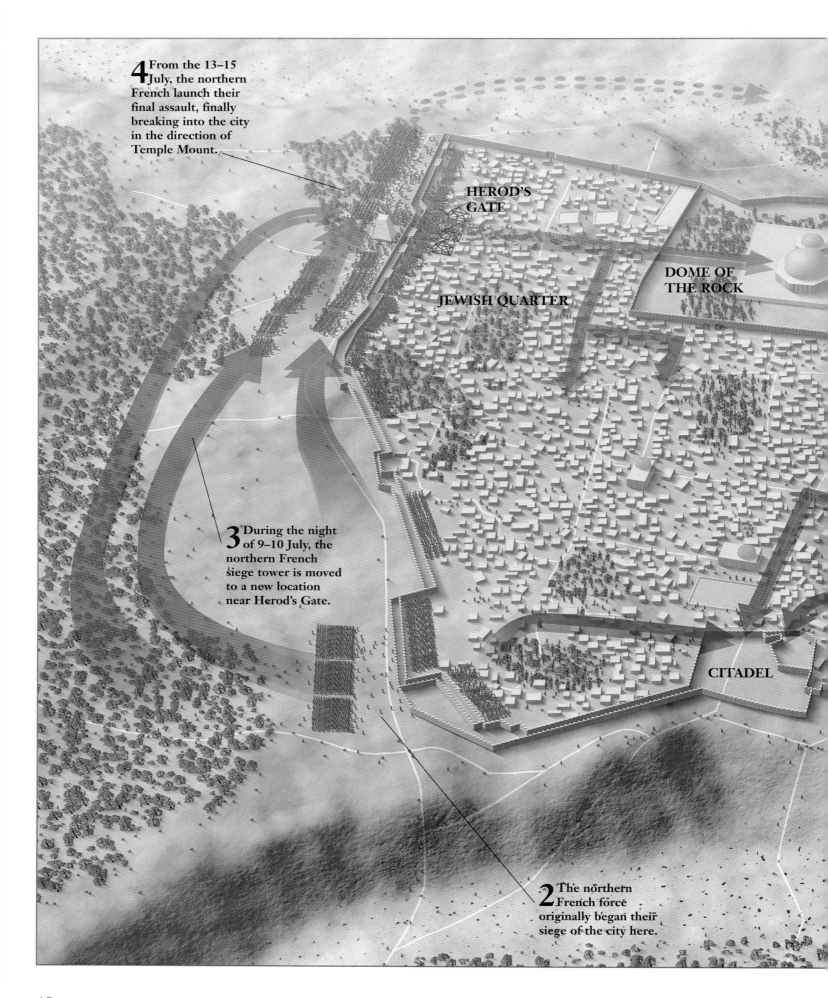

4 From the 13–15 July, the northern French launch their final assault, finally breaking into the city in the direction of Temple Mount.

HEROD'S GATE

DOME OF THE ROCK

JEWISH QUARTER

3 During the night of 9–10 July, the northern French siege tower is moved to a new location near Herod's Gate.

CITADEL

2 The northern French force originally began their siege of the city here.

JERUSALEM
1099

1 Route of crusader penitential procession on 8 July, ending at the Mount of Olives.

6 As word spreads that the crusaders have broken into the city, the Fatimid garrison flees to the citadel, where they are trapped and eventually slaughtered.

SIEGE ARTILLERY

ZION GATE

5 A second assault comes from the other side of the city from the Provençal troops, led by Count Raymond of Toulouse.

JERUSALEM

damage on the Muslims. As the Crusaders positioned the ram at the foot of the wall, the enemy worked desperately to burn it, with flaming arrows, fire pots and even Greek fire, while the Crusaders expended much of their precious water to protect it. Despite the defenders' efforts, the men operating the ram succeeded in bringing down a portion of the outer wall.

The inner wall was apparently too strong for the ram, and the space was very narrow, causing the ram itself to block the progress of the siege tower. So the Christians now set the ram alight themselves, while the defenders desperately tried to put out the flames. When the ram was finally destroyed, the Crusaders were able to move their siege tower close to the inner wall. The tower was a massive structure, standing about 15–17m (49–56ft)

high and looming above the wall. As was usual in such situations, the tower's purpose was to act as a platform for firing down on the wall's defenders, thus making it possible for other attackers to raise siege ladders and climb the walls in relative safety. The Muslim soldiers were well aware of their danger and aimed a large number of mangonels against the tower, but the Crusaders had covered the structure with woven osiers to buffer it from the shock of stones striking; they had also covered it with wet hides so that the defenders could not set it alight. As the tower reached the wall, the defenders even tried to tip it over, swinging a heavy beam against it that they had suspended with ropes between two of the wall's towers; the Crusaders, however, succeeded in cutting the ropes that supported the beam, using blades attached to long poles for the purpose.

Duke Godfrey and his brother Eustace commanded from the top of the siege tower, showing how much the Crusader plan depended on it. In its shadow, forces still on the ground were able to bring up a number of ladders. More unusually, some men in the siege tower also got onto the wall, climbing over on a tree trunk. Once on the walls, the Crusaders spread out, some of them opening the Josaphat Gate some distance to the east to admit their compatriots.

THE SOUTHERN ASSAULT

While the northern assault had the advantage of surprise over enemies who did not have time to reinforce the walls there, the southern assault, led by Raymond of Toulouse, had been forced to prepare in full sight of the enemy. While the northerners fought for the forewall on their side of the city, the Provencals continued to fill in the ditch before the southern wall, a necessary step before moving their siege tower forward. Their main defence against missiles from the walls would have been large shields made of woven branches. The defenders fought with fire, to very good effect. When, on the morning of 15 July, the Christians brought their petrariae (large stone-slinging engines) forward, the enemy made fireballs of fat, hair and other combustibles, and launched them against the Crusader machines, succeeding in

Joseph-François Michaud's 1875 History of the Crusades *idolized Duke Godfrey of Lorraine. In this illustration from Michaud's history, by Gustav Doré, Godfrey is shown leading his troops into the city.*

This illustration by M Meredith Williams (1910) shows the men from Duke Godfrey's siege tower battling their way onto the wall of Jerusalem, as their comrades mount scaling ladders.

Below: This simple mangonel was operated by torsion: the arm was pulled against the resistance of tightly coiled rope, which launched the missile when the arm was released.

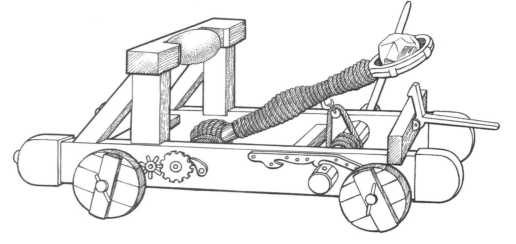

causing major fires in Raymond's camp. Unlike the defenders to the north of the city, they also succeeded in damaging Raymond's siege tower so badly that it could not be brought up to the wall.

The Provencal assault was flagging badly when word arrived that the northern attack was succeeding. The Provencals then launched a mad scramble for the wall with ladders and ropes, and they too succeeded in winning their way into the city. The surviving members of the garrison retreated before the Crusaders into the citadel, but

JERUSALEM

This nineteenth-century illustration catches both the beauty and the ugliness of Jerusalem's conquest: the ordered procession to the left contrasts starkly with the savagery of the soldiers who have just finished a massacre within the walls.

surrendered almost immediately when Raymond promised to protect them.

THE AFTERMATH

The battle was effectively over at that point. The Crusaders swept into the town and began an orgy of killing and looting. That in itself was typical when an army took a city by assault. Much of the native population in fact survived the initial Crusader onslaught – but three days later, the Crusader leaders ordered the massacre of all prisoners. The reason was simple: an Egyptian army was on its way, and the council of leaders determined to meet the enemy outside of the city. They simply could not leave a large number of enemies and potential enemies behind them in the newly conquered city. This logic, however, does not explain the slaughter of women and children as well as

adult men. Before leaving the city for Ascalon, where the Crusaders fought their last battle, the leaders had make an important decision: now that the holiest of cities was in Christian hands, who would rule and protect it? The churchmen argued that the first step should be the choice of a Latin patriarch.

The secular leaders, however, overrode them, deciding that one of their own should be the effective ruler: Godfrey of Bouillon, Duke of Lorraine. Godfrey refused to be crowned king of the place where Christ was crowned with thorns, but accepted the title 'advocate' of the Holy Sepulchre. Thus was established the Latin kingdom of Jerusalem (Godfrey's successor did not feel the same qualms about being named king), the focal point of Muslim–Christian struggle for the next two centuries.

Opposite: This Gustav Doré illustration (1875) is an imaginative re-creation of the siege engines employed at Jerusalem. Although inaccurate in details, it gives a good impression of the scale of the enterprise.

ASCALON
1099

IN MAY 1099 THE ULTIMATE OBJECTIVE OF THE CRUSADERS WAS IN SIGHT. IN THE PREVIOUS YEAR, THE CRUSADERS HAD WON SOME SIGNIFICANT VICTORIES, INCLUDING THE CAPTURE OF ANTIOCH AND THE SUBSEQUENT DEFEAT OF A LARGE TURKISH ARMY IN JUNE. AFTER CONSOLIDATING THEIR POSITIONS IN NORTH SYRIA, THE CRUSADERS WERE NOW POISED TO STRIKE AT JERUSALEM.

WHY DID IT HAPPEN?

WHO A Crusader army of 9000 foot and 1200 knights led by Raymond of Toulouse, Godfrey de Bouillon and Tancred faced Fatimid Egypt's and Vizier al-Afdal's force of perhaps 20,000 men.

WHAT The Crusaders, upon learning of the arrival of the Egyptian army at Ascalon, left Jerusalem and moved to attack the Fatimid forces in their camp outside of Ascalon.

WHERE Just north of the port town of Ascalon, some 80km (50 miles) west of Jerusalem.

WHEN 12 August 1099.

WHY The Crusaders had recently captured Jerusalem from the Fatimids after a five-week siege. The Fatimids, unable to lift the siege, sent an army to drive the Crusaders from the city. Rather than be besieged in turn, the Crusaders marched out and surprised the Egyptians at Ascalon.

OUTCOME The Egyptians, caught out by the speed of the Crusader advance, were poorly coordinated. The Crusaders routed the enemy field army, but were unable to capture Ascalon itself.

The army was well placed to make its final push, although there were a number of factors that left the Crusaders in a very difficult position. One was the attrition incurred during the campaigns fought in North Syria. The Crusader army had dwindled to perhaps fewer than 15,000 trained fighting men, including no more than about 1500 mounted knights. There had also been casualties amongst the Crusader leaders, the most notable being the death of the senior clergyman on the expedition, the Papal legate Bishop Adhemar of Le Puy. His loss meant that there was no churchman of sufficient standing to keep the princes working together and focused on the objectives put forth by Pope Urban II.

As a result, the natural rivalries between the Crusade leaders were free to play themselves out, to the detriment of their military situation. One of the most serious emerged in the wake of the Christian victory at Antioch, where Prince Bohemond had secretly arranged for the capture of the city and thus claimed it for himself when it was taken. This caused major difficulties for the Crusaders.

This later depiction of the battle shows the Crusaders as fifteenth-century French knights and footmen, equipped with much heavier armour than their counterparts in the First Crusade. The illustration does, however, seem to depict the state of the battle when the Crusader cavalry complete the rout of the Egyptian foot soldiers.

FATIMID MILITIAMAN

By the time of the First Crusade, the Fatimid Egyptians had suffered a military decline but they nonetheless possessed a relatively large military force. The heart of the Fatimid armed forces was a large body of infantry armed with spears (as shown here) bows or even flails. The infantry came from a variety of peoples including Berbers and other north Africans, Armenians, Ethiopians and Daylami tribesmen. These were supported by Arab and Berber light cavalry as well as more heavily armoured horsemen, with both man and horse protected. The units of the army were organized into units based on ethnicity and divided into companies of 100 men.

The first problem was that it abrogated the terms of the treaty that the Crusaders had brokered with the Byzantine Emperor Alexius I. Bohemond's justification was that the Byzantines, who did not send any troops to aid the Crusaders during some of the more dangerous times at Antioch, had withdrawn their support and thus deserted the Crusade – thereby no longer being worthy of the vows taken by the Crusader leaders. Whatever his justification, Bohemond's actions ensured that there would no longer be any aid for the Crusader army from the Emperor Alexius.

The second problem caused by Bohemond's seizure of the city was the discontent it caused among the other princes, in particular with Raymond, the Count of Toulouse. The Crusade's leaders seemed more concerned with their own internecine quarrels than pursuing the quest to liberate Jerusalem, and rifts were growing between them and the rank and file of the army, who were still very much driven by the desire to liberate the city.

The first several months of 1099 saw a distinct absence of purpose among the various Crusader contingents. But by early spring, Raymond of Toulouse, who now fancied himself as the Crusade leader, garnered considerable support from the commoners in the army for an advance into Palestine. He was also able to reconcile two other key leaders in Godfrey de Bouillon and Tancred and join their forces to his own – in part, at least, owing to the growing support for Raymond's plans among their own followers. The tables were turned on Raymond in May while he laid siege to Akkar, when Godfrey and Tancred forced him to abandon the operation as they left and advanced towards Tripoli. At this point the Count of Toulouse faced the erosion of his own forces as his men left to follow the rest of the army towards Jerusalem.

These events had shown a serious weakness in the Christian army, namely, that there was no cohesive leadership. Without the influence and authority of someone like Adhemar of Le Puy, individual princes jostled for position, with any one leader only able to assert himself for a brief time at best.

THE CAMPAIGN

The Crusaders' earlier successes in Anatolia and North Syria had weakened the Turks to the extent that the Fatimids in Egypt were able to take the advantage by capturing and occupying Jerusalem. The Fatimid Egyptians and Crusaders would both benefit from the defeat of the Turks, so had engaged in diplomacy to this end. It was clear, however, that once the Fatimids occupied Jerusalem that any settlement was now no longer acceptable, at least to the Crusaders. But a conflict with Fatimid Egypt posed serious problems for the

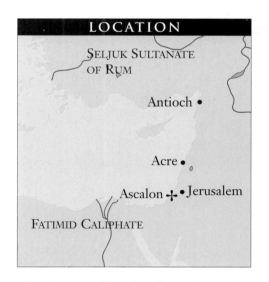

LOCATION

SELJUK SULTANATE OF RUM

Antioch •

Acre •

Ascalon ✛ •Jerusalem

FATIMID CALIPHATE

After the capture of Jerusalem, the crusaders, fearing the arrival of a large Egyptian army at Ascalon, decided to attack the strategically located port rather than allow themselves to be besieged in Jerusalem, since the city's supplies had been exhausted by their own siege.

This gold and enamel reliquary cross (reverse side open), is Byzantine, and dates from the early eleventh century. The cross is hinged at the top and bottom; the cap on one end of the top hinge unscrews so that the two sides can be opened to reveal a relic; it, possibly, once contained a fragment from the True Cross. The reverse depicts the Virgin Mary standing with her hands before her chest in an attitude of prayer. To her right is a bust of St Basil the Great and to the left a bust of St Gregory Thaumaturgus.

miles) from Jerusalem, they had the opportunity to move quickly before the Fatimids could react. While the Egyptians had a garrison in the city, it was not large, consisting of some regular Fatimid troops, most likely infantry, including at least some Ethiopians, and supported by locally raised militia. A body of 400 cavalry had been sent by the Vizier al-Afdal to bolster the garrison, but this seems to have been the limit of available forces. The real relief army had to be raised in Egypt and that would take time, since although there was a sizable force kept in the capital, troops also needed to be recalled from scattered outposts. Therefore, if the Crusaders could move quickly, they could reach Jerusalem long before the arrival of a relief force.

The Crusaders took advantage of this and moved from Tripoli to Jerusalem by the coastal road in just over three weeks, approaching the city on 7 June. The Crusaders were fortunate in that the Fatimid forces in Jerusalem did nothing to impede them during their advance along the coast. This was no doubt due in part to the Egyptian garrison's relatively small size – few troops could be spared for such harrying operations. The arrival at Jerusalem was an important moment for the Crusaders and the culmination of an expedition that had begun almost three years earlier. With the final goal in sight, their morale was high.

THE ATTACK ON JERUSALEM

As they invested the city, the Christians captured messengers sent to the garrison promising the arrival of aid in short order. Given the army's jubilant mood and the possibility of such a relief force, the princes quickly organized for a direct assault. This hasty attack was launched on 13 June, less than a week after their arrival, but it was not well planned or supported. For example, due to a shortage of available wood, there was but a single siege ladder ready; as a result, the attack was easily repulsed.

The Crusaders began to invest the city but found themselves faced with some serious problems. Their army was too small to completely surround the city. This was exacerbated by the squabbling among the leaders, which led to the army deploying

princes. The Fatimids, although no longer at the apogee of their power, were a formidable force with a large and powerful standing army. Moreover, their army was also a sophisticated military machine that included heavily armoured horsemen, light cavalry and a variety of infantrymen including archers, spearmen and Azoparts (Ethiopians equipped with heavy flails).

The Crusaders had little hope of support now that the alliance with the Byzantines had been broken, but they did, however, have the advantage of strategic surprise. The Fatimids had such an advantage of strength and position that the Crusaders' rejection of a diplomatic settlement was unexpected. Given that the Crusaders had all of their forces concentrated at Tripoli, some 354 km (220

THE OPPOSED FORCES

CRUSADERS (estimated)

Knights/Men-at-Arms:	1200
Infantry:	9000
Total:	**10,200**

FATIMIDS (estimated)

Cavalry:	5000
Infantry:	15,000
Total:	**20,000**

into what was in effect two separate forces. The north French under Godfrey, Robert of Flanders and Tancred formed along the city's north wall, while the Provencals under Count Raymond camped under the city's southern defences.

The Christian forces spent the next three weeks or so preparing for another assault. There was still a sense of urgency given the imminent arrival of a Fatimid army, so the Crusaders quickly built ladders and siege engines, including two large towers, as well as mangonels to clear the defenders from the walls. The assault began on 13 July and continued for the next two days. Eventually, the Crusaders breached the walls and rampaged through the city, slaughtering the defenders. Those that survived were massacred on 17 June, when the Crusaders killed all Muslims remaining in Jerusalem.

CRUSADER ARGUMENTS

The Crusader victory was further diminished by the infighting that broke out in the wake of Jerusalem's capture. Numerous issues divided the Crusaders, including how the city would be ruled, who

CAMP FOLLOWERS

Every Crusader army on the move had with them numerous camp followers and pilgrims, often to provide for the needs of the knights and men-at-arms, who needed cooks, cobblers, blacksmiths, farriers and shepherds to look after any livestock. Although lightly armoured and armed, these men proved extremely useful in combat, since many were highly skilled slingers who had honed thier expertise since childhood. They were often employed to see off enemy skirmishing cavalry and could also provide an accurate volley of fire at the commencement of a battle or siege.

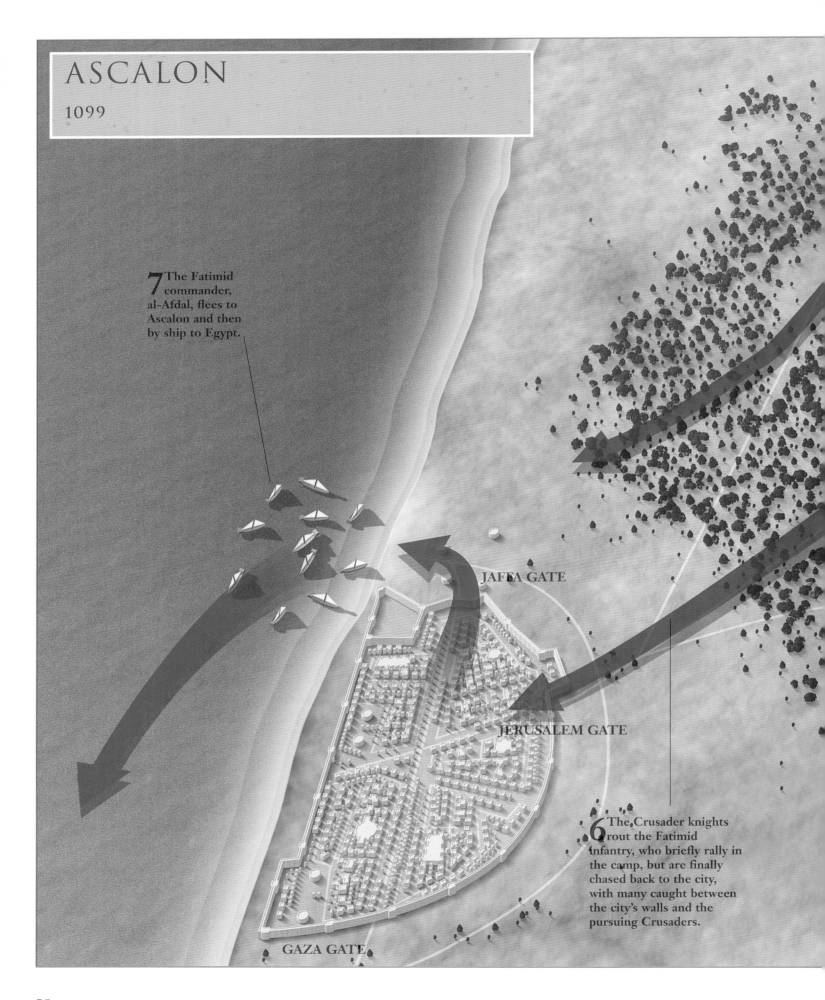

ASCALON

1099

7 The Fatimid commander, al-Afdal, flees to Ascalon and then by ship to Egypt.

JAFFA GATE

JERUSALEM GATE

6 The Crusader knights rout the Fatimid infantry, who briefly rally in the camp, but are finally chased back to the city, with many caught between the city's walls and the pursuing Crusaders.

GAZA GATE

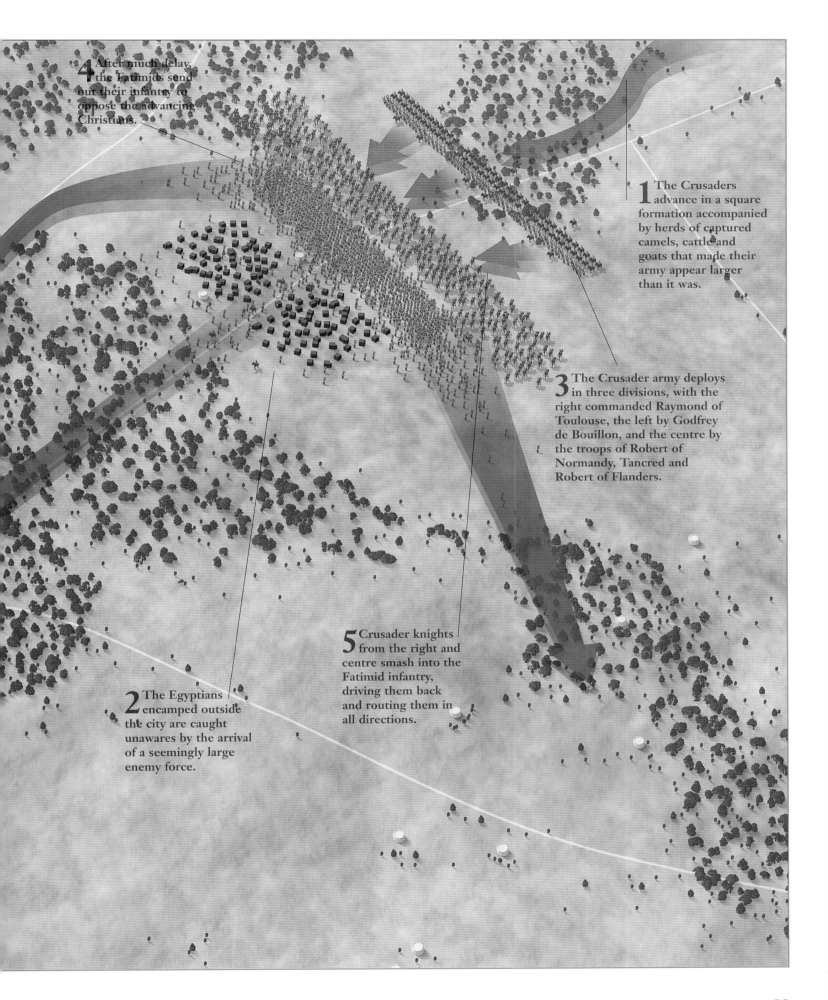

4 After much delay, the Fatimids send out their infantry to oppose the advancing Christians.

1 The Crusaders advance in a square formation accompanied by herds of captured camels, cattle and goats that made their army appear larger than it was.

3 The Crusader army deploys in three divisions, with the right commanded Raymond of Toulouse, the left by Godfrey de Bouillon, and the centre by the troops of Robert of Normandy, Tancred and Robert of Flanders.

2 The Egyptians encamped outside the city are caught unawares by the arrival of a seemingly large enemy force.

5 Crusader knights from the right and centre smash into the Fatimid infantry, driving them back and routing them in all directions.

Opposite: This wooden engraving from the late fifteenth century depicts Godfrey of Bouillon, ruler of Jerusalem from 1099 to 1100. He is symbolically crowned with relics from the Passion of Christ: the crown of thorns, the cross and the whip.

would serve as Patriarch, and who would control key fortifications. Tensions between the army's two major leaders continued to grow when Raymond of Toulouse was offered the crown. He refused and Godfrey was instead named Jerusalem's 'Advocate'.

In the midst of this internal strife, the Fatimid forces established themselves in the port city of Ascalon, some 80km (50 miles) to the west of Jerusalem. A minor skirmish was fought between the Fatimids and a group of Crusaders under Tancred on 7 August. On learning of this battle, Godfrey and Robert of Flanders set out to join Tancred and engage the enemy. Count Raymond did not immediately set out with the other princes, but instead waited for confirmation of the enemy's location from his own troops, an indication of how frayed relations had by now become between the Crusader leaders. The next day, 10 August, he and Robert of Normandy

set out to join the rest for the impending battle with the Egyptians.

DEPLOYMENT

The two Crusader hosts joined up near Ramla, about 40km (25 miles) northwest of Ascalon. On 11 August, they set out in search of the enemy. The Crusaders were wary of being ambushed by the Egyptians and so formed themselves into nine groups, arrayed in a square formation, three groups wide and three deep, so that they could easily face an enemy attack from any direction.

That evening, they discovered large herds of animals, apparently, according to captured guards, collected to help feed the Fatimid army. The Crusaders were also told that the herds had been deliberately placed so that the Crusader force might scatter to collect them.

On 12 August, under strict orders not break formation in order to forage, the Crusaders headed towards Ascalon. They brought the captured animals with them, which had the unanticipated but beneficial effect of making their Crusader army seem larger than it actually was. They found the main body of the Fatimid army encamped outside Ascalon's north wall.

These horsemen are typical of the Anglo-Norman and northern French crusader cavalry. Heavily armoured with mail hauberks and kite shields, and armed with heavy spears intended primarily for thrusting, as well as a variety of hand weapons, they were dangerous when charging an enemy.

ASCALON

This undated illustration after a glass painting on the Abbey of St Denis, Paris, depicts the battle between the Crusaders and Muslims at Ascalon, 1099.

THE BATTLE OF ASCALON

As the Crusaders approached the Fatimid camp, they deployed in line of battle, with Raymond of Toulouse on the Crusader right wing and his own right flank towards the sea. The centre was held by Robert of Flanders, Tancred and Robert of Normandy. The Crusaders' left was held by Godfrey de Bouillon, who was positioned in such a way that he could interdict any troops attempting to sally out of Ascalon and prevent them from joining the Fatimid main body. The Christian infantry, both archers and spearmen, were placed in a line in front of the mounted knights.

The appearance of the Crusader army caught the Egyptians off guard. There was a period of inactivity in the Fatimid camp, and one tradition holds that the Fatimids believed that the omens were not favourable for an attack. But, eventually, the Egyptians did begin to advance from their camp. The force that came out against the Crusaders was composed primarily of infantry,

This rather romanticized depiction of the battle of Ascalon shows the Crusader leaders directing their troops outside the walls of Ascalon, the main battle raging in the background. The armour and dress in this illustration is from a much later period.

although there was a small body of light cavalry on the Egyptian right flank. This implies that the Crusaders had achieved tactical surprise and that the Fatimid heavy cavalry were not armed, armoured or mounted for battle. The infantry were therefore sent out to allow them to prepare.

The Egyptian infantry advanced and engaged the Crusader foot. A hotly contested battle ensued with heavy casualties inflicted on both sides. Particularly fearsome were the Fatimid Azoparts with their heavy flails, which smashed through shields and armour. The Egyptian light cavalry attempted to outflank the Crusader line but were driven off by Godfrey's men.

The battle was a close-fought affair until the Christian knights from the right wing and centre attacked, scattering the Egyptian infantry and pushing into the Fatimid camp. Though the Muslims launched a brief counterattack, it was defeated by the arrival

of Godfrey and his men at the encampment. At this point a general rout ensued, with many of the Fatimids trapped between the Crusaders and the city walls.

By sending only part of their army out to fight, the Egyptians had allowed the Crusaders to concentrate their forces against this unsupported group and overwhelm them.

Although the Fatimid army outside the city had been routed, the garrison still held Ascalon itself. But once again, a Crusader victory was spoilt by the lack of unity within their army. Count Raymond began negotiation with the commander of the town, but he and Godfrey fell into an argument over who was actually to control the port. Having learned of the quarrel between these two leading princes, the town's commander decided to hold out and broke off negotiations. The end result was that Ascalon would remain in Muslim hands for another 54 years.

HARRAN
1104

THE FIRST CRUSADE (1095–1099) HAD CRASHED THROUGH THE MIDDLE EAST, LEAVING THE CRUSADERS IN CONTROL OF THE KEY CITIES OF EDESSA, ANTIOCH AND JERUSALEM. THE CRUSADERS CREATED THE PRINCIPALITY OF ANTIOCH, RULED BY BOHEMOND, WHILE THE KINGDOM OF JERUSALEM AND THE COUNTY OF EDESSA WERE RULED BY KING BALDWIN I (1100–1118). BOHEMOND AND BALDWIN WOULD LEAD THEIR RESPECTIVE ARMIES TO DEFEAT AT HARRAN.

WHY DID IT HAPPEN?

WHO Prince Bohemond I of Antioch (1098–1111), supported by Prince Tancred of Gallilee (1072–1112), Lord Joscelin of Turbessel (1098–1131) against the Seljuk Atabeg Jekermish of Mosul and the Artukid Prince of Mardin, Sokman.

WHAT Harran ended the Crusaders' reputation for 'invincibility'.

WHERE The battle may have taken place on the River Balikh, some 12km (7.5 miles) from Harran, or on a plain opposite the small town of ar-Raqqah two days' march from Harran.

WHEN 7 May 1104.

WHY Bohemond of Antioch and Count Baldwin I of Edessa (also King of Jerusalem) wished to expand their territories, secure them against Muslim attacks and split the Seljuk states of Syria, Iraq and Anatolia – all to be achieved by taking Harran.

OUTCOME Muslim victory ensured that Edessa remained an isolated outpost surrounded by enemy-held territory, eventually falling in 1144 to Atabeg Zengi of Mosul.

With the Seljuk Empire and the Fatimid (Shia) Caliphate of Egypt in a weakened state, it seemed that the remaining Muslim states of Aleppo, Damascus and Mosul were ripe for the plucking.

Led by Count Raymond of Toulouse, an army of some 20,000 Crusaders (mainly north Italians or Lombardians), had set out from Europe in 1100, crossed Byzantine territory and entered the Sultan of Danishmend's lands, where, in early 1101, the Crusaders were quite literally slaughtered. The Danishmend army was composed of light cavalry who employed hit-and-run tactics. Using their bows and arrows with devastating effect, the Danishmend Turks never allowed themselves to get entangled in close combat with the more heavily armed Crusaders. Four-fifths of Raymon's army lay dead on the bloody fields of Mersivan.

As if this was not bad enough, a second Crusader army, led by the Duke of Aquitaine and Duke Welf of Bavaria, arrived in Asia Minor only to be wiped out at the disastrous battle of Heraclea in September 1101.

These calamitous defeats left the Crusaders' military reputation in tatters and

This romanticized allegorical portrait of Prince Tancred of Galilee shows the prince dealing with a group of 'ladies' in an enchanted forest.

their Muslim enemies filled with renewed vigour. But the Mersivan and Heraclea disasters were far more important than that, since they closed forever the overland route from Europe to the Holy Land via the Byzantine Empire. Thus, all European colonists and reinforcements for the Latin states would have to be shipped across the Mediterranean. In the long run, this ensured these states were starved of both and could not prosper.

The battle of Harran three years later only reinforced this trend and was the final nail in the Crusaders' reputation for military invincibility.

ANTIOCH AGAINST BYZANTIUM AND ALEPPO

The brand new Crusading states of Jerusalem-Edessa and Antioch were now obliged to revenge these reverses if they were not to see their enemies' morale soar. The first to act with precipitous violence was Prince Bohemond of Antioch, who invaded and annexed a slice of Byzantine Cilicia – thus ensuring the enmity of the formidable Emperor Alexius I Comnenus (1081–1118). Bohemond's foolish hatred of Byzantium split the Christians and ensured that the Byzantines would not rally to the Crusaders in the holy war against their common enemy.

As Bohemond saw it, he had not committed any blunder, but had cleared his back, allowing him, in March 1104, to turn his army against Emir Radwan of Aleppo (1095–1113).

A fortress on the road between Antioch and Aleppo (Basarfut) fell to Bohemond but his further progress was hampered by the Arab tribe of Beni Ulaim. However, Bohemond's deputy, cousin and Lord of Turbessel, Joscelin of Courtenay (d.1131) managed to cut communications between Antioch and the Euphrates River.

PRELIMINARY MOVEMENTS

Aleppo seemed ripe for the plucking but compared to Mosul it was a mere nuisance for the Crusaders. But if the powerfully fortified city of Harran on the Balikh River could be captured, this would not only open the road through the Jezira region to Mosul but would also divide the Seljuk Turk states in the region.

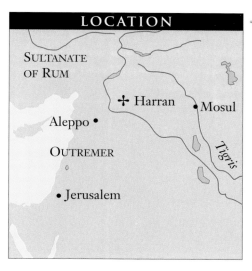

LOCATION

SULTANATE OF RUM

✝ Harran · Mosul

Aleppo ·

OUTREMER

Tigris

· Jerusalem

Harran lies in the western part of the strategically crucial al-Jezira region north of the River Euphrates and is a crucial way station between the northern Crusader states of Outremer and the capital of the Atabegs of Mosul.

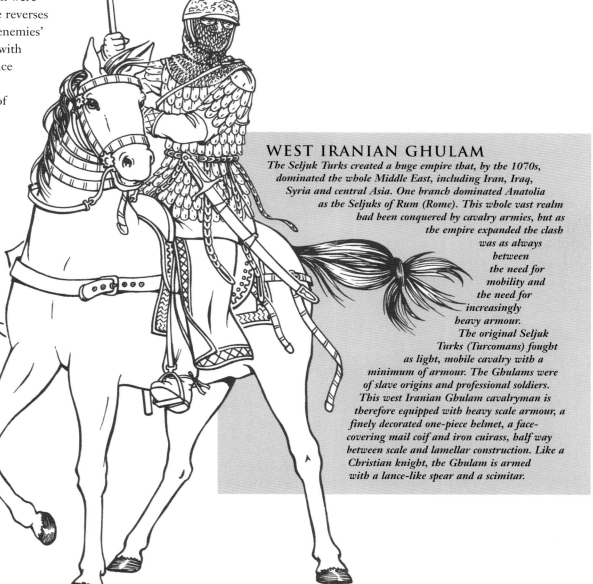

WEST IRANIAN GHULAM
The Seljuk Turks created a huge empire that, by the 1070s, dominated the whole Middle East, including Iran, Iraq, Syria and central Asia. One branch dominated Anatolia as the Seljuks of Rum (Rome). This whole vast realm had been conquered by cavalry armies, but as the empire expanded the clash was as always between the need for mobility and the need for increasingly heavy armour. The original Seljuk Turks (Turcomans) fought as light, mobile cavalry with a minimum of armour. The Ghulams were of slave origins and professional soldiers. This west Iranian Ghulam cavalryman is therefore equipped with heavy scale armour, a finely decorated one-piece helmet, a face-covering mail coif and iron cuirass, half way between scale and lamellar construction. Like a Christian knight, the Ghulam is armed with a lance-like spear and a scimitar.

Fine romanticized nineteenth-century 'portrait' of King Baldwin or Baudouin II of Jerusalem and Count of Edessa (1118–1131). His family was in fact of 'modest' non-royal origins as Counts of Flanders and had struck it lucky in Outremer.

THE OPPOSED FORCES

SELJUK-ARTUKID TURKS

Sokman's Turcoman cavalry:	7000
Jekermish's Seljuk cavalry:	3000
Infantry, if any:	unknown
Total:	**c. 10,000**

CRUSADERS

Heavy cavalry:	3000
Infantry and archers:	9000
Total:	**12,000**

Mosul too was in poor political shape after the death of its ruler, the Atabeg Kerbogha, in 1102. The Grand Seljuk Sultan Mohammed had appointed his relative Prince Jekermish as the new Atabeg. Jekermish's rival, Prince Soqman (Sukman) of Mardin plunged Mosul into a pointless war of succession that left this state in no shape – or, at least, so it seemed – to fight the Crusaders. (Damascus had been similarly paralysed since the death in early 1104 of the Emir Daqaq.)

In the face of mortal danger, sense did prevail on the Turkish side and the two rivals eventually struck a temporary and insincere truce. They forged Soqman's Turkish light cavalry and Jekermish's Kurds, Arabs and Seljuk Turks into an army of sorts and chose to invade Edessa.

This pre-emptive strike united the Crusaders under the supreme command of King Baldwin of Jerusalem. His less than reliable nephew, Prince Tancred of Galilee, joined the attack on Harran. Bohemond's Antiochene army were joined close to Harran by Tancred and Baldwin. The Crusading army numbered 9000 infantry and 3000 knights. They faced around 12,000 Turkish cavalry-archers.

THE FALL OF HARRAN

Civilian morale in Harran – already low after what had happened to Jerusalem – plummeted yet further with every kilometre that the Crusaders moved closer on the Balkh River and the city. The civilians opened up talks as soon as possible and they chose, quite sensibly, to surrender before the city fell and was brutally sacked.

But all was not well. The Citadel still held out, and its garrison, knowing that they would be given short shrift, were determined to fight to the death rather than surrender to the 'infidel' besiegers. Furthermore, Bohemond and Baldwin fell out over who was now master of Harran – a premature and dangerously wasteful exercise given that Soqman and Jekermish's united Turkish army were closing in.

They would have been well advised to heed a warning from the past since Harran was perilously close to Carrhae, where the Roman Consul Crassus and his legions had been wiped out by the Parthians. These eastern warriors, like their Seljuk-Turk successors, fought nimbly on horseback with archers, and used mobility to surround and destroy their slower and more ponderous western enemies. History was, unfortunately for the Crusaders, about to repeat itself.

But where was it about to be repeated and how was the battle fought? If we trust the Edessan chronicler, Matthew, the battle was in fact a series of skirmishes spread out over two days over a wide area around Harran and the Balikh River. His fellow Christians, Albert of Aachen and Fulcher of Chatres, claim the battle took place on a river plain opposite the small Jezirah town of ar-Raqqah – a whole two days' ride from Harran. Finally, just to add to the general confusion, one Muslim chronicler, Ibn al-Athir, claimed the battle took place 12km (7.5 miles) away – possibly at ar-Raqqah.

THE BATTLE

The exact location and date of the decisive battle of Harran (ar-Raqqah) is far less important than the factors that led the Crusaders to be defeated and the fatal outcome of the battle.

The Turks' mounted cavalry had the advantage of mobility, speed and agility, although that came at the expense of armour and weaponry that was far lighter than their enemy's. If they were to get tangled up in close, deadly combat against the knights and infantry of the Crusaders, they would be torn to pieces.

King Baldwin's Edessans massed on the left and had the task of attacking and engaging the Turkish army in preparations for the final knockout blow. This would be administered by Bohemond's Antiochene army, who were hidden out of sight behind a low hill, and would only enter the battle at the decisive moment, when the Turks were pinned down by the Edessans.

Unfortunately, the Crusaders' plan mirrored that of their Turkish foe, who added a feigned 'flight' from the battlefield

These scenes from the First Crusade date from 1490. In the foreground of the main image, a mounted knight is unhorsed and killed in a mêlée of hand-to-hand fighting, with (left) a man wielding a two-sided battleaxe. The inset (bottom left) shows Peter the Hermit (c. 1050–1115) pleading for help from the Byzantine Emperor Alexius I (1048–1118).

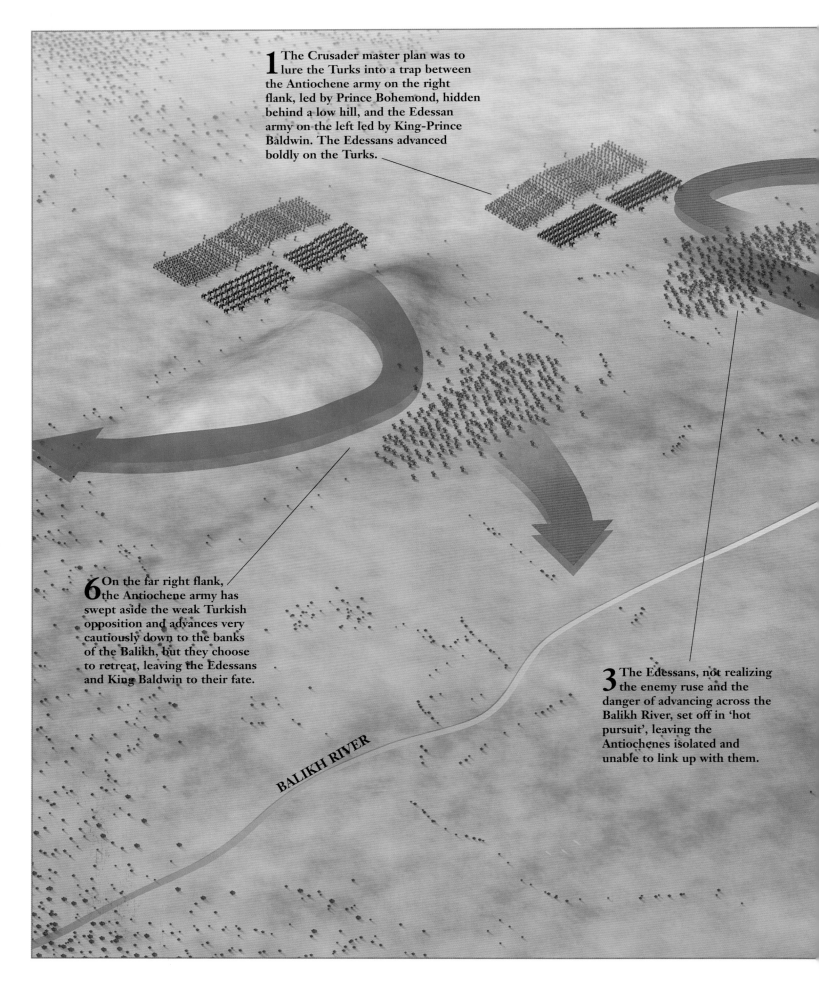

1 The Crusader master plan was to lure the Turks into a trap between the Antiochene army on the right flank, led by Prince Bohemond, hidden behind a low hill, and the Edessan army on the left led by King-Prince Baldwin. The Edessans advanced boldly on the Turks.

6 On the far right flank, the Antiochene army has swept aside the weak Turkish opposition and advances very cautiously down to the banks of the Balikh, but they choose to retreat, leaving the Edessans and King Baldwin to their fate.

BALIKH RIVER

3 The Edessans, not realizing the enemy ruse and the danger of advancing across the Balikh River, set off in 'hot pursuit', leaving the Antiochenes isolated and unable to link up with them.

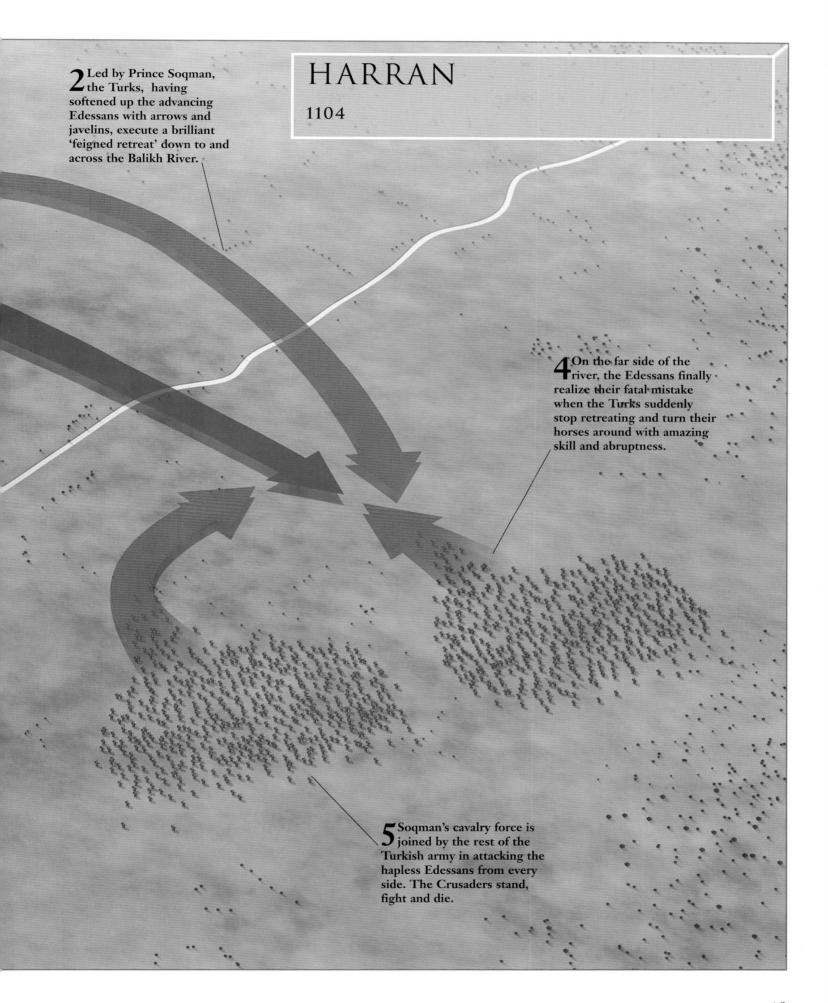

HARRAN

1104

2 Led by Prince Soqman, the Turks, having softened up the advancing Edessans with arrows and javelins, execute a brilliant 'feigned retreat' down to and across the Balikh River.

4 On the far side of the river, the Edessans finally realize their fatal mistake when the Turks suddenly stop retreating and turn their horses around with amazing skill and abruptness.

5 Soqman's cavalry force is joined by the rest of the Turkish army in attacking the hapless Edessans from every side. The Crusaders stand, fight and die.

Count Joscelin de Courtenay built the powerful Crusader Castle of Montfort in order to control and defend the Crusader state of Galilee, which he ruled with a firm hand. Even today, the site is impressive lying as it does on a massive, high peak in the middle of a wilderness.

to lure the Crusaders into a deadly trap. Soqman's Turcomen (Artuq) cavalry attacked the Crusaders' left (Edessans), showering them with arrows, javelins and a few jabbing attacks on the fringes of their formation. Then, with what must have seemed to their enemy amazing dexterity, they turned and fled across the Balikh River.

A prudent Crusader commander used to Turkish field tricks would have stayed put or would have advanced cautiously up to the near bank of the river. There, he would have stood and awaited the Antiochenes before moving across the river and advancing to the far side.

Baldwin, however, was unable to control his commanders and troops when their blood was up, and was also probably swept along by the moment and the temptation of crushing the Turks without his rival prince's intervention. For whatever

reason, Baldwin failed to control his army – and paid a high price.

This mainly Frankish (French) army gave hot pursuit across the river. Water splashed, horses whinnied, and men shouted and cursed. They hoped not only to gain salvation by killing the infidel foe, but also to find booty in the enemy camp or high-ranking prisoners to ransom.

Having crossed the Balikh, the Edessans lost touch with their right flank and plunged into the brush and grass-filled fields on the other side. It was only when their vision and heads cleared that the Edessans saw, to their horror, the rest of the Turkish army arrayed before them. They had walked into the same trap they had set for the Turks.

With an almighty roar of 'Allah-u Akbar' ('God is Great'), the Turks mounted a full-scale cavalry attack upon the outnumbered, outwitted and surrounded Edessans. They noted that the Crusaders at least fought like lions but were eventually cut down where they stood. Few prisoners were taken as the Edessan army was completely destroyed.

Bohemond had meanwhile advanced cautiously, sweeping aside the few Turks he faced, only to reach the river as the calamity on the other side unfolded before his shocked eyes. Bohemond had no wish to destroy his army in defence of his rival, and chose, wisely but cynically, to retreat as quickly as he could. In Baldwin's and Edessan eyes, this was calculated treachery. From Bohemond's point of view, it was simple common sense.

By acting as swiftly as he did selfishly, Bohemond managed to save his army from a bloodbath, but as they passed Harran the still active Turkish garrison came out and set after the retreating Antiochenes with such enthusiasm that they killed their fellow Turks pursuing the 'Nazarines'.

What remained of the tattered Edessans fled down to the eastern riverbank, trying to cross or swim where they could. Bernard, the Archbishop of Antioch, it was claimed mischievously by his enemies, was in such a panic that the 'cut his horse's tail off' so that no Turk could catch it. Baldwin and Joscelin, defended by their Armenian mercenaries, made it to the riverbank before they were finally captured by Soqman's cavalry.

THE AFTERMATH

Their capture led to a fatal rupture between the two Muslim princes. Jekermish, unhappy about his share of the prisoners, raided Soqman's camp and carried off Bohemond. Wisely, Soqman chose not to retaliate and chose instead to withdraw from the war.

This left Jekermish to capture the fortress of Shahbaqtan before he encircled and lay siege to Edessa. Tancred, Regent of Jerusalem and Edessa, had repaired the city's fortifications and prepared its defences in time. But it was very much thanks to the city's Armenian population that Edessa did not fall into Seljuk hands.

Overconfident, Jekermish had failed to protect or guard his camp properly. This allowed Tancred to make a dawn raid that shattered the Seljuks, with Jekermish fleeing in wild panic with his remaining troops. Harran had been avenged; Jekermish had been humiliated and he was forced to offer Baldwin in return for a Seljuk princess. Tancred, well rid of Baldwin, took a ransom payment instead and delivered the princess safely to Jekermish.

SETBACKS

Antioch was just as hard pressed as Edessa. During the summer of 1104 a Byzantine army, led by General Monastras, recaptured Tarsus, Adana and Mamistra that Bohemond had taken from Alexius I six months earlier. None of the other Latin states of the Holy Land rushed to aid Bohemond, not even when the Byzantines retook the strategic port of Latakiah (Lattakieh).

Desperate, Bohemond called a Council of State in September, appointed Tancred as Regent of Antioch and departed for his lands in Apulia, Italy. From here, Bohemond plotted his revenge against the Byzantines but his attempt to take an Adriatic port ended in defeat. In September 1107, Alexius imposed the Treaty of Devol on the luckless Bohemond, who retired to his estates in Apulia, where he died in 1111, a broken man. Joscelin eventually became ruler of Edessa in 1118, in support of

Baldwin I's son, Baldwin II, taking the throne of Jerusalem. In 1123 both he and Baldwin were captured by the Turks but he managed to escape and, two years later, at Azaz, defeated the Atabeg of Mosul. He had finally and fully avenged the humiliation of Harran.

Joscelin died in 1131 from wounds received during a siege of a small fortress northeast of Aleppo.

Baldwin I was eventually released from captivity, no thanks to Bohemond or Tancred, but when he sought to re-establish himself as King and Count of Jerusalem and Edessa, Tancred fought against him in a short, sharp civil war. Tancred died in 1112.

A brooding Prince Bohemond I of Antioch as depicted in this nineteenth-century French engraving, when the Crusaders made for popular artistic themes. The real Bohemond was more a man of action than of contemplation.

SARMADA
1119

THE BATTLE OF SARMADA IS ALSO KNOWN AS THE FIELD OF BLOOD, AND FOR GOOD REASON. LESS THAN 200 OF THE 3700 CRUSADER SOLDIERS ESCAPED WITH THEIR LIVES.

WHY DID IT HAPPEN?

WHO Crusader forces from the Principality of Antioch under Roger of Salerno (d. 1119), numbering about 3700. They were opposed by a larger force of Turks under Ilghazi (d. 1122).

WHAT The Crusader force was surrounded and attacked by a superior enemy.

WHERE Kadesh was a rich and powerful fortified city that offered an excellent outpost to defend an empire, or from which to expand.

WHEN 1119.

WHY The Crusaders responded to an invasion of their territory by the Turks, resulting in a meeting engagement.

OUTCOME The Crusader force was massacred, with few survivors.

One of the armies of the First Crusade established itself in Jerusalem in 1099, and, after beating off attempts to dislodge it, had gradually consolidated its hold. Although Pope Urban II (c. 1035–1099), who had instigated the crusade, died before hearing of its success, the mission was apparently accomplished. The holy city was in Christian hands.

However, the Christian hold on the region was somewhat tenuous. Armies sent to reinforce the occupation of Jerusalem in 1100–1101 were defeated before they got anywhere near the holy city. Worse, the Byzantines, who had assisted the Crusaders, were becoming disenchanted with the whole business. The crusading Franks were supposed to have returned territory they took to Byzantine rule but had not done so.

The Franks, meanwhile, were not at all impressed with the degree of support they were receiving, and did not like the way the Byzantines were trying to retake their traditional territories. This all detracted from the real business at hand – the constant battles to keep and expand control of the Holy Land.

Despite a variety of setbacks and a defeat at Harran in 1104, the Franks were able gradually to expand their holdings in the Holy Land and elsewhere in Muslim territory during the years 1100–1119. Acre fell to them in 1104 and Tripoli in 1109. Beirut and Saida were captured in 1110 and Tyre in 1124.

This left the Crusaders in control of a considerable stretch of territory and a lot of critical coastline through which supplies

In this twelfth-century French manuscript illustration, Muslim cavalry and Crusader knights engage in hand-to-hand combat. In reality, Muslim cavalry rarely engaged up-close with the more heavily armed and armoured European knights unless they had a significant numerical advantage, preferring instead to harass at a distance with missile fire.

and reinforcements could be brought in. Attempts by the local Muslim leaders to retake their territory were a regular feature of the period and conflict was more or less constant, rising and falling in intensity at various times.

DEFEAT AT HARRAN

At first the Crusaders had seemed invincible, brushing aside attempts to stop them with headlong charges of armoured horsemen backed up by infantry and lighter cavalry. The latter were mainly Turcopoles ('sons of Turks') recruited from the region and converted to Christianity. Armed with bows and lances and with light armour, if any, their superior mobility allowed them to protect the flanks of the heavy cavalry.

This combination of forces had worked well at first, and attempts by Muslim troops to meet the knightly charges head on resulted in defeat. The Muslim leaders were learning how to defeat the Crusaders, however, and at Harran the invaders suffered their first major reverse.

That battle had been a clash between Crusaders besieging the city of Harran and Seljuk Turks coming to its relief. After a series of small skirmishes, in which the Crusaders were victorious, a major battle developed. During this action one wing of the Crusader army rushed impetuously into action and was soundly defeated, although the rest of the force retired and escaped.

Harran served to demonstrate not only that the Crusaders could be beaten, but also how it could be done. The battle had political consequences too, deepening the rift between the crusading Franks and the Byzantines. The latter even took advantage of the situation and recaptured some of their territory.

Nevertheless, the Crusaders managed to expand their territory despite the constant conflict. With the death of Radwan of Aleppo in 1113, a period of relative peace descended. At this time the main Crusader provinces were Edessa, under Baldwin II (1118–1131), Tripoli under Pons (c. 1098–1137), and Antioch. Roger of Salerno was regent of Antioch on behalf of Bohemond II (1108–1131).

By 1117, Aleppo was under the rule of Ilghazi of the Ortoqid dynasty, and the stage was set for further conflict. Roger of Salerno had perhaps passed up an opportunity to smash Aleppo during the disruption caused by Radwan's death. Now Aleppo once again had strong leadership and was in a position to respond when Roger's forces took Azaz in 1118.

The capture of Azaz provided the Crusaders with a route to attack Aleppo, and this could not be tolerated. Ilghazi responded in 1119 by invading the Principality of Antioch. Roger of Salerno was advised to ask for help from Pons and from Baldwin, who was now King of Jerusalem, but for reasons of his own he declined. Perhaps he thought he could not afford to wait for assistance to arrive.

OPENING MOVES

Roger assembled his forces at Artah, not far from Antioch. He was advised to remain there by Bernard of Valence, the Latin

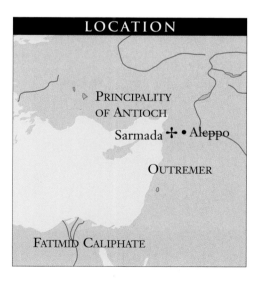

LOCATION

PRINCIPALITY
OF ANTIOCH

Sarmada ✛ • Aleppo

OUTREMER

FATIMID CALIPHATE

The Crusader states in the Holy Land were always in danger, and the narrow coastal strip saw many armies passing through it at one time or another. The pass at Sarmada was a logical approach route for an army marching on Aleppo.

SARMADA

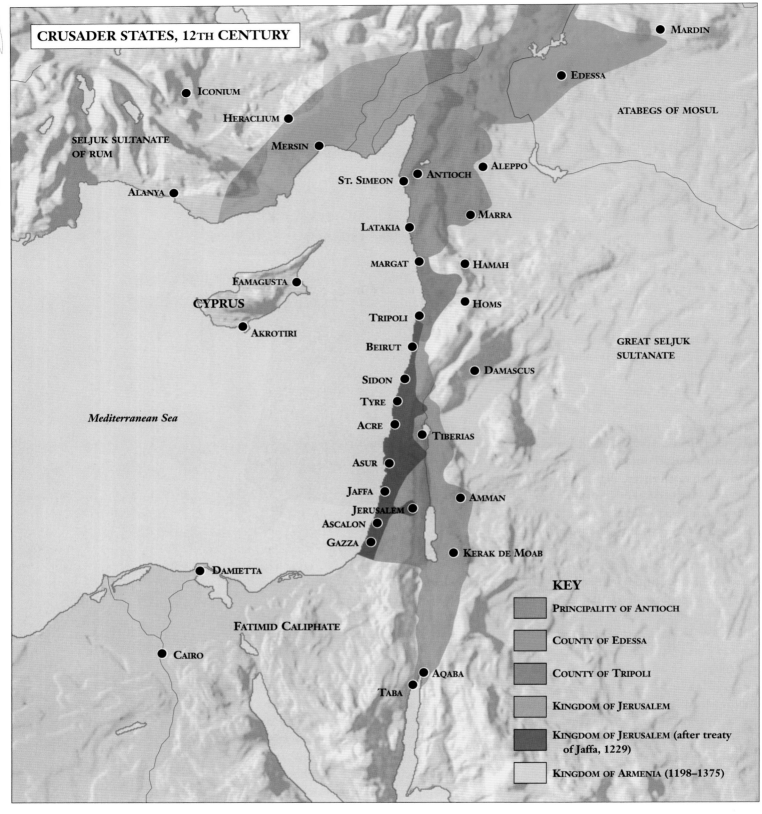

CRUSADER STATES, 12TH CENTURY

MARDIN

EDESSA

ATABEGS OF MOSUL

ICONIUM

HERACLIUM

MERSIN

ALEPPO

SELJUK SULTANATE
OF RUM

ALANYA

ST. SIMEON ● ANTIOCH

MARRA

LATAKIA

MARGAT

HAMAH

FAMAGUSTA

HOMS

CYPRUS

TRIPOLI

AKROTIRI

BEIRUT

DAMASCUS

GREAT SELJUK
SULTANATE

SIDON

TYRE

Mediterranean Sea

ACRE

TIBERIAS

ASUR

JAFFA

AMMAN

JERUSALEM

ASCALON

GAZZA

KERAK DE MOAB

DAMIETTA

FATIMID CALIPHATE

CAIRO

AQABA

TABA

KEY

PRINCIPALITY OF ANTIOCH

COUNTY OF EDESSA

COUNTY OF TRIPOLI

KINGDOM OF JERUSALEM

KINGDOM OF JERUSALEM (after treaty
of Jaffa, 1229)

KINGDOM OF ARMENIA (1198–1375)

This map shows the rather complex relationship between the Christian and Muslim states in the Middle East in the twelfth and thirteenth centuries, when the Crusader states reached their greatest extent.

Patriarch of Antioch. Ilghazi would have to reduce the fortress of Artah in order to advance on Antioch or else risk being attacked in flank or rear by Roger's army. Again Bernard suggested a defensive strategy, waiting for assistance in the security of the fortress.

Roger would have none of it. It is possible that he was overconfident, as the Crusaders had tended to win most engagements by simply attacking headlong as soon as possible. There are some parallels with the British situation in India centuries later. There, too, a vastly outnumbered occupying force generally defeated its enemies by a headlong attack, no matter what the odds. However, the British would have two major advantages in India. First, they possessed superior weapons and were better trained than their opponents. More importantly, they had the myth of invincibility on their side. Roger had neither. After Harran, the Muslims knew that Crusaders could be beaten, and while Roger's force was differently armed to its opponents, there is serious doubt as to whether it was better armed.

THE OPPOSING FORCES

Roger of Salerno commanded a force of about 3700 men, of whom around 700 were mounted knights and men-at-arms, and the remainder a mix of Turcopoles and infantry. The cavalry were the main striking force. Typical of Crusader knights and men-at-arms, they were covered in heavy armour and armed with lances and swords. Each man was the most powerful military force that an individual could be, but that is exactly what the knightly contingent was – a collection of individual warriors rather than a disciplined fighting force.

The infantry and Turcopoles were there simply as supports for the main striking force and to protect the knights in camp or on the march. These men were neither well trained nor very highly valued. In battle, it was the knights who decided the issue by charging at the enemy and defeating him. Infantry were considered to be little more than hangers-on, or at best a mobile obstruction to rally behind before launching the next charge.

The exact numbers of the Muslim force are not known, but it is likely that they outnumbered the Crusaders by a large margin. Muslim armies of the period tended to be more lightly equipped than their Crusader opponents but were more mobile as a consequence. In order to take advantage of that mobility, a certain level of discipline was also required, allowing the various parts of the army to operate as a coordinated force.

Thus the opposing forces were very different. If the Crusaders could land a blow with the sledgehammer that was their mounted knights, whatever was struck would be destroyed. But the sledgehammer could not be swung many times before exhaustion set in, and meanwhile the Muslim forces would be nibbling away at the Crusader army with arrows and fast mounted charges by lighter cavalry, waiting for the decisive moment to charge in and finish the matter.

AMBUSH AT AL-ATHARIB

Roger of Salerno began his advance, moving to meet the Muslim army. As he reached the pass of Sarmada, he learned that one of his forts, located at al-Atharib, was

THE OPPOSED FORCES

CRUSADERS (estimated)	
Knights/men-at-arms:	700
Infantry:	3000
Total:	**3700**

MUSLIMS (estimated)	
Total:	**10,000**

Although more lightly equipped than the knights opposing them, the cavalry of the Muslim army was determined, experienced and well armed. Equally well able to harass an enemy with minor attacks or make a massed lance charge, these horsemen were a powerful military asset in the right hands.

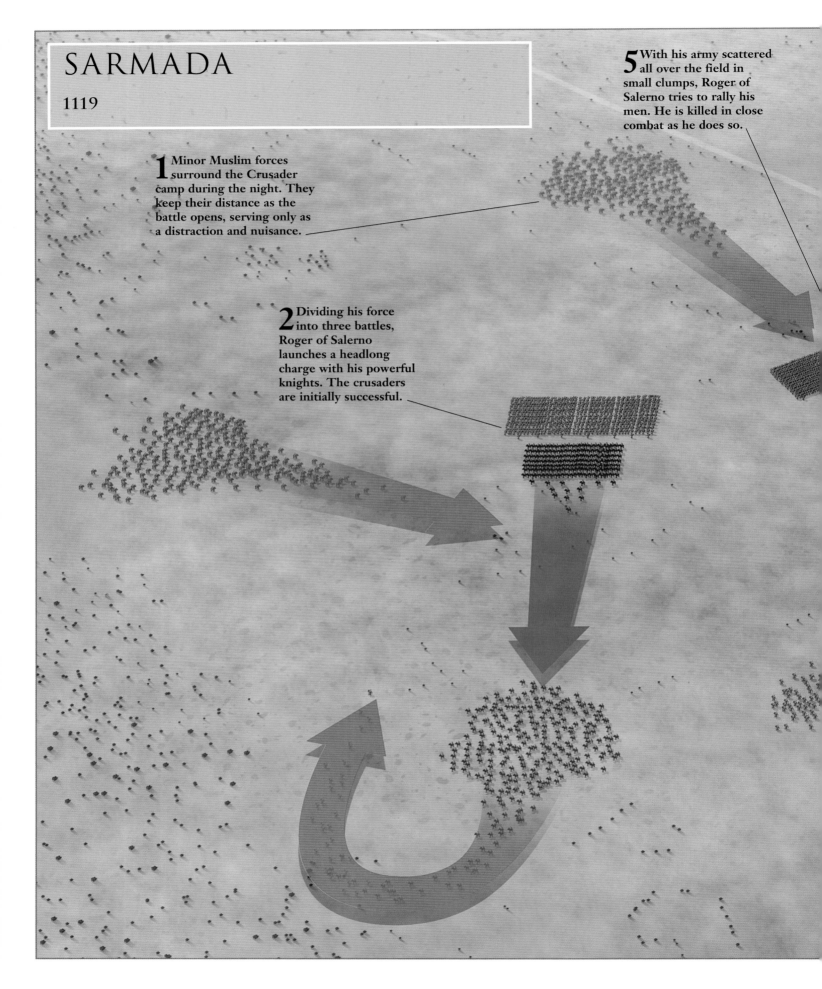

SARMADA

1119

1 Minor Muslim forces surround the Crusader camp during the night. They keep their distance as the battle opens, serving only as a distraction and nuisance.

2 Dividing his force into three battles, Roger of Salerno launches a headlong charge with his powerful knights. The crusaders are initially successful.

5 With his army scattered all over the field in small clumps, Roger of Salerno tries to rally his men. He is killed in close combat as he does so.

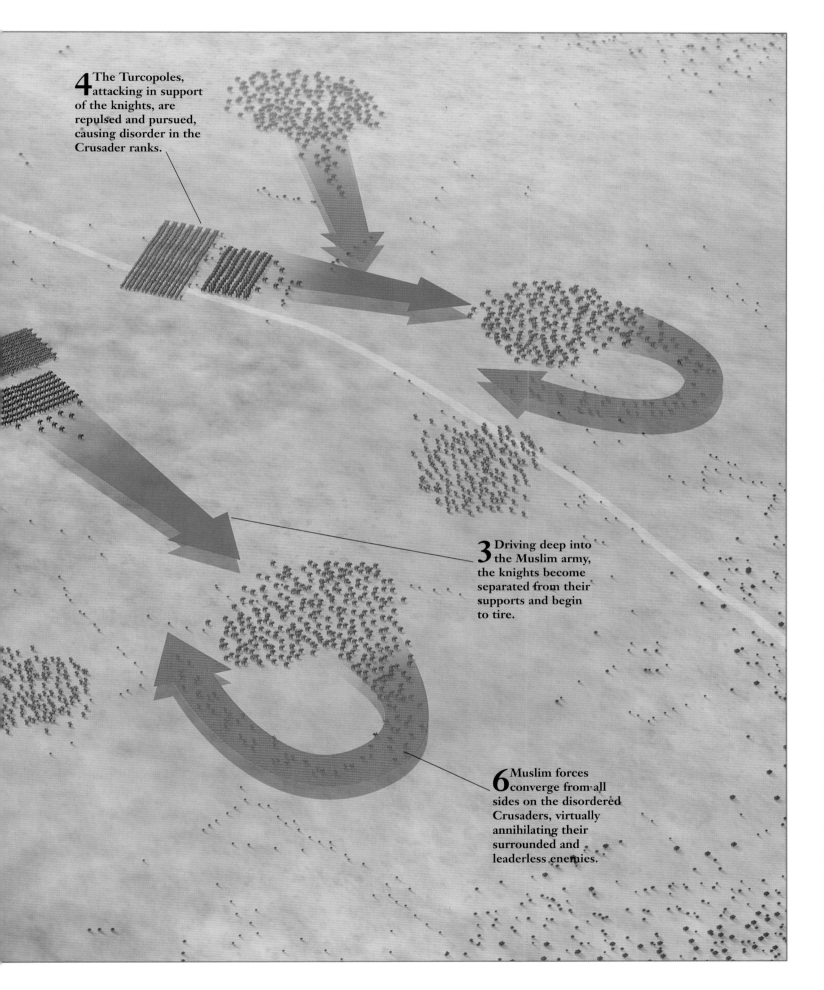

4 The Turcopoles, attacking in support of the knights, are repulsed and pursued, causing disorder in the Crusader ranks.

3 Driving deep into the Muslim army, the knights become separated from their supports and begin to tire.

6 Muslim forces converge from all sides on the disordered Crusaders, virtually annihilating their surrounded and leaderless enemies.

SARMADA

under siege, and decided to do something about it.

Roger sent out a small force under Robert of Vieux-Pont to break the siege. Rather than meet the Crusaders head on, the wily Ilghazi ordered a retreat, and Robert's force pursued, joined by forces from the fortress.

However, this was not a real retreat at all, but a feigned withdrawal of the sort favoured by the Muslim armies to draw out and tire their impetuous foes. Among the nobility of Europe, caution was another word for cowardice, and a commander who failed to lead his men in a headlong assault would lose their confidence. Thus Robert really had no choice but to pursue, and indeed at that stage in the campaign he simply may not have known about the favourite tactics of his foes.

Thus Robert's men were drawn ever further from support, supply and the security of the fort, and when the time was right Ilghazi turned and launched his own attack. The Muslim fighting man of the period was much better disciplined than the Europeans, and thought nothing of being ordered to flee for many kilometres before turning to fight. This pragmatic attitude gave Ilghazi an easy victory over Robert's relief force, as a prelude to setting out to meet the main Crusader army.

DISPOSITIONS

During the night of 27–28 June the Muslim army moved into position, surrounding the

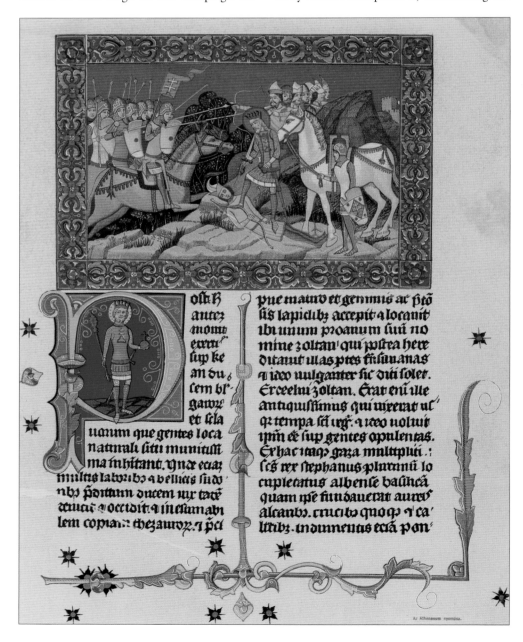

An eighteenth-century illumination depicting the Crusades. By the time this depiction was made, the crusades had become something of a romantic legend whose complex (and sometimes sordid) details had been largely forgotten.

camp of the smaller Crusader force. Roger of Salerno was probably not unduly worried. He was a Christian knight about to give battle in the Lord's name. Victory was his by right, and surely nothing could withstand the head-on charge of his knights?

Roger split his force into three 'battles', as was common practice at the time. These forces were under the command of Geoffrey the Monk, Guy Fresnel and Roger himself. Meanwhile, the Muslim army was being addressed by Abu al-Fadl ibn al-Khashshab, who was armed for battle but wearing the turban of a lawyer.

This slightly incongruous combination detracted nothing from his oratory as he reminded the assembled soldiers of their duty and role in the coming clash. By the time he was finished, according to contemporary historians, many of the warriors were in tears and went to battle inspired to great deeds.

THE BATTLE OF SARMADA

Not unexpectedly, things at first went well for Roger of Salerno. The initial charge of his knights met with success and drove the enemy back. However, a Muslim army was not like a European one. European armies could be rather brittle, shattering under the hammerblow of seeing their knights defeated or even just driven back.

Fighting power was more evenly distributed in the Muslim armies and discipline was good enough to absorb any blows to morale. A setback in one area would not necessarily dismay the men fighting elsewhere.

Besides, even as the Crusaders drove forward, they tired fast. Weary men mounted on blown horses became increasingly separated from their supports, and the tide began to turn. Robert of St Lo, leading the Turcopoles, was driven back into the main line of the Crusader force. This caused severe disruption, and the Muslims were coordinated enough to take advantage of it.

The Crusader army began to break up, and small groups were quickly overwhelmed by superior numbers. Roger of Salerno tried to rally his men, fighting under a huge jewelled cross that was his personal banner, but it was to no avail. He was struck down by a blow to the face as his army disintegrated.

There was nowhere to run. The Crusaders had started the battle surrounded and were now scattered all over the field in disorganized clumps. The Muslims concentrated against first one and then another of these, slaughtering the Crusader army until virtually nothing was left of it.

Only two of Roger's knights survived. One, Raynald Mazoir, was able to reach the fort at Sarmada but was later taken prisoner. Other prisoners were taken, while a handful of men were able to make off and reach safety. In the end, some 3500 of the 3700 Crusaders engaged were killed, giving the battle its name – Ager Sanguinis, or 'Field of Blood'.

AFTERMATH

Bernard was left to prepare a hasty defence of Antioch, which probably would have been in vain. However, Ilghazi did not attack. King Baldwin of Jerusalem and Count Pons arrived in time to eject Ilghazi from the region, and Baldwin took control of Antioch.

The Principality of Antioch was crippled by the catastrophic defeat of Roger and his army, and never really recovered. Although the Battle of Azaz, which took place a few years later in 1125, was a victory that allowed the Crusaders to reclaim some of their prestige, the myth of their invincibility, which had served them so well for so long, had been shattered forever.

The Muslims now knew without a doubt that they could beat the Crusaders in the field, and they would do so repeatedly in the years to come.

A Crusader footsoldier and sergeant. The spearman's thick gambeson of quilted cloth offered excellent protection against arrows but was uncomfortable to wear in the hot Middle Eastern climate. The sergeant's armour is backed by a similar garment worn underneath the mail.

LISBON
1147

THERE IS LITTLE QUESTION THAT THE SECOND CRUSADE WAS ONE OF THE MOST DISASTROUS MILITARY CAMPAIGNS EVER. YET AT ITS OUTSET NONE COULD HAVE PREDICTED THAT THE TAKING OF LISBON WOULD BE THE ONLY SIGNIFICANT CHRISTIAN SUCCESS OF THE CAMPAIGN.

WHY DID IT HAPPEN?

WHO Northern European Crusaders under a group of minor nobles, along with local Christians, against the inhabitants of Lisbon and their mainly Muslim defenders.

WHAT The Crusaders besieged the fortified city until the eventual surrender of the defenders.

WHERE Lisbon, in Portugal.

WHEN 1 July to 21 October 1147.

WHY The European Crusaders were persuaded to divert from their journey to the Holy Land and help Afonso Henriques cement his claim to the throne of Portugal by taking this wealthy port from the Muslims.

OUTCOME The defenders surrendered on terms, although that did not prevent the sacking of the city.

Zengi's conquest of the Crusader County of Edessa in 1144 was certainly a setback for Christian efforts to capture the Holy Land, their first major reversal of military fortune since the First Crusaders took Jerusalem in 1099. But it was not unanswered. The two most powerful kings of Christendom – Conrad III of the Holy Roman Empire and Louis VII of France – responded to the call to go on the Second Crusade. Their armies and other soldiers who 'took up the cross' to reinforce the resident Crusaders added many thousands to their numbers.

But it was more than an increase of soldiers that was needed in the Holy Land.

Poor leadership scuttled this Crusade from the very arrival of Conrad and Louis in Jerusalem. The two kings were unified in their military purpose but this differed from that of the resident Crusaders, whom the kings clearly blamed for the defeat of Edessa because they had treated the Muslims too lightly. Meanwhile, the resident Crusaders, while they initially welcomed these reinforcements, soon began to resent their presence, especially as the new arrivals ignored their experience.

Disagreements between the two were essentially rooted in different approaches to strategy. The plan the resident Crusaders proposed was to take the army north to

Afonso I Henriques, King of Portugal (c. 1109–1185). It was at the behest of Afonso Henriques that a fleet of northern Crusaders en route to the Holy Land landed and besieged Lisbon. This successful endeavour not only added the rich city of Lisbon to Afonso's realm, but also made him a European hero, the only victorious leader of the Second Crusade.

IBERIAN CHRISTIAN MERCENARY

Medieval Spain has been described as a 'Society Organized for War'. Almost all males, including those destined for Church service, were trained in warfare. They did this primarily to provide a militia to defend their villages from Muslim raids, but they also could be used as troops for the Reconquista (reconquest) of Spain. While most returned to their normal occupations during times of peace, some became professional soldiers, willing to fight for whoever could pay them. These frequently included Muslim leaders who paid the mercenary soldiers to fight for them against other Muslim leaders – in Al-Andalus and North Africa – and sometimes also against Christians.

Aleppo, the capital city of the Seljuk Turkish Sultan Nur-ad-Din, who had succeeded his father, Zengi, after the latter's assassination in 1146. By doing so they would be striking directly at the conqueror of Edessa and would be able to regain that County almost immediately, along with Aleppo, one of the great Muslim cities of the Middle East. But Conrad, Louis and the other new Crusaders saw a closer target in Damascus, a city led by a Muslim ally of the Crusaders, Mujir ud-Din Abaq, who was an enemy of Nur-ad-Din. In fact, Nur-ad-Din and his father, Zengi, before him had been actively trying to capture Damascus since at least 1140.

The European kings prevailed, and on 24 June 1148 the Second Crusaders marched on Damascus. However, even before reaching the city, the two kings began to argue over who was to take credit for the victory that never came. For not only did the attack of Damascus fail, but the citizens of the town were so enraged at the disloyalty of the Crusaders that they removed their own leader, Abaq, and submitted to Nur-ad-Din. Following this defeat, Conrad III immediately set out for home. Louis VII stayed on in Jerusalem, but by summer 1149 he had also returned to Europe.

However, not all the Second Crusaders made it to the Holy Land, and nor did they all take part in the horrendous defeat at the siege of Damascus. A large group of northern European Crusaders from England, Scotland, Normandy, Brittany, Flanders and the Rhineland had set sail from Dartmouth on the southwest coast of England on 19 May 1147, hoping to meet up with the rest of the Crusaders in the Holy Land. However, on the way they made a decisive detour: to Lisbon on the western Iberian coast.

LISBON: WEALTHY CITY

Founded at the natural harbour produced by the conjunction of the Tagus River and the Atlantic Ocean, Lisbon has existed as a city since at least 1200 BC when the Phoenicians established a trading post there. Nearly 2400 years later the city had endured occupations by Carthaginians, Romans, Visigoths and Muslims. These latest conquerors had first occupied Lisbon in 711 when it became one of the early sites attacked by Moroccan and Arabic armies who had travelled across the Straits of Gibraltar as part of the Islamic conquest of

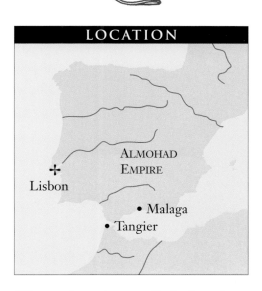

Lisbon was the most important Muslim city retaken by Christians before the beginning of the thirteenth century. However, its fall did not lead to further reconquest, as the Spanish Christian kings were rarely united in any Crusade.

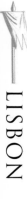

LISBON

Meeting of the Chapter of the Knights Templar under Robert de Bouguignon, held in Paris in the presence of Louis VII of France and Pope Eugene III, 22 April 1147.

THE OPPOSED FORCES

CRUSADERS (estimated)

Total: **25,000**

LISBON INHABITANTS (estimated)

Total: **50,000**

the Iberian Peninsula. No doubt because of all these conquerors, Lisbon's population was very diverse. Christians, Muslims and Jews lived together, although in separate districts. The Muslim district, the Alfama, still exists: the only medieval neighbourhood to survive the earthquakes in 1531 and 1755. People were also free to practice their own religions, although there is no doubt in Lisbon that, as elsewhere in the medieval Islamic world, in order to gain any political status or military rank, one had to be a practising Muslim.

Prosperity was not a question of religious orientation, however, for medieval Lisbon was a generally wealthy city. The wealth came from the harbour, one of the busiest in medieval Europe. Ships came to Lisbon from everywhere: Northern Europe, Mediterranean Europe, Islamic Africa, the Byzantine Empire and the Middle East. On any given day the city's warehouses were filled with grains, cloths, spices, furs, wool, gold, silver and ivory. Such prosperity also meant a huge population. First-time visitors were stunned by Lisbon's size, prosperity and diversity. Raol, whose chronicle *De expugnatione Lyxbonensi* (*The Capture of Lisbon*) is an eyewitness report of the siege of 1147,

wrote with amazement at what he saw when first visiting Lisbon:

> At the time of our arrival the city consisted of 60,000 families paying taxes, if you include the adjacent suburbs... The city was populous beyond what can readily be believed; for, as after its capture we learned from their alcayde, that is, their governor, it contained 154,000 men, without counting women and children... The buildings of the city were so closely packed together that, except in the merchants' quarter, hardly a street could be found which was more than eight feet wide.

RECONQUEST

Most of medieval Iberia had been conquered as part of the eighth-century Muslim expansion. But some parts at the very top of the Peninsula had stayed in Christian hands, leading to constant calls for *Reconquista* (reconquest) of the land. Border warfare was continual, and fortifications were constructed on both sides. One of these surrounded Lisbon. Raol describes it:

> The hilltop is girdled by a circular wall, and the walls of the city extend downward

on the right and left to the bank of the Tagus. And the suburbs, which slope down beneath the wall, have been so cut out of the rocks that each of the steep defiles which they have in place of ordinary streets may be considered a very well fortified stronghold, with such obstacles is it girt about.

Formidable as they were, if Lisbon was to fall, these fortifications had to be taken.

There are reliable contemporary accounts of the siege of Lisbon and the Crusaders who fought it. Raol, whose words have been quoted above, was an English eyewitness to the siege and wrote a lengthy and comprehensive chronicle of it. A shorter account comes from the so-called 'Lisbon Letter', written by a priest from the Rhineland to Arnold, the Archbishop of Cologne. Both men differ on certain details and aspects of the siege, and they are obviously biased towards the troops from their own region, but when used together they provide a fairly complete rendering of what occurred.

The Crusaders who arrived at Lisbon had answered the call to take the cross with the same enthusiasm as did those who travelled with Conrad III or Louis VII. Their numbers were quite large. Raol tallies the fleet at 164 ships while the Lisbon Letter rounds it off at 200. They were led by a group of lesser nobles – Arnulf, Count of Aerschot, Christian, the Castellan of Gistel, Hervey de Glanvill, Simon of Dover, Andrew of London and Sacher of Archelle – who likely would have turned command of their soldiers to the royal leadership of the Second Crusade once they arrived at the Holy Land. Undoubtedly it was for the unity of their goal and for safety that they left from England and travelled together.

The journey from England across the Channel and along the coasts of western France and northern Iberia was made without difficulty. Leaving in May meant

that the harshest winter and spring weather had passed. According to the eyewitnesses, the Crusaders' ships also made very swift progress, arriving at the Iberian Peninsula in less than a month. The Crusaders had gone frequently ashore during this trip, to restock water and victuals or to escape from storms, and they were always welcomed and entertained by local political and ecclesiastical leaders. Their numbers also undoubtedly increased when new recruits also took on the cross.

CRUSADERS PERSUADED

When they stopped in Porto on 16 June, the bishop of the town, Pedro II Pitoes, convinced the Crusaders to change their goals – at least temporarily – in order to assist Afonso I Henriques, who claimed the throne of Portugal, in conquering (or, in Crusader terms, reconquering) Lisbon. Why did the Crusaders agree to do this?

Christian cross from St. Catherine's Monastery on Mt. Sinai. The cross became the symbol 'taken' by all Crusaders. It was said to have been attached to their surcoats and painted on their shields, and it made their military campaigns pilgrimages.

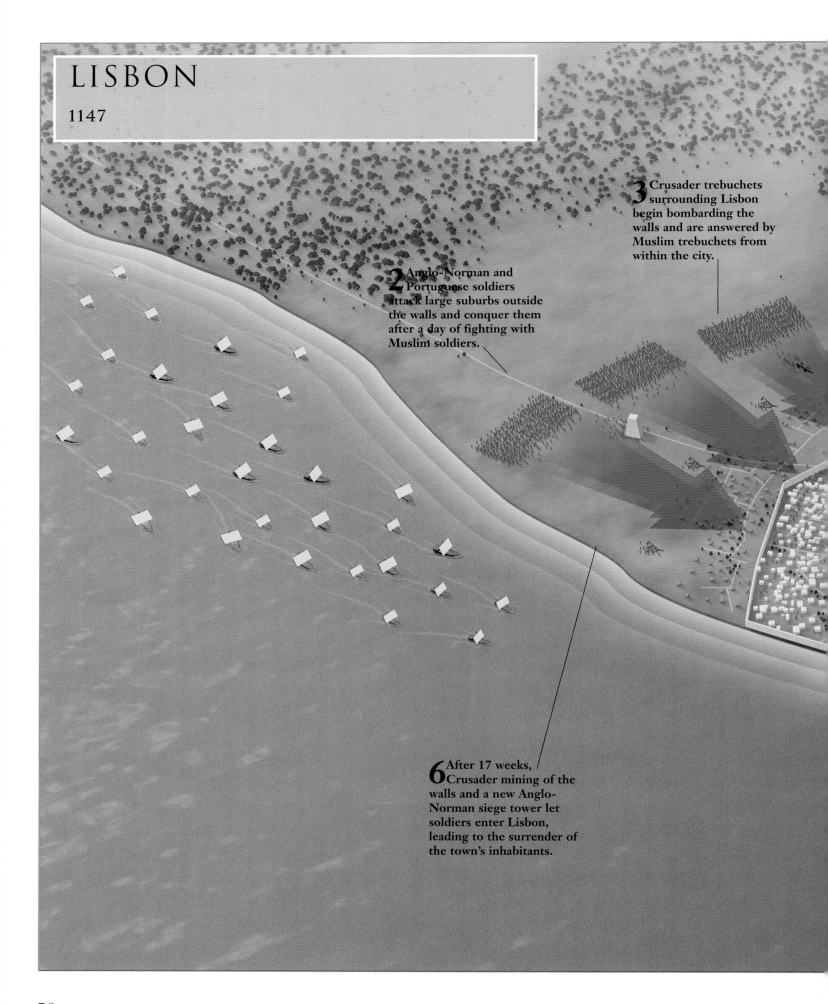

LISBON

1147

2 Anglo-Norman and Portuguese soldiers attack large suburbs outside the walls and conquer them after a day of fighting with Muslim soldiers.

3 Crusader trebuchets surrounding Lisbon begin bombarding the walls and are answered by Muslim trebuchets from within the city.

6 After 17 weeks, Crusader mining of the walls and a new Anglo-Norman siege tower let soldiers enter Lisbon, leading to the surrender of the town's inhabitants.

4 An Anglo-Norman siege tower bogs down in the mud as it moves towards the western walls and is demolished. A German siege tower is more successful in approaching the eastern walls, but few soldiers are able to cross over the walls before it too is destroyed.

1 On 1 July 1147, having arrived north of Lisbon three days earlier, the Crusaders, accompanied by Afonso Henriques' Portuguese troops, move to within 'a stick's throw' of the city's walls.

5 Crusaders try to use their ships as siege towers to cross over the walls from the Tagus River but take so much damage from Muslim trebuchets that they withdraw.

LISBON

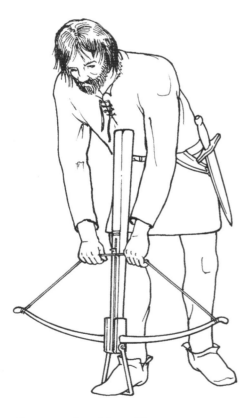

European archers of the twelfth century were crossbowmen. These weapons provided a long-range threat that could be delivered by lower-class and unskilled soldiers. Accuracy was determined primarily by the bow mechanism and not by aiming, so training was only required to load the crossbow. Because they were not directly engaged in combat, and no doubt because of their relative poverty, crossbowmen were rarely armoured.

It will likely never be known. The Lisbon Letter is silent on the matter, while Raol indicates that the decision was made only after a lengthy sermon by the bishop assured them that fighting against the Muslims in Spain was as important as fighting them in the Holy Land. Since the beginning of the *Reconquista* in the eleventh century Portugal had been seen as a part of the Kingdom of Leon-Castile, and in 1147 the King of Leon-Castile was Alfonso VII. By this time, however, Alfonso's interest lay much further to the east, and elsewhere in his kingdom local barons were free to strive for power and political legitimacy. In Portugal one such was Afonso Henriques, son of Alfonso VII's illegitimate half-sister, Teresa, and Count Henry of Burgundy. Afonso Henriques had declared himself King of Portugal in 1139 following his victory over Muslim forces at the battle of Ourique, using this as military legitimacy for his right to rule Portugal. Once king he began to endear himself to Christians in Portugal and throughout Europe. He built monasteries – especially for Cistercians – and churches, and he sent ambassadors to the papacy to declare his allegiance. To further assert his independence from Alfonso VII and the rest of Spain he wed Mafalda of Savoy, daughter of the very influential Count Amadeo III of Savoy.

It was once thought that Afonso's interception of the Crusader fleet at Porto happened by chance; that he asked for their assistance simply because the opportunity presented itself. Now it is known that Bernard of Clairvaux, the fiery Cistercian preacher who had incited so much participation in the Second Crusade, alerted the Portuguese king to the travel of the northern Crusaders and assured him that he and the Pope (by virtue of his prominence) supported the detour to Lisbon. No doubt word of this support was passed on to the Crusader leaders by the Bishop of Porto, making their decision to besiege Lisbon much easier.

LISBON BESIEGED

On 1 July 1147, the siege of Lisbon began. The Crusaders had arrived three days earlier north of the city, meeting up with a number of Afonso Henriques' troops, who were ostensibly positioned there to protect their landing. They all moved to the walls of the city, within 'a stick's throw' according to Raol, where they met some resistance, although not enough to keep them from setting up their camp and establishing their siege lines.

After some negotiations between the Crusaders and Afonso about who was to do what, the siege began. The Anglo-Normans were positioned to the west of the city walls, the Flemings and Germans on high ground to the east, and the Portuguese to the north. Initial attacks were made on the large suburbs to the west of the city outside the walls. Bows and crossbows were fired by both sides and heavy hand-to-hand fighting ensued. By sundown the Crusaders had captured their target, with their opponents retreating behind the walls.

The easy part of the siege had concluded, and the Crusaders were now faced with the walls themselves. Lisbon was a heavily populated city and it is likely that the Crusaders could have starved the citizens and garrison into submission in a few months. However, that would have delayed their journey to the Holy Land, and most still considered the siege of Lisbon a temporary stop on the way to the Middle East. Delay also risked the arrival of a Muslim relief army. But Lisbon's walls were tall and strong, and direct assaults on them were dangerous. So the Crusaders resorted to siege engines of all kinds, especially trebuchets.

CATAPULTS AND TOWERS

The Crusader trebuchets at the siege of Lisbon were of the type known by the modern term 'traction' trebuchets but referred to at the time as 'mangonels', 'Balaeric slings', or 'perrieres'. The ones used at Lisbon were quite large. They seem to have been designed with a rotating beam placed on a fulcrum, supported by a wooden tower and base. The beam was positioned unevenly on the fulcrum, with the larger end holding a sling where projectiles, generally large stones, were placed. On the opposite, shorter, end of the beam, 40 to 125 ropes were attached, which were pulled by a team of soldiers estimated to number somewhere between 40 and 250.

EVGENIO TERZO 170

EVGENIVS · PP · III · PISANVS

Pope Eugenius III was Pope from February 1145 to July 1153. It was during his reign that the Second Crusade was called in response to the fall of the Crusader County of Edessa. Two kings, Louis VII of France and Conrad III of the Holy Roman Empire, responded by launching what became one of the most unsuccessful military endeavours in history. Only the siege and capture of Lisbon by a combined force of Portuguese soldiers and northern European Crusaders brought victory to the Christians.

Experimental archaeology has shown that, by pulling in unison, the team could generate a force that threw a projectile weighing anything between 1 and 60kg (2–130lb) in a relatively flat arc for a distance of 78–122m (255–400ft) before landing with significant force.

The Muslim defenders answered these trebuchets with their own smaller stone-throwing versions, but damage to the walls from Crusader fire was substantial enough that they also risked a number of sallies to try to destroy the attackers' weapons. On one occasion they were successful in burning five of the German trebuchets, but the overall impact of these raids was negligible. The Crusaders' ability to fire heavy projectiles at the city remained largely unhampered.

With their trebuchets, the Crusaders were hoping to breach the walls or to force a submission by the city's inhabitants. They also tried to enter the city by other means. On three occasions large siege towers were constructed to enable attacking troops to overlook the walls and climb across the top of them. One of these was a 29m (95ft) tall tower built by the Anglo-Normans, which proved too heavy to get near the walls, becoming bogged down in the mud before it was close enough for a bridge to reach from it to the walls.

After four days of constant bombardment by three Muslim trebuchets, the tower was destroyed. A second, more successful, tower was built later in the siege by the Germans. Standing only 25m (83ft), according to the 'Lisbon Letter', it was

LISBON

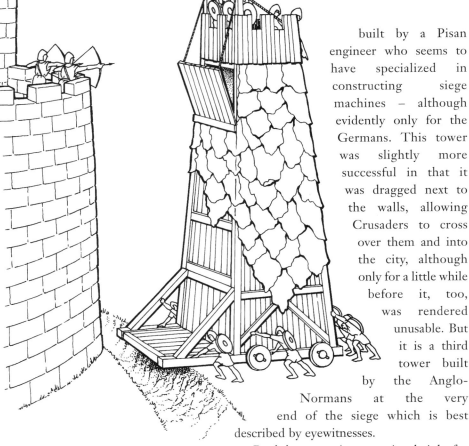

built by a Pisan engineer who seems to have specialized in constructing siege machines – although evidently only for the Germans. This tower was slightly more successful in that it was dragged next to the walls, allowing Crusaders to cross over them and into the city, although only for a little while before it, too, was rendered unusable. But it is a third tower built by the Anglo-Normans at the very end of the siege which is best described by eyewitnesses.

Raol does not give a precise height for this tower but he does say that attached to it were 'penthouses' and wicker mantlets that protected the Crusaders pushing it towards the walls as well as those walking behind it. It also had several levels from which large numbers of archers were able to shoot at opposing soldiers and drop water on any burning material that hit the tower.

Siege towers were difficult to build and operate, and they were vulnerable to attacks by fire from the besieged. Consequently, they were used only by the most determined besiegers. At Lisbon, the Crusaders built quite intricate siege towers. Early towers proved ineffective, but a later siege tower, built by Anglo-Norman soldiers, helped them to gain access to the city.

Mining a wall was an ancient and common way of passing it. The idea was to tunnel under the wall, supporting the roof of the tunnel with props. When complete, the props were fired and the tunnel collapsed, bringing the wall down with it. The attackers at ground level could then get in.

On 20 October, the tower was pushed next to the southwestern wall, with the Crusaders planning to use it to climb into the city. However, their attack was stalled when the tide came in and cut the tower off from the troops planning to make the assault. The following day Muslim soldiers sortied out of the city to attack the tower, while their trebuchets rained stones onto its upper levels. For 36 hours the battle raged before it was decided in the Crusaders' favour.

The Crusaders also tried to use their ships as towers to climb over the city's seaward walls, but after a couple of these vessels took significant damage from Muslim trebuchets they were sailed away. In addition, rams were used to attack the walls, but with little effect.

MINING THE WALLS

Ultimately, it was the oldest siege technique that did the most damage: mining. From the very outset of the siege, Crusader miners began digging under Lisbon's walls. This was not easy. Much of the ground beneath the walls was stone and digging through it was extremely difficult and time consuming. Most of the mines that were dug eventually ended up being stopped by difficult ground or successfully countermined by Muslim miners. Finally, on 16 October, one of the Germano-Flemish mines made it under the walls. According to the 'Lisbon Letter', it was an enormous mine, with huge halls and five entrances, and had taken more than a month to build.

As they were dug, mines like this would be shored up by wooden supports. Once the attackers were ready, the timber would be burned, causing the mine to collapse and bring down the stone walls above. In this case, the collapsing mine created a large breach in the walls through which a few Crusaders gained access to the city, but the breach was soon blocked by timber cut for this very purpose, and the Crusader assault was halted.

DEFENDERS LOSE HEART

The city had large numbers of Muslim defenders, and throughout the 17-week siege the citizens were more than willing to help the garrison with men and supplies. Their hope lay either in the Crusading army becoming discouraged at the size of their task and giving up, or in the arrival of a relief army. Their morale increased when they saw that many of the Crusading Portuguese soldiers left about midway through the siege, an act seen as traitorous by Raol, although it may only have been the reality of the harvest requiring the non-professional soldiers to return to their farms.

However, the defenders' morale must have declined severely when in August it was observed that the Crusaders had brought their ships on to dry land, lowered their masts and stowed the sails and cordage in the hulls. Clearly, they were prepared not to sail off to Jerusalem but to winter in Lisbon. However, the biggest blow to Muslim morale came when a messenger arrived from the Governor of Beja, Sidray ibn Wazir, bearing the news that there would be no relief. Although the messenger was captured by the Crusaders, they more than gladly let him go to deliver his message.

SURRENDER

On 21 October, food supplies were dwindling and winter was approaching. With Anglo-Norman Crusaders preparing to use their large siege tower to cross over the walls on the west, and German and Flemish Crusaders preparing to use ladders to scale the towers on the east – some Lotharingians had even made it onto the tower, claims the 'Lisbon Letter' – the Muslims asked for peace terms, which were granted. The citizens were to surrender hostages to Afonso Henriques, who promised that none of the citizens or soldiers in Lisbon would be killed, and the city would not be ransacked.

The Crusader leaders, anxious to get on their way, agreed. Their troops, however, were not to be pacified so easily. Within a very short time rumours went out that there was a large amount of riches hidden in the city and that the common troops were to have none of it. Crusader soldiers rushed through the gates of the city and began sacking it. A priest from Bristol even led a group of 400 sailors against Hervey de Glanvill, blaming him for accepting the surrender, while a large number of Germans and Flemings attacked the Portuguese camp, demanding that they hand over the hostages. Before calm could be restored, Lisbon had been ransacked and a number of citizens killed – including the Mozarabic Christian Bishop of the city.

AFTERMATH

By the following spring, most of the Crusaders had left Lisbon. Some travelled to their homes overland and others by sea. Some travelled to and participated in the siege of Tortosa in Spain, which lasted from July to December 1148. A large number continued on to the Holy Land, where, upon their arrival in mid-summer, they discovered that the Second Crusade was over and had failed. The capture of Lisbon had been its only success.

ALMOHAD FOOT SOLDIER

The largest number of soldiers in the Almohad army were light infantry raised from the villages and towns of Spain and Morocco. They had little training in warfare and were not armoured, although many carried shields. Despite this, their generals often placed them at the front of their battle lines, where they became the first to encounter an enemy charge. This tactic has led some historians to accuse Muslim military leaders of sacrificing these soldiers, as they often failed against their better-trained and armoured opponents; they did, however, weaken them, making them vulnerable to other, heavier Muslim units.

MONTGISARD
1177

MONTGISARD WAS A MASSIVE DEFEAT FOR SALADIN, FROM WHICH HE
ONLY JUST ESCAPED WITH HIS LIFE. IN MANY WAYS THIS WAS THE CLASSIC
CRUSADER VICTORY, WON BY A HEADLONG VIOLENT CHARGE AGAINST
SUPERIOR NUMBERS. NEVER AGAIN, THOUGH, WOULD SUCH A SMALL
FORCE SHATTER A HUGE HOST IN THIS MANNER.

WHY DID IT HAPPEN?

WHO A Crusader army containing
almost 600 knights and several
thousand common soldiers under
Baldwin IV, versus approximately
30,000 Muslim troops under
Saladin.

WHAT The Crusaders surprised
their opponents and, after a brief
hesitation, charged headlong at
them.

WHERE Near Montgisard.

WHEN 25 November 1177.

WHY Part of the ongoing war
between Crusaders and Muslim
states in the Holy Land.

OUTCOME The Muslim force was
routed, suffering further casualties
in its subsequent retreat.

Warfare in the medieval period was characterized by sieges and raids more than pitched battles, and indeed many of the battles that occurred were as result of a relief attempt. Army movements tended to be directed at a critical objective with the intent of capturing it (usually by siege), or else were attempts to intercept such a move. It was generally by the capture or salvation of strong places that the political landscape was changed, rather than as a result of decisive battles in the field.

Of course, if a battle led to a force being able to besiege a fortress unimpeded, then this had much the same effect, but most critical medieval battles were important due to their effects on the campaign-winning siege rather than deciding the matter in their own right. Montgisard was something of an exception, in that the Muslim army was so massively defeated that the battle itself became significant for many years.

Another factor in medieval warfare, particularly but not exclusively in the

Relics such as the True Cross could inspire highly religious troops to incredible heights of bravery, as they represented little short of the actual presence of God on the Crusaders' side.

Crusades, was the role of religious fervour and the significance of holy relics. Whether troops really were imbued with the power of their God, or simply motivated to reckless courage by the belief that they had divine influence on their side, religious relics played an important part in the wars of the period.

In some cases a battle turned on the effects the presence of a holy relic had on friendly troops, and it is hardly surprising that leaders who had access to relics (or objects claimed or supposed to be holy relics) often had them incorporated into a banner that could be seen from anywhere on the battlefield.

This was particularly important in the Holy Land, which was itself of religious significance and the source of relics. One such was the True Cross, thought to be the actual cross upon which Christ was crucified and which was stained with holy blood. The True Cross had been incorporated into a standard adorned with jewels and gold and capable of imbuing those who fought under it with tremendous power.

The Crusaders needed all the help they could get. Split into factions under regional rulers, the kingdom they had carved out was under constant attack by displaced Muslims, and the Crusaders were frequently defeated in the field.

King Baldwin IV (c. 1161–1185), the titular leader of the Crusaders, was suffering from leprosy, and his subordinates were looking for a suitable husband for his sister Sibylla. Their first choice, William of Montferrat, died of malaria in 1177 soon after the marriage. The search for another prospect was yet another divisive issue among the Crusader leaders.

This was not a time for the Christian leaders to be arguing among themselves. In 1175, Saladin had attempted to bring Aleppo under his control and been thwarted by a Crusader army. He tried again in 1176 and conquered much of the region, though he was not able to take the city itself. Now, in 1177, Saladin was positioned to try again.

THE CAMPAIGN OPENS

Saladin was planning a new offensive against the Crusader Kingdom of Jerusalem, marching out of Egypt with 26,000 men under his direct command. The Crusaders had intended to attack Saladin in Egypt and had arranged a joint campaign with forces from Byzantium and others fresh from Europe. These plans had to be abandoned in favour of a response to Saladin's thrust, and so the Crusader army assembled to meet the Muslim force.

The Crusaders were led by the leper king of Jerusalem, Baldwin IV, accompanied by the Bishop of Bethlehem, in whose care was Baldwin's holy banner, the True Cross. With him was Raynald of Chatillon, who had spent many years as a Muslim prisoner before being released in 1176. Now married to Stephanie of Oultrejourdain, Raynald was no longer an adventurer but a Crusader lord. Under their banner marched some 500 knights with several thousand infantry in support.

SALADIN GAINS THE UPPER HAND

Baldwin's plan was to meet the advancing Muslim force at Ascalon and halt them there. He would have support from forces based at Ascalon and could rely on the city to provide logistical support for his army, a matter of critical

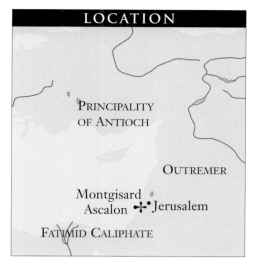

The Crusader victory at Montgisard was a major setback in Saladin's attempts to reduce the power of the Crusader states.

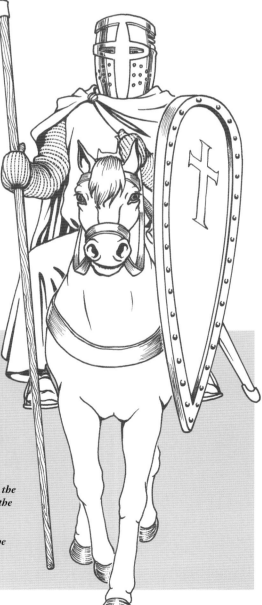

TEMPLAR KNIGHT

The epitome of European military might, the armoured knight represented the maximum fighting power that could be delivered by one man. Well protected in his armour and made reasonably mobile by his horse, the knight combined the shock of the lance charge with the staying power of his skill with hand weapons.

While all knights were skilled and highly motivated, those belonging to special orders like the Templars were particularly capable. Knights of the Temple were both monks and knights, and were deeply religious as well as being highly trained. Their order was formed to protect pilgrims to the Holy Land, and saw the defeat of all threats to Christians in the region as a holy mission.

The castle of the counts of Flanders can still be seen today in Ghent, Belgium. Castle-building was both an art and a science in the medieval period, and fortifications like this one were both a refuge and a base of operations. Just as importantly, they were symbols of prestige and power.

THE OPPOSED FORCES

CRUSADERS (estimated)
Crusader Knights:	500
Templar Knights:	80
Infantry: Several Thousand	
Total:	**3,000**

AYYUBID MUSLIMS (estimated)
Mostly cavalry	
Total:	**30,000**

importance in the prevailing conditions. However, the plan went awry.

The Knights Templar, staunch enemies of Saladin, had promised to send assistance. Eighty of their number were marching to Ascalon but were challenged by Muslim troops and forced to seek refuge in Gaza. There, they were besieged and apparently unable to contribute to the campaign.

Meanwhile, Baldwin attempted to confront Saladin but was instead trapped within the city of Ascalon by Saladin's superior force. After some inconsequential fighting, Saladin concluded that Baldwin's force was too small to break out of the city. He left a covering force to keep Baldwin bottled up and pushed onwards with his

campaign. Ramla fell quickly to his host, and both Arsuf and Lydda were taken under siege. Unless they could be relieved – unlikely, with both major Crusader forces trapped under siege themselves – the two cities would fall sooner or later.

THE CRUSADERS FIGHT

Saladin reasoned that even if Baldwin did manage to get out of Ascalon, his force was too small to risk going after Saladin's massive army. In this, he miscalculated. Whether through religious faith, overconfidence or sheer desperation, Baldwin made the decision to break out of Ascalon. He fought his way through the blockade and began his move to confront

Saladin. Meanwhile, the Knights Templar had come to a similar decision and, prompted by a timely message from Baldwin, they forced their way through the troops besieging them in Gaza. Once out of the city, they headed for Saladin's army with the intent of giving battle.

This tiny band of knights represented a formidable fighting force. They were well armoured and highly skilled with their weapons. In addition, they were motivated by religious fervour and were fighting an enemy of their god. Unusually, their horses were also trained to fight, lashing out with hooves and teeth against anyone getting too close.

The Templars were few in number, but dangerous all the same. Like all knightly forces, their main capability was the headlong charge to deliver a hammerblow to the enemy. If they could make contact with the enemy, they would bring a tremendous amount of force to bear at the critical point and perhaps break an entire

In this classic depiction of the Christian knight as noble defender of his people, St George (in a Greek-style helm, reflecting the Classical tastes of the Victorian artist) tackles the fearsome dragon. Legends say that at the battle of Montgisard Baldwin led the charge from the forefront with St George and the True Cross beside him.

MONTGISARD

1177

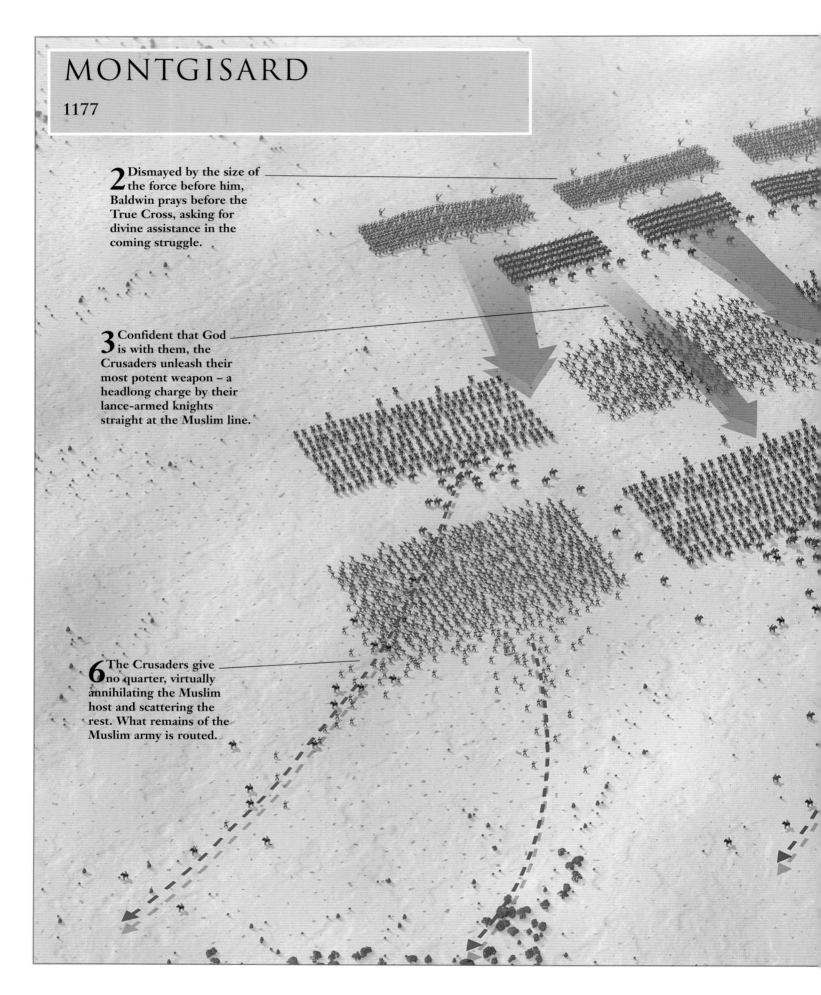

2 Dismayed by the size of the force before him, Baldwin prays before the True Cross, asking for divine assistance in the coming struggle.

3 Confident that God is with them, the Crusaders unleash their most potent weapon – a headlong charge by their lance-armed knights straight at the Muslim line.

6 The Crusaders give no quarter, virtually annihilating the Muslim host and scattering the rest. What remains of the Muslim army is routed.

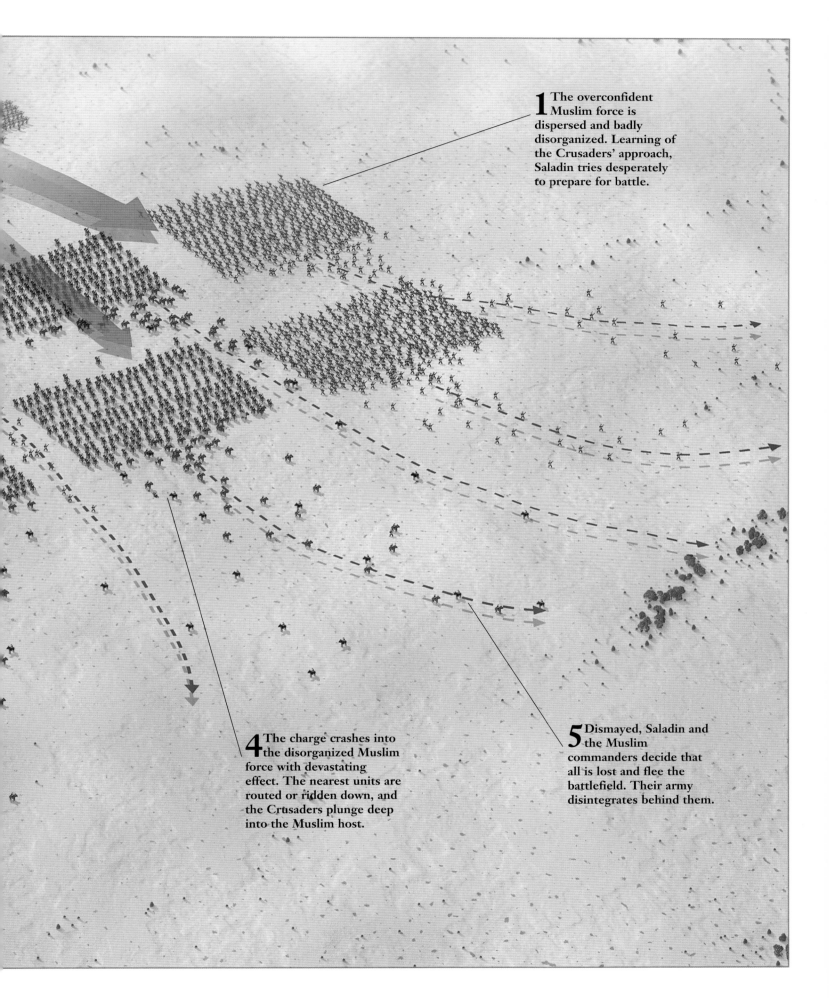

1 The overconfident Muslim force is dispersed and badly disorganized. Learning of the Crusaders' approach, Saladin tries desperately to prepare for battle.

4 The charge crashes into the disorganized Muslim force with devastating effect. The nearest units are routed or ridden down, and the Crusaders plunge deep into the Muslim host.

5 Dismayed, Saladin and the Muslim commanders decide that all is lost and flee the battlefield. Their army disintegrates behind them.

Raised from childhood as religious warriors, the Mamluks were extremely skilled and determined soldiers. Although lighter equipped than European knights, they were formidable opponents. The figure on the left is armed with the traditional cavalry bow and small 'buckler'-style shield, while the figure on the right holds a cavalry lance and larger shield.

it. Under the right conditions, that confidence, coupled with heavy blows of sword and lance, could carry an enemy before it.

DISPOSITIONS

Saladin himself set the scene for his defeat at Montgisard. He was sure that his enemies could not challenge him, and thus allowed his army to become excessively dispersed. To some extent it was necessary to spread out somewhat, in order to forage for supplies, and to avoid trying to force too many troops through the same regions. Saladin, however, took this too far.

With no real threat in sight, Saladin allowed his forces to forage and pillage over a wide area. The latter improved morale, as troops took booty to enrich themselves, and also damaged the enemy in many ways. Anything taken from enemy territory was of course lost to them, and in addition there was a clear message being sent – the Crusaders cannot protect their own territory and must therefore be weak. The pillaging could also be seen as punishment for allowing the Crusaders to dominate the people of the region.

army by shattering its key unit or bringing down its leaders.

The Templars certainly believed that this was possible. Their tactics – if charging head on at the enemy can be considered as tactics – were based on the dream of Saint Bernard, who claimed that a small force could destroy a much larger one in this manner. The Templars' fighting style was thus approved by the very highest authority and as a result they had great confidence in

However, with foraging parties out all over the countryside and troops detached for two small sieges, Saladin was badly overstretched. This would only matter if a significant opponent appeared to offer battle. At Montgisard near Ramla, that is exactly what happened.

THE ARMIES MEET

Baldwin's army had made a junction with the Templars, bringing the main striking force available to Baldwin to 580 mounted knights. They were supported by several thousand infantry, armed mainly with spears and bows, but the main strength of the Crusader army was its heavy cavalry. The day would be won or lost by their actions. Saladin was caught completely by surprise, with his army scattered and, perhaps more importantly, he was in a complacent frame of mind. Suddenly, everything had changed; he was facing a major battle and he knew he was unprepared for it. Saladin started the battle badly off balance.

It is rightly said that 'victory is found in the mind of the enemy commander; defeat lies within yourself'. In other words, winning a battle is to some extent a matter of convincing the opposing leader that he is defeated. Saladin was already some of the way there. However, Baldwin was also dismayed. Baldwin saw the vast force ranged against him and became unsure of himself. His army was greatly outnumbered and the Crusaders had been defeated several times in recent history. His chances did not look good. There was nothing for it, though. Baldwin had to fight and defeat Saladin to save the Crusader kingdom. And he did have God on his side.

Baldwin dismounted and prostrated himself before God, as represented by the Bishop of Bethlehem and the True Cross. The Crusader king prayed for victory in the coming battle, asking for divine assistance in driving the infidel from the Holy Land. He then made a brief oratory to his troops and led them forward to fight.

THE BATTLE

Baldwin was now in a confident, or at least aggressive, frame of mind. He was advancing at the head of his host under the banner of the True Cross. The Templars had come to his assistance and God was with him. Baldwin had good reasons to believe that he might win the day; Saladin, however, did not.

Saladin was probably not very effective as a commander at Montgisard. He had been caught on the hop and was facing a very aggressive opponent. Saladin was trying to avoid defeat while he pulled in his dispersed forces and made a plan. Meanwhile, Baldwin was launching an all-or-nothing bid to win the battle.

One reason why Crusader charges often failed was the clever manoeuvring of opposing forces so that their initial charge hit empty air. Then, as the knights were drawn on in pursuit of their retreating target, other

Crusaders march carrying the True Cross. Several major relics were present in the Holy Land – after all, they originated there – but none was more significant than the True Cross. Those who marched under it considered themselves to be God's chosen instruments.

Saladin in his later years. He was both wise and ruthless, compassionate and fearsome, and truly one of the great military leaders of history. That he lived to become such was in part due to his wise choice of a fast mount for the battle of Montgisard. Years later, he would refer to the battle disdainfully as 'so great a disaster'.

units would close in and shoot them full of arrows before a final hand-to-hand assault overwhelmed the tired survivors.

At Montgisard, overall tactical direction was lacking in Saladin's army and the Crusader charge hit home. Less than 600 lances smashed into the Muslim army, but the line was broken and the infantry followed up their knights' success with a determined advance. The knights themselves pressed forward, losing momentum but driving the enemy before them as St Bernard had dreamed.

In the Muslim army, it seemed that all was lost. Had the commanders on the spot managed to rally their followers they might have counterattacked and overwhelmed the Crusaders. But it was not to be: Saladin's

men had started the battle off balance and were now presented with what looked like a resounding Crusader victory in progress. Once they decided that they were losing, it swiftly became reality and the Muslim army disintegrated.

It was always as one side broke that heavy casualties were inflicted, and Montgisard was no exception. The wars of the Holy Land were bitter, with prisoners frequently executed by both sides, and as a result there was no quarter given by the victorious Christians. Wounded men were despatched as the victors advanced over them, and the survivors were scattered wherever they could flee.

Saladin himself escaped the carnage on the back of a particularly swift camel, but not before his elite bodyguard was slaughtered. He gathered what he could of his army and began the long retreat back to Egypt.

SALADIN'S RETREAT

Baldwin did not mount much of a pursuit at first. The remnants of the Muslim army and siege forces were all over the countryside and they had to be dealt with. He did set out after Saladin and entered the Sinai Peninsula but was not able to bring the defeated Muslim army to renewed battle. He had, however, already won a spectacular victory.

Saladin's army struggled through torrential rains to try to reach the safety of friendly territory. However, like other defeated armies, his force was plagued by raiders along the way. In this case it was Bedouin tribesmen taking advantage of the defeated army to harass and ambush its units wherever possible, and to steal whatever they could.

At last Saladin reached Egypt, where he regrouped his devastated army. In the battle and subsequent retreat his force had suffered 90 per cent casualties, a quite incredible figure.

AFTERMATH

Recognizing that he had won a decisive victory, Baldwin ordered a monastery to be erected on the site of the battle. It was dedicated to St Catherine of Alexandria since the battle had been won on her feast day. Saladin was not able to resume hostilities the following year, and though he did return to the fray in 1179, the intervening year of relative peace was the first for a long time. The achievement of wringing out of the enemy even a single year without major conflict was duly recognized and celebrated by Baldwin's supporters and the Knights Templar.

King Baldwin IV died in 1185, while Saladin continued to lead the struggle to repel the Crusaders from the Holy Land for many more years.

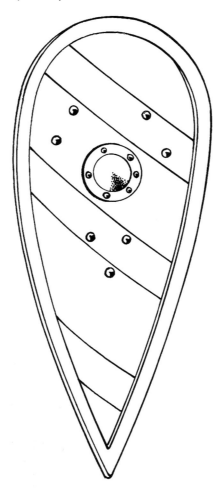

Above and below: The round shield, which could be made from either wood or metal, was very popular among Muslim soldiers – especially among cavalry – because of its light weight and easily handled shape. The smallest of this type of shield was called a buckler, and could be used as a kind of hand-held offensive weapon.

Above: This large, triangular wooden shield was commonly used by infantry, especially the Byzantine and Muslim forces the Crusaders often faced. The holding device was on the inside of the central boss.

Above The 'kite' style cavalry shield was used by Northern French and Anglo-Norman men-at-arms from the eleventh to the twelfth century. The shape protected both torso and legs.

HATTIN
1187

THIS BATTLE HERALDED A NEW EFFECTIVENESS OF COMMAND FOR THE MUSLIMS UNDER SALADIN, RESULTING IN THE EVENTUAL RECAPTURE OF JERUSALEM. HATTIN MEANT THAT THE CRUSADERS WOULD NEVER AGAIN HAVE AS MUCH TERRITORY AND POWER AS THEY HAD PREVIOUSLY.

WHY DID IT HAPPEN?

WHO Some 50,000 Muslims under Saladin (1138–1193) against a force of about 32,000 Crusaders under Guy of Lusignan (King Guy of Jerusalem, c. 1150–1194).

WHAT Saladin lured the Crusader armies forward, away from their water supplies, until they were pinned down and surrounded in a shallow valley. Thirst and harassing fire eventually exhausted the Crusaders and left them unable to resist the final Muslim assaults.

WHERE The Horns of Hattin, near Tiberias on the Sea of Galilee.

WHEN 4 July 1187.

WHY Saladin assembled a large army to punish the Crusaders for repeated breaches of a truce and for attacks on trade caravans.

OUTCOME Most of the Crusaders were killed or captured, allowing Saladin to go on and eventually retake Jerusalem.

On 4 July 1187, the Crusades changed, and the change was felt not only in the Holy Land, but also throughout Syria, Egypt, Byzantium and Europe. It seemed as if the Christian God's wheel of fortune had fallen while the Muslim God's wheel had risen. And this was due solely to the military genius of one man: Saladin.

Later European writers would think highly of Saladin. Some even wondered if he was secretly Christian, celebrating his heroism, chivalry and mercy – three obvious 'Christian' traits – especially as the great Crusade leader, Richard the Lionheart, had left the Holy Land without defeating Saladin, and that could only have happened, they reckoned, if Richard knew that he was leaving it in Christian hands. The celebrated Italian poet, Dante, knew better, but Saladin still impressed him so much that he placed the Islamic Sultan among the 'Virtuous Pagans' on the rim of and not inside hell, in the company of Plato, Aristotle and Virgil, Dante's guide through the underworld.

TURKISH POWER GROWS

The story of Saladin and the battle of Hattin began many years before 1187. At the end of their successful First Crusade the Crusaders had established only a very weak northeastern border in the County of Edessa. Edessa was the oldest of Crusader principalities, but it was not well protected, being quite a distance from the other kingdoms and with no natural defences guarding it. By 1144, the Seljuk Turks had recovered sufficient strength that a unifying leader, Zengi, was able to attack Edessa, and the County fell quickly.

Among the leaders of the Turkish army that conquered Edessa was Zengi's son, Nur-ad-Din, who inherited his father's power and title after Zengi died rather

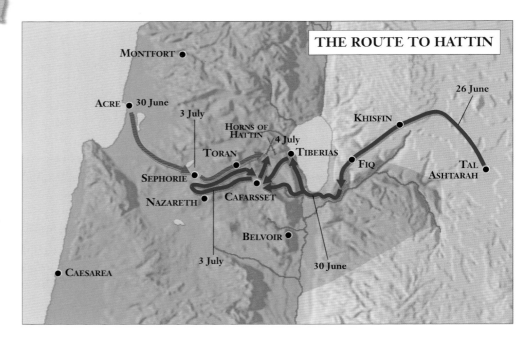

THE ROUTE TO HATTIN

The map shows the movement of the two armies up until the decisive battle of Hattin on 4 July 1187. Saladin's troops shadowed the Crusader army for some days, only choosing to engage when the Christian force was at a significant disadvantage, low on supplies and water.

mysteriously in 1146 while on campaign against Damascus. Nur-ad-Din altered his father's strategy, directing his army around Damascus towards Egypt. As such there was no direct threat to the remaining Crusader principalities, but the loss of Edessa panicked them nonetheless, and they immediately called for a Second Crusade.

The call to 'take the cross' in the Second Crusade proved almost as popular as that for the initial Crusade. A large number of soldiers responded, among them two kings, Conrad III of Germany and Louis VII of France. But numbers meant nothing. Almost immediately after reaching the Holy Land they began quarrelling with the resident Crusaders, who resented the arrogance of the new arrivals. Principally they differed on how to fight Nur-ad-Din: the resident Crusaders wished to take the Crusade army north to Aleppo, the capital of Nur-ad-Din's lands; the Second Crusaders targeted a closer site, Damascus, a city controlled by the Muslims, but enemies of Nur-ad-Din and allied to the resident Crusaders. In the end, the status and will of the two kings prevailed, and on 24 June 1148 the Crusaders advanced on Damascus.

But soon after the armies began their attacks on the strong city walls, Conrad and Louis began to bicker over whose forces were to do what. Conrad III quickly set out for home, with Louis VII leaving a bit later. By summer 1149, almost all the Second Crusaders had returned to Europe, having suffered one of the biggest defeats of the Middle Ages.

Nur-ad-Din took immediate advantage of the Crusaders' defeat and retreat from the Middle East. Damascus fell in 1154, with the rest of Syria following. At the same time, Nur-ad-Din also sent armies to Egypt and against Crusader holdings along his frontiers. The latter were soon successful, capturing the castles of Harim and Inab, and winning the battle of Inab against the forces of Antioch.

But it was the defeat of Egypt that handed Nur-ad-Din his greatest military achievement. The Seljuk Turks and Fatamid Egyptians had been fighting for a century. Taking advantage of internal conflicts in Egypt as well as attacks against the Fatamids

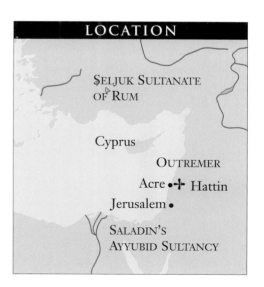

TEMPLAR KNIGHT
(TWELFTH CENTURY)
The Knights Templar is the popular name for the members of the Poor Fellow-Soldiers of Christ and of the Temple of Solomon, a military monastic order founded in the Holy Land around 1119. They were essentially fighting monks who took the vows of poverty, celibacy and obedience like other monks, but also promised to defend the Crusader principalities against Muslim attacks.

Their headquarters was on the Temple Mount in Jerusalem, but Templars could be found in towns and castles throughout all of the Holy Land and in Europe. The Templars became famous throughout the Crusading period as strong and enthusiastic warriors who did not seek quarter, an attitude that led to the execution of those captured by Saladin at the Battle of Hattin. But equally famous was their wealth and the secrecy of their initiation rituals, which led to the suppression of the order in the early fourteenth century.

by armies of the kingdom of Jerusalem and the Byzantine Empire, in 1168 Nur-ad-Din added this land to his territorial holdings.

SALADIN'S RISE

It was during the Egyptian conquest that Saladin rose to power. Shirkuh had been Nur-ad-Din's commanding general or vizier, against the Fatamids, and Saladin was his nephew and lieutenant. When Shirkuh died in 1169, only months after he had entered Cairo at the head of a victorious army, Saladin succeeded him. Saladin seems not to have been Nur-ad-Din's first choice for this leadership role, but the Sultan's distance from him – he was in Damascus – allowed the young general the time to convince the other leaders and the rest of the army in Egypt that he was right for the job. He was named vizier and then, two

LOCATION

SELJUK SULTANATE OF RUM

Cyprus

OUTREMER

Acre ✦ Hattin

Jerusalem

SALADIN'S AYYUBID SULTANCY

King Guy of Jerusalem set out to relieve the castle at Tiberias, but was cut off from his water supply by Saladin's larger Muslim army. The battle took place around two rocky outcrops – the Horns of Hattin.

HATTIN

No relic in medieval Christianity equalled that of the True Cross. Reputed to have been found in Jerusalem during the fourth century by St Helena, Constantine's mother – as depicted in this late medieval illumination – several pieces existed by the time of the Crusades. The piece held in the Kingdom of Jerusalem was taken with the Crusading armies to the Battle of Hattin, where it was captured by Saladin.

Saladin followed his victory at the Battle of Hattin with the capture of Jerusalem. Among the terms of the city's surrender was the ransoming of all Christians who could pay and the freeing of those who could not, mercy that would later make him a symbol of chivalry in Europe. However, in this nineteenth-century illustration, Saladin is shown reviewing the Christians forced from Jerusalem with more of an attitude of triumphal conqueror than is recorded in contemporary sources.

This, however, did not bring him peace. Aleppo and Mosul held out against Saladin's control. Eventually, both came to him with relatively little violence, in 1176 and 1186 respectively, but not before Saladin had survived two attempts on his life by members of the elusive cult of fanatics whose use of hashish in ceremonies gave them their popular name 'Hashshashins' (now known as 'Assassins'). Their willingness to kill for money gave them their occupation.

During this period Saladin and the Crusader kingdoms co-existed rather well with each other. The only time when large armies from the two Middle Eastern powers clashed, at Montgisard on 25 November 1177, the Crusader forces of King Baldwin IV of Jerusalem (c. 1161–1185) and the Knights Templar defeated those of Saladin. But both sides had taken a pounding and thus the year following this battle a truce between them was declared. It would last for ten years.

THE TRUCE IS BROKEN

When the truce was broken in 1187, it was not Saladin's doing. Unlike the Muslim sultanate, which at this time was absolutely governed – both politically and religiously – by Saladin, the Crusader principalities had a number of rulers, and many more influential political and religious voices. The traditional supreme leader of the Crusaders had been the King of Jerusalem, but in the 1180s King Baldwin IV was in the final throes of leprosy, which would cause his death in 1185.

Despite leading the armies at Montgisard, Baldwin had always pushed for peace, perhaps understanding that while they had been victorious there, the Crusaders could never hope to succeed in

years later, Sultan, giving him political as well as military leadership.

From 1171 to 1174 there was an uneasy peace between the Nur-ad-Din and Saladin. In theory, Saladin ruled only in Nur-ad-Din's name, but in actuality there was no question who was the future of Islam in the Middle East. Saladin made great military gains, enlarging his lands south down the Nile and across the Red Sea into Yemen. Nur-ad-Din's military campaigns against the Crusader Kingdoms in 1171 and 1173 came to naught. Saladin brought prosperity and unity to Egypt and Nur-ad-Din's internal control was weakening. Had Nur-ad-Din not died of a sudden illness in 1174, there would likely have been civil war between the two Muslim leaders.

Instead, Saladin was able to march east to Damascus, entering there in peace the year of Nur-ad-Din's death. Marrying Nur-ad-Din's widow gave him further legitimacy.

THE OPPOSED FORCES

CRUSADERS (estimated)

Cavalry:	4000
Infantry:	8000
Total:	**12,000**

MUSLIMS (estimated)

Cavalry (inc. archers):	5000
Infantry:	10–13,000
Total:	**15–18,000**

HATTIN

1187

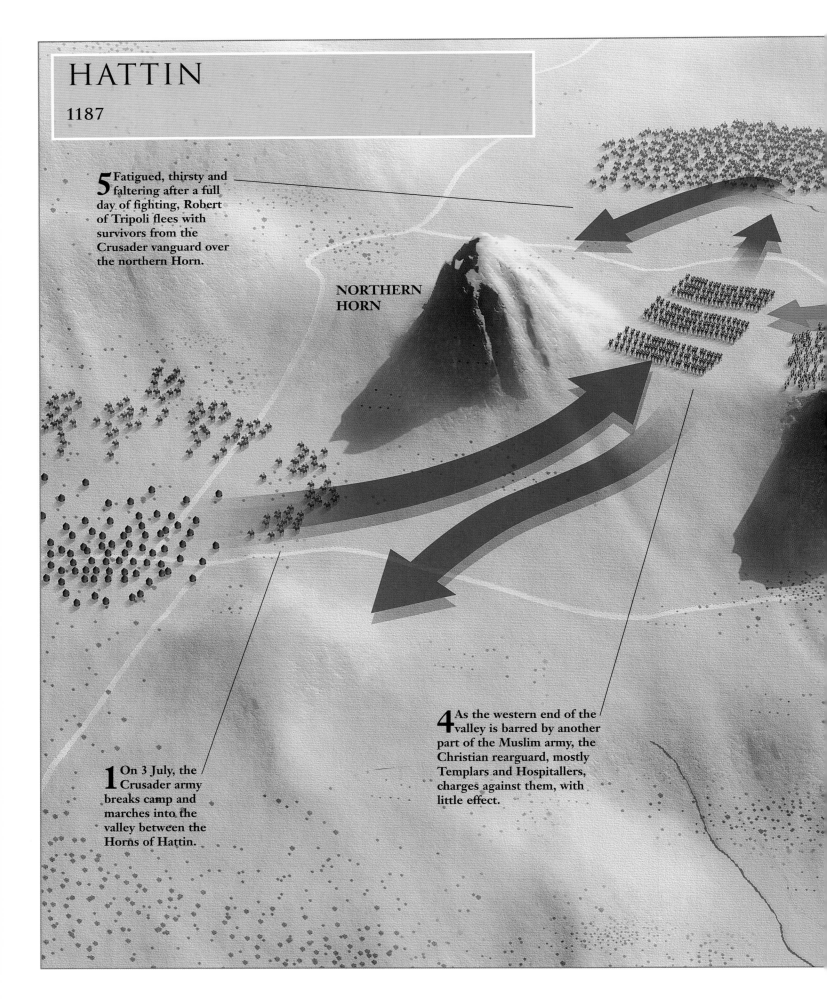

5 Fatigued, thirsty and faltering after a full day of fighting, Robert of Tripoli flees with survivors from the Crusader vanguard over the northern Horn.

NORTHERN HORN

4 As the western end of the valley is barred by another part of the Muslim army, the Christian rearguard, mostly Templars and Hospitallers, charges against them, with little effect.

1 On 3 July, the Crusader army breaks camp and marches into the valley between the Horns of Hattin.

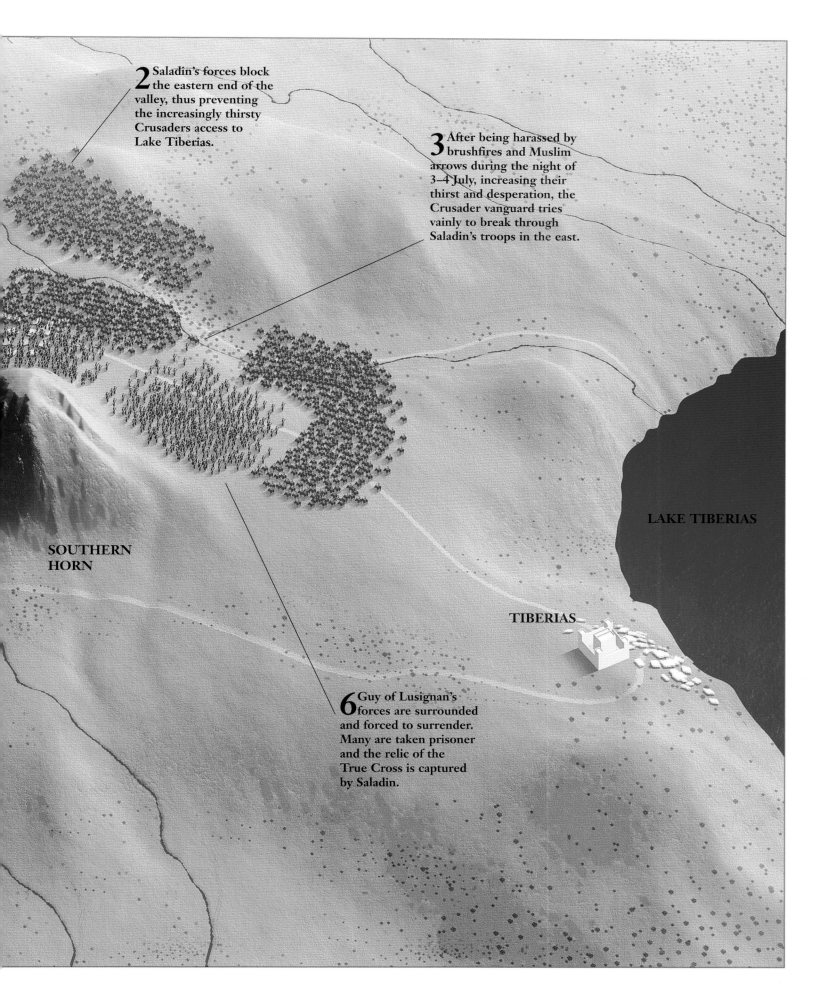

2 Saladin's forces block the eastern end of the valley, thus preventing the increasingly thirsty Crusaders access to Lake Tiberias.

3 After being harassed by brushfires and Muslim arrows during the night of 3–4 July, increasing their thirst and desperation, the Crusader vanguard tries vainly to break through Saladin's troops in the east.

LAKE TIBERIAS

SOUTHERN HORN

TIBERIAS

6 Guy of Lusignan's forces are surrounded and forced to surrender. Many are taken prisoner and the relic of the True Cross is captured by Saladin.

destroying the large numbers of soldiers that were potentially available to Saladin. During his failing years and following his death, Baldwin's regent, Count Raymond III of Tripoli, chose to follow the King's wishes. But he was constantly opposed by the Master of the Templars, Gerard of Ridfort, on whose side was also found the bellicose voices of Reynald of Chatillon and Guy of Lusignan, who, while not princes themselves, had married well – Guy to Sibylla, Baldwin's sister, and Reynald to Stephanie of Milly, the widowed heiress of Oultrejourdain. At the death of Baldwin these latter individuals gained sway when in an election to replace the heirless King of Jerusalem, the Crusader barons chose Guy over Raymond. Guy of Lusignan, now king, would lead the Crusaders at the disastrous Battle of Hattin.

REYNALD OF CHATILLON

But the true villain of Hattin was not Guy but Reynald (or Reginald) of Chatillon, one of his lieutenants there. When he arrived in the Holy Land in 1153, Reynald was only a penniless adventurer of little European status – the second son of a lesser, quite poor French noble, Henry, Lord of Chatillon – but with a confidence and restlessness that, in the Middle East, could make up for low birth.

Within only a short time, Reynald had gained both wealth and title by marrying the recently widowed Constance of Antioch. However, never one to be satisfied with his prosperity, in 1155 Reynald set out to gain more by attacking Cyprus. Initially he was successful, ravaging and plundering the island, but he could not hold on to it. (Indeed, later, he was forced to pay the Byzantine emperor for the damages caused during this attack.)

As pugnacious as he was, before 1160 Reynald seems never to have fought Muslim soldiers; and his encounter that year did not turn out at all well for him, as he was captured by Nur-ad-Din's troops while raiding Muslim habitations near Marash. For the next 17 years he was held captive in an Aleppo prison. Yet, even this did not thwart his ambition – or his recklessness. Once released in 1176, and with his former wife dead, he married Stephanie of Milly,

the widow of Humphrey II of Toron, and through her became master of the seigniory of Oultrejourdain. This seigniory also meant ownership of the important castles of Kerak and Montreal, located southeast of the Dead Sea, which controlled trade routes between Egypt and Damascus. From these locations Reynald began to prey on Islamic trade… and, no doubt, to 'pick a fight'.

Thus Reynald forced Saladin to notice him. On several occasions the two came to

Right: Lower Galilee, Israel – the Horns of Hattin mountains. This photograph gives an excellent impression of the terrain: scrub with patches of rubble and rocky outcrops – sufficient to hinder free movement of the mounted Crusaders but not to impede the arrows of the Muslim horse archers.

blows, and although most of these conflicts were small and indecisive, Reynald was generally successful.

It seems that Saladin was unwilling to lead a large army against this lone Crusader and thereby violate the truce between himself and the other Crusaders. On the other hand, Saladin may simply have been biding his time, waiting to use a more substantial violation as a means of motivating his diverse army to a unified

military response – a difficult task for even this most successful military leader.

TRUCE IS VIOLATED

That 'substantial violation' came in 1182 with Reynald's extremely poorly conceived and widely unsuccessful attempt to attack Mecca from the Red Sea. This folly ended quickly when one of Saladin's lieutenants captured Reynald's ships on the coast of Sudan after they had been blown across the

HATTIN

Krak des Chevaliers: Throughout the twelfth and thirteenth centuries the Crusaders built large stone castles to protect the borders of their principalities. One of the largest of these, known as the Krak des Chevaliers, was built by the Hospitallers in the early twelfth century. Measuring nearly 140 x 210 metres (459 x 689ft) in area and with stores and cisterns that could sustain a garrison for five years, this castle was nevertheless besieged several times and fell twice to Muslim armies.

sea from their target. Direct participants did see Mecca, however, as they were taken there and publicly beheaded. Anger towards a common enemy, the Crusaders, by Muslims of all religious and ethnic varieties soared. Nor was it quelled when Saladin besieged Kerak Castle during the marriage celebrations of Reynald's stepson, Humphrey IV of Toron, to Isabella of Jerusalem, raising this siege only after receiving promises of peace from Raymond III of Tripoli.

Reynald of Chatillon was not a man to sit idle though, and in 1186, after allying with Guy of Lusignan, Raymond's adversary, Reynald again began to attack trade caravans passing near his castles. In one of these rode Saladin's sister. Why did Reynald assault a caravan that clearly showed insignia indicating that it contained a relative of the great Sultan? Was this simply part of Reynald's reckless character? Or, is it possible that Saladin purposely sent his sister into such an obviously dangerous situation? Can it be that he was ready to make his move against the Crusaders and that he knew that he could provoke a war by

tempting Reynald of Chatillon with such a rich caravan?

Whatever the answer, the attack certainly triggered further conflict. Guy of Lusignan and Raymond of Tripoli attempted to regain peace with the Sultan, but by the following year, 1187, Saladin had invaded the Latin Kingdom of Jerusalem.

THE SPRINGS OF CRESSON

Mustering of armies could begin early in the year in the Holy Land, and Saladin started gathering his forces shortly after March 1187, bringing troops together at his camp

Opposite: One of the greatest generals of history, Saladin rose to power in Egypt when he succeeded his uncle, a lieutenant of Nur ad-Din, as military governor. When Nur ad-Din died in 1174, Saladin succeeded him as Sultan. Over the next two decades he directed his armies against the Crusaders, eventually capturing almost the whole of the Kingdom of Jerusalem following the Battle of Hattin and the siege of Jerusalem. The combined armies of the Third Crusade could not decisively defeat the Sultan or even regain the city.

As depicted in this late medieval illumination, one of the most famous incidents in the Battle of Hattin was Saladin giving a cup of water to the captured Guy of Lusignan, King of Jerusalem, following the battle. By doing so, the Sultan indicated to Guy that his life would be spared. Reynald of Châtillon was not so fortunate. When Guy passed the cup to Reynald, Saladin slapped the cup from his hand, indicating that he would not have similar mercy. Saladin then beheaded Reynald.

from as far away as Egypt and Syria. Over the next couple of months groups of these were sent on raids into Crusader territory – including one against Reynald's Kerak Castle on 26 April – as Saladin took note of their responses and vulnerabilities. Eventually, he marched his army around Lake Tiberius.

Hearing of Saladin's advance, the Templar Grand Master, Gerard de Ridefort, summoned all of the nearby Templar troops – almost all of those in the Holy Land – as well as secular infantry and cavalry, and rode

to intercept the Muslim force. On 1 May 1187, a small engagement was fought at the Springs of Cresson. Initially, the Christians held the upper hand, catching the Muslims by surprise.

However, the Christians were greatly outnumbered – 1000 Crusaders facing more than 7000 Muslims by one account – so when the Muslims counter-charged, the Templars were quickly surrounded. Almost all of the knights were slaughtered and their infantry scattered throughout the countryside.

June the Muslims crossed the lightly-defended Jordan River, camping at Cafarsset (Kafr Sabt). Two days later, Saladin attacked the town of Tiberias, the town that controlled Lake Tiberias. The town was not well protected – most of its garrison having left to join the main Crusader army – and surrendered within hours of being besieged. It was likely not an important goal for the Sultan, and the attack was also likely a tactic used by him to try to lure the Crusaders from their well-provisioned camp at Sephorie.

THE CRUSADERS ADVANCE
Sephorie's main attraction was its supply of water; a commodity that no army could do without for long. Saladin understood this – as did all military leaders – and both he and the Crusaders knew there was little water between Sephorie and Lake Tiberias. Nor could the Crusader army carry enough water to sustain them should a long battle be fought.

At least for a while Guy of Lusignan was patient. Others in his army were not, however. On 3 July, under pressure from Gerard de Ridefort and Reynald of Chatillon, Guy marched his army east towards Tiberias and Saladin's forces. The Crusaders marched in three divisions, with Raymond of Tripoli commanding the vanguard, Guy of Lusignan in the centre, together with the Holy Cross relic, guarded by the Bishops of Acre and Lidde (Lydda), and the Hospitallers and Templars, under command of Ridefort, in the rearguard. The march was only about 25km (16 miles), but it was hot and dusty. And with every step the Crusaders and their mounts became more and more thirsty.

Saladin knew almost immediately that the Crusader army was on the move – intelligence gathering was never difficult for Muslim generals in a Holy Land occupied by European Christians. He withdrew to Cafarsset and gathered his forces. The move also forced the Christians to march north into the valley of Hattin, guarded at the end by two large rises known as the Horns of Hattin.

By marching through the valley, they could reach Lake Tiberias the following day. It was a good strategy: if the Crusaders

could reach the lake, they would be supplied with water.

But Saladin had other plans for them. He reached the eastern end of the Hattin valley and cut it off before the Crusaders could march through it. At the same time, he sent another part of his army to the other end of the valley and blocked it. The Crusaders were trapped in between.

IN THE VALLEY OF HATTIN
During the night of 3–4 July Saladin harassed the Crusaders, setting fire to brush on the northern side of their camp so that the dry wind parched their already dry throats and blew the smoke into their eyes. Drums also beat throughout the night giving the Crusaders little rest. On the other side, the Muslims were supplied with water by camels carrying it from the lake.

Saladin began the morning of 4 July at dawn with intense archery fire into the beleaguered Crusaders. The brushfires still spewing smoke meant that the arrows could not be seen until the last moment. Panic spread quickly among the Christian soldiers. But Saladin held his main forces back. He was still wary of the Crusaders, especially the heavy cavalry of the Hospitallers and Templars, which had proven in the past to be formidable foes. At Hattin they were also emboldened by the presence of a fragment of the Cross, the most holy of Christian relics and one that reminded all of sacrifice. Saladin also wanted to know which way the Crusaders were going to try to break out of the valley: would it be to the east and the water of Lake Tiberias or to the west and a return to the springs at Sephorie?

While this was happening, the Crusader leaders were meeting. The decision was made to march to the lake, behind Raymond of Tripoli's troops, and they slowly set out. As soon as Saladin saw this from his vantage point high on the valley ridge, he moved part of his army down into the valley and out across the eastern end to block Raymond's march. The remainder of his troops then moved into the other side of the valley behind the Crusaders and began pursuing them. The Crusader rearguard, composed mostly of Hospitallers and Templars, turned to face them.

His troops had been victorious, but it is clear that this was not how Saladin planned to conquer the kingdom of Jerusalem. He pulled back and regrouped, with a larger strategy in mind. Saladin seemed to understand that he needed a large, fairly decisive battlefield victory that he could quickly follow up with an attack on Jerusalem.

By the end of June Saladin decided to make his move, marching to Al Qahwani on the southern coast of Lake Tiberias and setting up camp. On or slightly after 30

A romanticized version of the surviving Crusaders surrendering to Saladin after the Battle of Hattin (painting by S Tahssin). Saladin offered to spare their lives if they promised not to fight further against him. When the Templars and the Hospitallers refused to take this oath they were executed.

Quickly, these two ends of the Crusader army became embroiled in combat. In the centre, Guy of Lusignan could not decide which end to support. Raymond of Tripoli sent word that he was on the point of breaking through the Muslim troops. But at the same time messengers from the Hospitallers and Templars pleaded for assistance in holding out against their attackers. Initially, Guy of Lusignan decided to rush to Raymond's aid, but then changed his mind and marched back towards the rearguard. The Cross was with him.

The battle raged on. By midday, the hottest part of the day, Raymond of Tripoli's fatigued and thirsty troops at the east end of the valley began to falter. He made a desperate tactical decision: he would take his own soldiers out of the valley in whatever way he could, even if that meant climbing the northern Horn. Abandoning the others, his soldiers desperately fled from the field, and by doing so saved most of their lives. Most contemporary chroniclers called Raymond a traitor, while most modern commentators see his move as heroic.

At the other end the Crusaders fought on. They had now turned to the offensive. Instead of allowing themselves to be charged at, they began to make their own charges against the Muslims. Several cavalry charges followed, and when their horses fell, the cavalry charged with the infantry on foot. But Saladin's soldiers in position there were too numerous and the Crusaders were eventually pushed back until there was only a small group vainly defending the Holy Cross. Once this relic was captured, the remaining Crusaders surrendered and awaited the judgement of their conqueror, the Sultan Saladin.

AFTERMATH

Guy of Lusignan and Reynald of Chatillon both survived the fighting and were captured. Brought to the tent of Saladin, who according to his contemporary biographer was giving thanks to God for his victory, Guy was handed a cup of iced water to relieve his thirst. By this gesture, Saladin assured the defeated King of Jerusalem that he would not be killed. But when Guy passed the cup to Reynald, it was taken from him, and when the latter refused to convert to Islam, Saladin personally killed him with his own sword.

As Saladin told Guy: 'it is not the custom of kings to kill each other, but [Reynald] had overstepped the limit.' Most of the common soldiers were allowed their freedom, although their noble leaders were kept as prisoners. The Templars and Hospitallers were not freed, and after almost all of them had refused to convert to Islam they were executed and their corpses left unburied in the hot sun.

The road to Jerusalem lay open. Four days after the battle, the port of Acre fell and cut the Kingdom of Jerusalem off from the Mediterranean Sea. Over the next two months most of the rest of the coastline and surrounding countryside followed suit. Having cut Jerusalem off from any reinforcements, the Sultan began a siege of the city on 20 September.

Using some of the finest siege artillery known at the time, such as mangonels and trebuchets, he commenced a constant bombardment of the walls. The defenders of the city returned fire, but their artillery was too light and too little. At the same time, Muslim sappers began to undermine the city's walls. Crusader counter-mining was ineffective. Grossly outnumbered and hoping to save their lives, the inhabitants pressed for peace. Saladin agreed and on 2 October he victoriously entered the holiest, and the most bitterly fought over, city in the world.

Chertsey Tiles showing Richard the Lionheart fighting Saladin in battle. The duel between the two opposing military leaders of the Third Crusade was celebrated in history and romance. In these, Richard is always depicted as the victor, although as the two never fought each other on the battlefield such a result cannot be known for certain.

ACRE
1191

SALADIN'S VICTORIES AT HATTIN AND JERUSALEM LED TO THE THIRD CRUSADE. THREE KINGS TRAVELLED TO THE HOLY LAND TO REGAIN WHAT HAD BEEN LOST, BUT ALTHOUGH THEY CAPTURED ACRE AND DEFEATED SALADIN AT THE BATTLE OF JAFFA, THEY COULD NOT RECAPTURE THE CITY OF JERUSALEM.

WHY DID IT HAPPEN?

WHO Local Crusaders under Guy of Lusignan (King Guy of Jerusalem, c. 1150–1194) joined by the Third Crusade under Kings Richard I of England (1157–1199) and Philip II of France (1165–1233) against a Muslim army under Saladin (1138–1193).

WHAT Saladin's armies failed in repeated attempts to break the Crusader siege, and massive Christian reinforcements from Europe eventually caused the city to surrender.

WHERE The city of Acre, in the Gulf of Haifa, now northern Israel.

WHEN August 1189 to July 1191.

WHY The siege was a Crusader response to Saladin's attempt to retake the Holy Land and consolidate his earlier victories at Hattin and Jerusalem.

OUTCOME The fall of Acre and later Crusader victory at Arsuf ensured the survival of the Crusader state, although Jerusalem remained in Saladin's hands.

News of the defeat at Hattin and the loss of Jerusalem to Saladin in 1187 was greeted in Europe with stunned disbelief and fear. The City of God and a piece of the True Cross had fallen to infidels: unbelievers in the true religion and true God, who had defiled the sacred sites and relics. The anonymous author of *De expugnatione terrae sanctae per Saladinum* (*The Capture of the Holy Land by Saladin*) wrote: 'What can I say? It would be more fitting to weep and wail than to say anything. Alas! Should I describe with impure lips how the precious wood of the Lord, our Redeemer, was seized by the damnable hands of the damned? Woe to me that in the days of my miserable life I should be forced to see such things…'

Rationalizations started immediately. Blame was heaped on the resident Crusaders, whose sins many believed had caused the loss. Especially singled out was Eraclius, Patriarch of Jerusalem, who pushed for the negotiations with Saladin that led to the city's capitulation. Although this move had certainly saved the lives of the city's inhabitants as well as guaranteeing that Christian sites and relics there were preserved, many in Europe saw it as cowardice and corruption. The English cleric Ralph Niger concluded: 'Whence it happened that by the judgment of God the land was taken and the princes captured and those who in some way were able to flee went in dispersion.'

The Third Crusade was called, and a huge number of soldiers quickly responded. Among these were three kings – Henry II of England, Philip II Augustus of France, and Frederick I Barbarossa of the Holy Roman

Between the Second Crusade and Third Crusades a number of truces between Christians and Muslims were made, but neither side kept the peace for long, necessitating a constant vigilance by both.

Empire – and a soon-to-be king, Richard I, the Lionheart (he would succeed his father, Henry II, on 6 July 1189, before he had set out for the Holy Land). Monies were also raised, most famously by the 'Saladin Tithe' levied throughout England and English holdings in France in 1188. Supplies, arms and armour were collected, and transportation to the Holy Land arranged.

SALADIN CONSOLIDATES

In the Middle East Saladin was trying to consolidate his power, a task that was not easy. His empire had now grown to an unprecedented size. It stretched from Edessa in the east to Tunisia in the west, and from the Mediterranean in the north to Yemen in the south. Throughout that empire, there were numerous political and religious leaders who disputed Saladin's leadership and would try to rouse the local people against him. These required the Sultan to deploy his loyal military leaders and soldiers away from his army, which was attacking the remaining Crusader states.

In addition, despite him declaring his rule, a new dynasty, the Ayyubids, the people who lived in Saladin's lands, were ethnically and theologically diverse. Saladin himself was a Kurd, a Middle Eastern minority then as now, and thus he could not simply rely on troops from his own people. His forces were, and always had been, mixed. Seljuk Turks fought next to Egyptians who fought next to Syrians, Berbers, Nubians, Persians, Turkomans and Arabs; Shi'ites and Sunnis fought together, and they were in units even with Jews, Greeks and some Christians. Why did all of them fight for him?

In the Crusaders Saladin had created a 'common enemy', one that united the soldiers of his army. Even more important than his strategic or tactical acumen was Saladin's ability to get men to fight for him. This is the very essence of generalship: to make an army fight as one when its disparate parts would rather fight each other. Also, while two of the Crusader kingdoms had been eliminated – Edessa and Jerusalem – there were plenty of Crusaders left, and they still held many castles and fortified towns in the Holy Land. Saladin was winning more and more of the

Crusaders' territory, but often these were difficult sites to capture without protracted sieges which would take time; time that the Sultan knew was short.

Eventually, a new Crusade would be called and he would have to contend with far larger armies coming from Europe. Indeed, his moves following the conquest of the kingdom of Jerusalem show a strategic desire to capture as much territory as he could before new Crusaders arrived, to make it as difficult as possible to wrest Jerusalem from him.

By 1190, it was clear that Saladin's strategy was working. Many smaller fortresses and towns had fallen to him, especially in the kingdom of Jerusalem, which had been largely denuded of troops.

SYRIAN AMIR
This Syrian nobleman wears a knee-length mail hauberk covered by a silk brigandine. He also wears a mail head covering and helmet and is armed with a sword. Although there were, no doubt, a large number of professional soldiers in Saladin's army, many of whom were very experienced in warfare, the majority of his forces were light infantry drawn from all the lands of his realm. These soldiers joined him out of societal obligation and religious belief, and they were united by Saladin in fighting a common enemy, the Crusaders. This may have been his greatest achievement as a general.

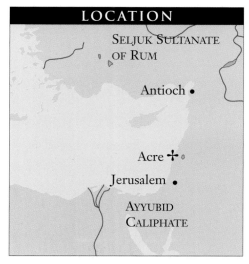

LOCATION

SELJUK SULTANATE OF RUM

Antioch •

Acre ✝ ◦

Jerusalem •

AYYUBID CALIPHATE

At its extent, Saladin's caliphate stretched from Egypt to Asia Minor, from the Mediterranean Sea to the Indian Ocean. The Crusader states were surrounded.

109

ACRE

Beginning in August 1189, the city of Acre was besieged by Crusaders. For most of this time the besiegers came from other Christian states. However, their numbers increased dramatically in May and June 1191 when first the French and then the English Crusaders joined the siege, pushing the city to capitulate in July.

But when he moved against larger, better-fortified towns and cities, Saladin's plan faltered. He was successful at decreasing the size of the principality of Antioch, virtually pinning it to the coastline, but did not have the strength to attack the city itself. Tripoli was even stronger, with Saladin making little headway at decreasing the size of this principality.

FAILURE AT TYRE

It was, however, Tyre and Acre that gave the Sultan his worst military headaches. In November 1187, a month after Jerusalem fell, Saladin began a siege of Tyre but could not take it. The walls were not the only reason Tyre held out, however. Credit must also be given to the man who led the resistance to Saladin there: Conrad of Montferrat. Born sometime in the mid-1140s as the second son of William V, Marquess of Montferrat, Conrad had to find his own fame and fortune – as did many younger sons of medieval nobles. He did so

by fighting throughout the eastern Mediterranean from his late teens into his thirties, and his abilities and intelligence as a soldier and leader of soldiers became widely known.

The anonymous chronicler of the *Brevis Historia Occupationis et Amissionis Terrae Sanctae* (*A Brief History of the Occupation and Submission of the Holy Land*) was especially impressed:

> Conrad was vigorous in arms, extremely clever both in natural mental ability and by learning, amiable in character and deed, endowed with all the human virtues, supreme in every council, the fair hope of his own side and a blazing lightning-bolt to the foe, capable of pretence and dissimulation in politics, educated in every language, in respect of which he was regarded by the less articulate to be extremely fluent.

In 1187, Conrad decided to join his father, who was fighting in the Holy Land. But by the time he arrived at St Elias Castle, where his father resided, William of Montferrat had been captured at the battle of Hattin. Conrad retreated with the castle's inhabitants to the better-protected Tyre – then negotiating a surrender with Saladin – and being the most experienced general, he was given the task of defending the city. Under Conrad's leadership, Tyre not only held out against the forces of Saladin, but became the focal point of resistance to him.

CRUSADERS BESIEGE ACRE

By August 1189, the number of Crusader soldiers that had gathered in Tyre had risen to more than 7000. Guy of Lusignan, freed by Saladin in 1188, tried to join them, but immediately clashed with Conrad, whose authority he tried to assume.

However, the still titular King of Jerusalem was able to convince the troops in Tyre to follow him in an attack on Saladin's forces in Acre. At Hattin, Guy had proved that he was no tactical genius; it now looked as if he had no strategic ability either.

Guy did make it to Acre, but almost as soon as the Crusaders set up their siege lines, Saladin attacked them. Yet, surprisingly, the siege lines held, and not

THE OPPOSED FORCES

CRUSADERS (estimated)
Guy of Lusignan:	400 cavalry
	7000 infantry
Reinforcements:	53,000
Total:	**60,000**

SALADIN (estimated)
Total:	**80,000**

only through this attack but through many Muslim attacks between autumn 1189 and summer 1191.

In the meantime, the Third Crusaders were on their way from Europe. Frederick Barbarossa was the first to set out. Surprisingly quick to muster his troops and supplies, considering how large the Holy Roman Empire was, in May 1189 Frederick set out on what would be a short but very eventful Crusade. He chose to travel with most of his army overland – although some of his subjects did sail directly to the Holy Land from Italy – and by late August he had entered the Byzantine Empire. Relations between Frederick and Isaac II Angelos, the Byzantine Emperor, were always strained as they both claimed the same parts of Italy. The Byzantine Emperor could not put the forces into the field that the Holy Roman Emperor could, but conflicts between the two slowed the Imperial army down. These

This illumination depicts the siege of Acre, from the Chroniques de France ou de St. Denis. *The* Chroniques de France *was compiled between the thirteenth and fifteenth centuries, beginning in the reign of Saint Louis, who wished to preserve the history of the Franks. It was continued under his successors until completed in 1461.*

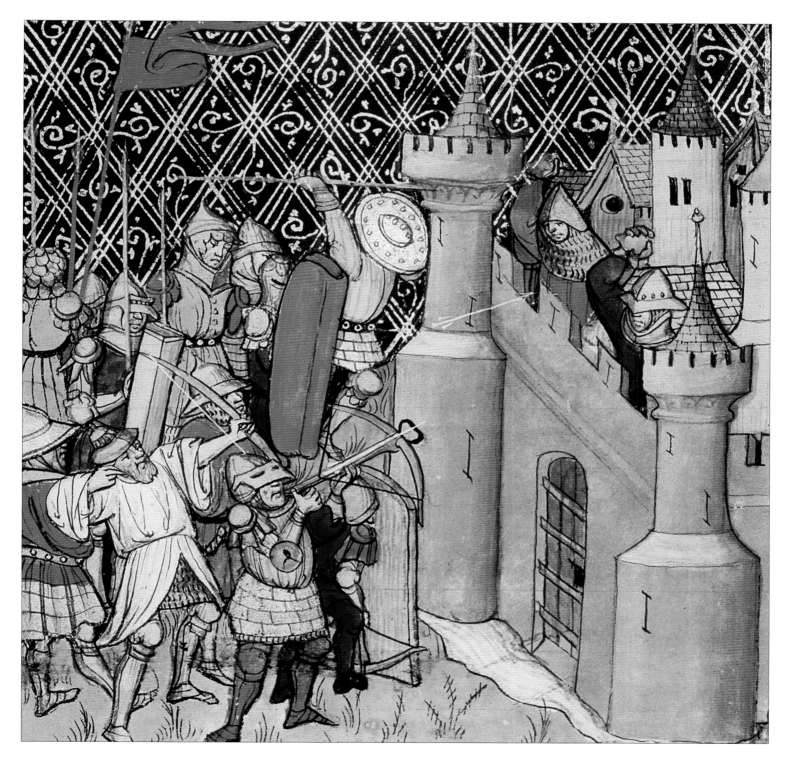

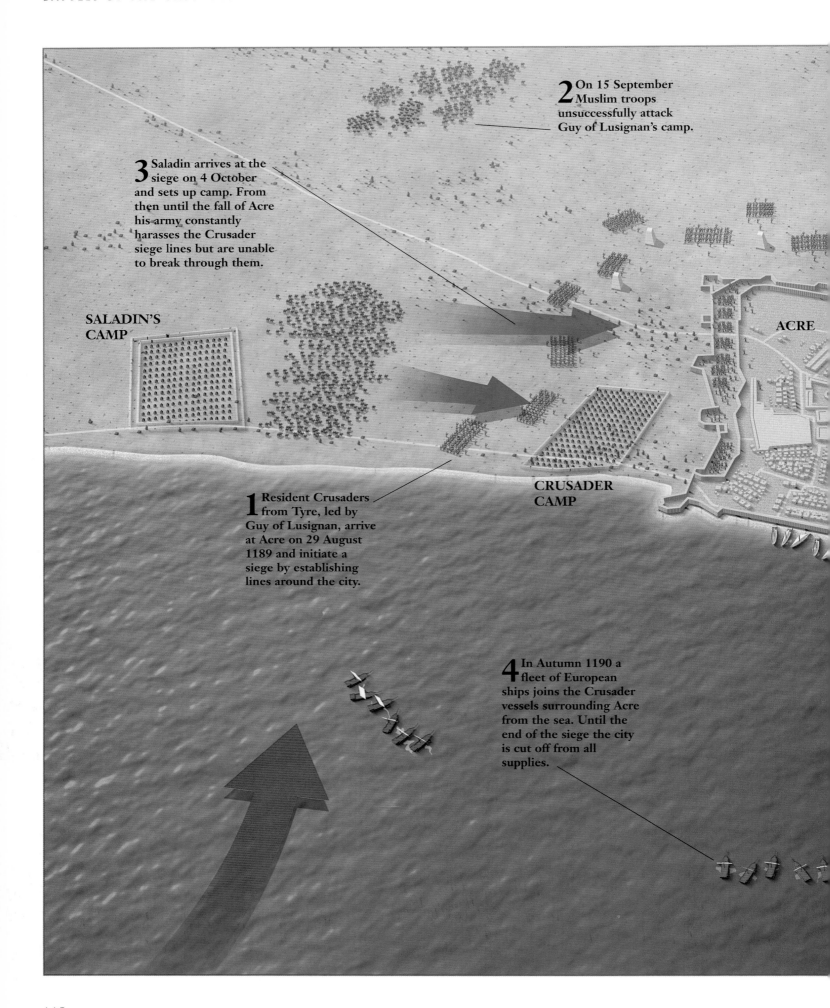

2 On 15 September Muslim troops unsuccessfully attack Guy of Lusignan's camp.

3 Saladin arrives at the siege on 4 October and sets up camp. From then until the fall of Acre his army constantly harasses the Crusader siege lines but are unable to break through them.

SALADIN'S CAMP

ACRE

CRUSADER CAMP

1 Resident Crusaders from Tyre, led by Guy of Lusignan, arrive at Acre on 29 August 1189 and initiate a siege by establishing lines around the city.

4 In Autumn 1190 a fleet of European ships joins the Crusader vessels surrounding Acre from the sea. Until the end of the siege the city is cut off from all supplies.

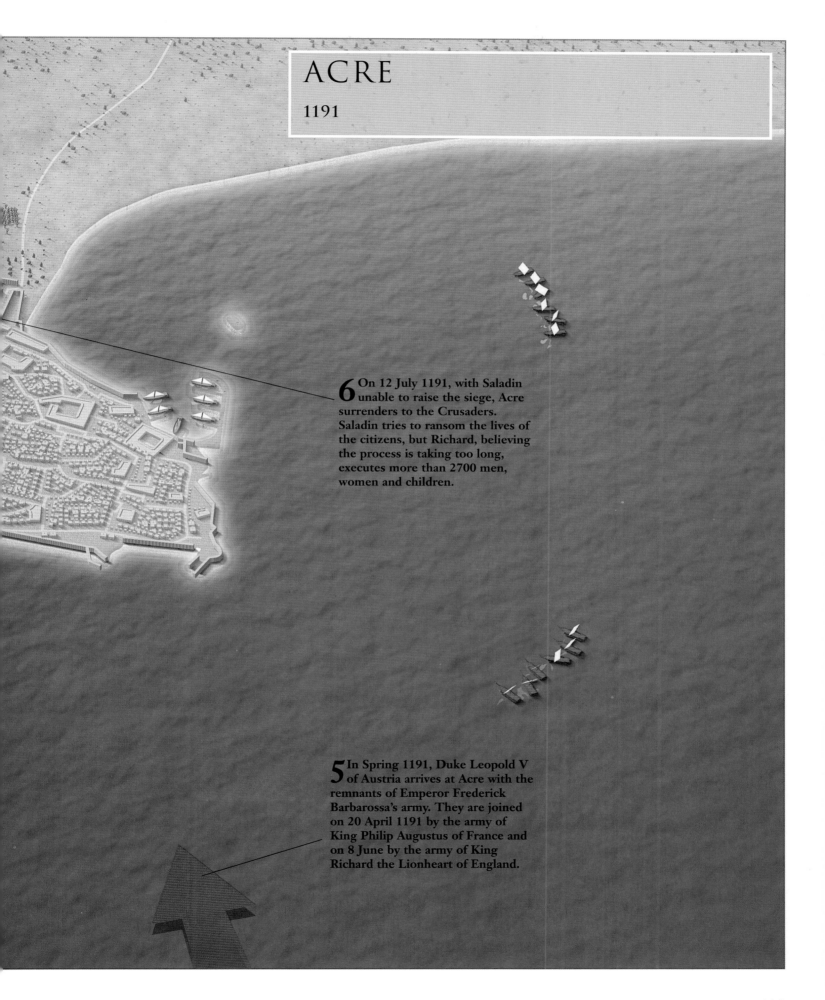

ACRE
1191

6 On 12 July 1191, with Saladin unable to raise the siege, Acre surrenders to the Crusaders. Saladin tries to ransom the lives of the citizens, but Richard, believing the process is taking too long, executes more than 2700 men, women and children.

5 In Spring 1191, Duke Leopold V of Austria arrives at Acre with the remnants of Emperor Frederick Barbarossa's army. They are joined on 20 April 1191 by the army of King Philip Augustus of France and on 8 June by the army of King Richard the Lionheart of England.

ACRE

Turcopole Archer. There is some dispute among historians as to who the Turcopoles were. They fought for both the Muslims and the Crusaders, leaving some historians to believe that they were mercenaries, while many others think that they were Middle Eastern Christians whose allegiance was not always with the conquering Catholics. Their speciality was mounted archery.

Opposite: As depicted in this early fourteenth-century illumination, the Crusader capture of Acre was heralded throughout Europe, a sign that God was still with the Christians in their struggle against Islam in the Holy Land. Crusader knights, carrying shields and swords and wearing mail armour and great helms, were impressive warriors, though more accustomed to fighting in the cooler climates of Europe than in the hot Middle East.

delays may have kept the Emperor from ever reaching the Holy Land. His army did march through Byzantium into Seljuk Rum, but no further. On 10 June 1190, while swimming in the River Göksu, Frederick Barbarossa drowned. Most of his army decided to return home, although some pressed on and would form up under the leadership of Leopold V, Duke of Austria.

SALADIN FAILS TO BREAK IN

By this time the siege had been progressing, or not progressing, depending on your perspective. The Crusaders had not broken

into the city, but neither had the Muslims been able to raise the siege. Saladin had begun his attacks on the Crusader besiegers on 15 September 1189 and he had not stopped since then. Further Muslim troops had arrived from Egypt in late October 1189 but still made no headway. Saladin was forced to siphon off some of his troops to harry Frederick Barbarossa's army, but after the Emperor's drowning they had rejoined the Sultan's main force.

So why was Saladin, the victor of Hattin and Jerusalem, so unsuccessful at Acre? Historians have argued about this ever since. Some have suggested that the unity of his force was foundering, and certainly there is some validity to this. Saladin's biographers – there were two writing officially from his camp – openly discuss the dissatisfaction of his soldiers. In October–November 1190, Saladin even relented when asked by northern Iraqi troops for permission to return home.

Other historians have credited the Crusaders for their effective defence rather than blame Saladin for his lack of success at Acre. Perhaps the resident Crusaders knew that they were soon to be relieved. Pisan fleets had arrived at Tyre before Guy of Lusignan and his troops marched south and, no doubt, the sailors were able to report of the new enthusiasm to join the Crusaders that was spreading throughout Europe.

They may also have been able to inform them that the Holy Roman Emperor and the Kings of France and England had answered the call to go on the Third Crusade. During the following few months several more ships came to the Holy Land, bringing much-needed supplies and charting the new Crusaders' progress.

The death of Frederick Barbarossa and the demise of his Crusade brought disappointment, especially as the Emperor was one of the most famous warriors of the twelfth century. However, with younger royal generals on their way, carrying the sobriquets 'the Great' (Philip) and 'the Lionheart' (Richard), there was hope.

Hope, though, could only be maintained by effective generalship prior to the kings' arrival, and it is here where the true reason for Crusader success at Acre may be found. Conrad of Montferrat proved to be an excellent logistician and administrator, getting plentiful supplies delivered to Tyre and passed on to the Crusaders around Acre without much interruption from Saladin's forces. He also served admirably as a leader in the siege. But the real surprise was Guy of Lusignan, whose leadership at Acre kept his men strong in military power and morale.

The legacy of Hattin still hung over Guy's head, however, and when Philip Augustus and Richard the Lionheart arrived – in May and June 1191 respectively – he was moved to a subordinate command

position. Moreover, his kingship of Jerusalem, which had only been accorded to him by his marriage to Sibylla, ended at her death in July or August 1190, ironically passing to Conrad of Montferrat, who was married to Sibylla's half-sister, Isabella.

THE CRUSADERS' JOURNEY

Philip Augustus and Richard the Lionheart, despite unfounded modern rumours of a homosexual relationship, were never very good friends. However, for the sake of the Third Crusade, the two put on a public show of unity at Abbey Church of Vézelay (the Basilica of Mary Magdalene) in July 1190. The town of Vézelay stands on a lone mountain top in Burgundy, with the Romanesque Abbey Church at the very centre of it. The church, where the two kings met officially to 'take the cross', can be seen from the valley below for miles, and the sight of two large armies camped around it must have been most impressive. Of course, this was Philip and Richard's purpose.

From Vézelay, the two forces travelled separately through France, over the Alps, and from northern to southern Italy. That two such great kings would be able to raise such large armies meant to all that God was still on their side, and that Saladin's occupation of Jerusalem was to be only temporary. However, as soon as Philip and Richard arrived in Messina, Sicily, a few days apart in September 1190, their temporary friendship became strained. Bickering nearly turned into combat as the two armies wintered there. About the only thing they continued to agree on was their goal: to Crusade in the Holy Land.

Philip's French army left Messina on 30 March 1191 and Richard's Anglo-French troops on 10 April. The French travelled directly to Tyre, joining the siege of Acre on 20 May.

RICHARD'S DETOUR

Richard decided not to travel directly to the Holy Land but to visit a few Eastern Mediterranean sites, in particular Crete (end of April), Rhodes (1 May) and Cyprus (12 May). All were part of the Byzantine Empire. It is not known why Richard did this. One of the accounts of his Crusade, Benedict of Peterborough's, claimed that

SALADIN'S CAVALRY
Saladin's best tactical unit was his light cavalry. Not as well armoured as their Crusader counterparts and riding swifter Arabian horses, these soldiers swept down on their opponents while firing bows and throwing javelins. Then, just as quickly, they rode away. If the Crusaders did follow them, they and their steeds quickly became fatigued, making them more vulnerable to Muslim counter-attacks.

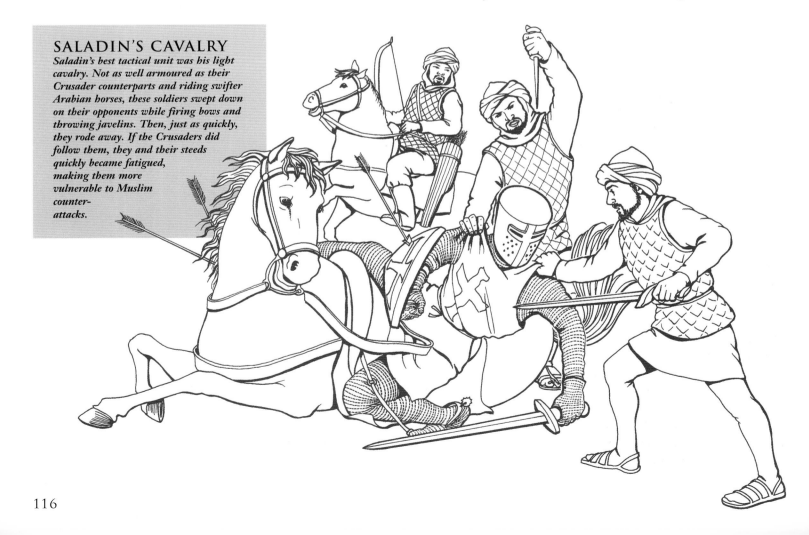

Richard had to land at Cyprus when three of his ships were driven there and destroyed by a storm. Richard's ensuing sack of the island is explained as retribution against the Byzantine Emperor after he absconded with the cargo on those ships and robbed the survivors, including the royal vice-chancellor.

Yet, one might question the accuracy of this account as a little too convenient an excuse for military activity against what was after all a Christian state. This is further confirmed by Neophytus, a non-English chronicler whose account nevertheless supports Richard's invasion; he justifies the English action because Emperor Isaac II Angelos had taken Cyprus from its rightful Latin Christian owners and had for seven years since ruled it tyrannically.

REINFORCEMENTS ARRIVE

When Richard arrived at the siege of Acre on 6 June 1191, delayed as he had been by his Eastern Mediterranean diversions, almost all of the Third Crusaders were there. Not only did these include Richard's Anglo-French soldiers, Philip's French soldiers and the remnants of the Imperial Crusaders, but others, too, had led armies to the Holy Land, including Henry III of Champagne, Count of Troyes, and Baldwin, the Archbishop of Canterbury. Troops from Cologne, Frisia, Bremen, Thuringia, Flanders, Brabant and Scandinavia were also present. At sea, these were supported by fleets – English, French, Imperial, Genoese, Venetian, Pisan, and Sicilian – perhaps the largest number of ships that had ever accompanied a Crusade.

How many Crusading soldiers were there? An accurate number will never be known. Peter of Bartholomew claims that the English army travelled on board 150 large ships and 53 galleys, but does not state the size of these vessels or give the numbers of men on them. It was large though – many thousands – that is certain, but it was never larger than the numbers that Saladin had with him, which also can not be calculated.

The siege of Acre had been waged for more than a year and a half before Philip and Richard arrived. The resident Crusaders had been doing quite well on their own, but once there the status of the

two kings quickly surpassed that of local leaders. English chroniclers remark that when Philip Augustus came to Acre he was warmly received by the besiegers, but only until Richard the Lionheart arrived. Then, in the words of the English chronicler, Richard Devizes, Philip 'became obscured and without consideration, just as the moon is wont to relinquish her lustre at the rising of the sun'. Perhaps not surprisingly, the French chroniclers do not say the same. What can be certain is that once the English king came to Acre less than two months after the French king, the two began once again to bicker over Crusader leadership.

During the siege Acre had been surrounded, blockaded by land and by sea. The naval blockade was especially effective, with Saladin unable to compete against the Crusader ships with his own fleet. On land, the Crusader siege was also strong. As with most medieval sieges, however, it seems that the besieged did receive some relief throughout the ordeal, especially as Saladin continually distracted the Crusaders with assaults. Reinforcements for the Muslim garrison even made it into the city and helped convince those in Acre to hang on.

Adding the new soldiers to the Crusaders around Acre, however, increased their number significantly, so much so that

This romantic image of Richard the Lionheart and Philip Augustus inspecting the defeated inhabitants of Acre ignores the fact that, by this time in the siege, Richard and Philip did not get along and would not have been in such proximity to each other.
More importantly, it ignores the massacre of at least 2600 of the besieged following the city's capture.

ACRE

Despite history's recognition of Richard the Lionheart and his English soldiers as the victors of Acre, both France and the Holy Roman Empire provided troops as well. In this later medieval illumination from the Speculum majus, the French king, Philip II Augustus, celebrates Acre's fall with the military leaders of his army.

Surrender negotiations were not only held between the besiegers and the besieged, but also between the Crusader leaders. Philip and Richard shared the captured Muslim ships and also the garrison's leaders – whom Saladin held to ransom. Prisoners were also exchanged.

But these were only Acre's notable and wealthy. The poorer citizens were left in Crusader hands, Richard the Lionheart's after Philip left Acre on 31 July. Perhaps Saladin believed that the Crusaders would respect the lives of the common people, innocent pawns in these wars, and would treat them with the same mercy that he had shown those who could not afford ransom after his capture of Jerusalem in 1187.

MASSACRE

Richard, however, did not let them go. Instead, on 20 August, he had them beheaded – men, women, and children – 2600 by his own reckoning. English rationalizers excuse the act by claiming that the English king was simply responding to Saladin's unwillingness to return the fragment of the Holy Cross; and besides these people had not surrendered immediately after being besieged, a violation of the laws of war. Other chroniclers are not swayed: Richard's actions were heinous, an egregious and cowardly war crime.

AFTERMATH

In August 1191, Philip Augustus returned home to France, where he promptly began attacking Richard the Lionheart's holdings there. Richard was determined to retake Jerusalem. After all, he had bested Saladin at Acre and felt that nothing could stop him from reaching the goal for which he had taken the cross. He marched his army down the coast into the former kingdom of Jerusalem. Saladin's army marched parallel to them further inland. The two armies finally met at Arsuf on 7 September, in a battle that is usually seen as a victory for Richard, with the Muslims being driven from the field. But it was far from decisive as Saladin simply moved further inland, still keeping his army between the Crusaders and Jerusalem.

For another year Saladin and Richard the Lionheart marched up and down the

it appears any holes in the blockade were closed and the citizens began to suffer heavy bombardment from trebuchets and other siege machines; the walls of the city were also undermined. The Crusaders were in fact now so numerous that they set up two siege lines, one that blockaded the city and a second that protected this blockade from Saladin. There was little the Sultan could do. Relief attacks were tried but they failed, and on 12 July 1191, just a little more than a month after the arrival of Richard the Lionheart, Acre surrendered.

Saladin, who had not given his permission for this capitulation but was powerless to do anything about it, was informed by a swimmer who had made his way through the Crusader lines.

coastline of the Holy Land. Richard continued to want a battle, but Saladin refused to give him one. The Sultan knew that Richard did not have the strength to pursue him inland. Also, Richard had neither the troops nor the patience to besiege another fortified site, although he did conquer some unfortified villages and towns, including Ascalon – where Saladin had destroyed the fortifications and removed the population. However, nor were the Muslims able to chase the Crusaders back to Acre.

Finally, in July 1192, Richard asked Saladin for negotiations, and although they were not concluded until September, he eventually agreed to leave the Holy Land. He would not surrender anything he had captured – including Acre – but he would also not be given anything new – including Jerusalem. His troops were free to visit the

Holy City, as was the English King, but Richard refused to do so unless he was its conqueror.

The siege of Acre did not end for Richard the Lionheart when he sailed into the Mediterranean on 9 October 1192. Shipwrecked on the Southern European coast, he chose to march through the Holy Roman Empire rather than France.

This might have been wise, except for the fact that the territory he crossed around Christmas was owned by his old ally, Duke Leopold of Austria. It seems that Leopold had not forgotten that when Acre fell and the Duke had tried to raise his flag to an equal level as that of the King of England, Richard had ordered his troops to tear it down and throw it from the wall. Richard was captured and held until 4 February 1194, for almost as long as he had been in the Holy Land.

Richard the Lionheart's fame grew after Acre and Arsuf. Even failing to regain Jerusalem seems not to have damaged his standing, nor did the follies of his return trip when he was captured and imprisoned for 16 months by Leopold V, Duke of Austria, whom he had insulted at Acre.

CONSTANTINOPLE
1203

VENETIAN SCHEMING AND CRUSADER GREED COMBINED IN AN ASSAULT ON THE GREAT CITY OF THE BYZANTINE EMPIRE, THE SUCCESS OF WHICH WEAKENED THE EMPIRE AND HASTENED ITS EVENTUAL DOWNFALL.

WHY DID IT HAPPEN?

WHO A Franco-Venetian army, led by the Doge of Venice, Enrico Dandolo (1122–1205), attacked the Byzantine Empire.

WHAT Constantinople had its formidable defences breached for the first time.

WHERE Constantinople (Istanbul).

WHEN July 1203 and April 1204.

WHY Dandolo used the French Crusaders to destroy the Byzantines and pave the way for Venetian and Catholic domination over its eastern (Orthodox) rival.

OUTCOME The Byzantine Empire never recovered, allowing it to fall to the Muslim Turks.

Since the final and fatal split of the Church in 1054 between the Papal (Catholic) Church ruled with an iron hand from Rome and the Eastern (Orthodox) Church protected by the Byzantine Emperor and the Patriarch of Constantinople, the two sides had been sworn enemies.

Having been defeated at the disastrous battle of Manzikert (1070), the Byzantines welcomed, to begin with, the Crusaders' formidable presence and onslaught on their

In 1204, as in 1453, the Blachernae section of the massive triple-walled Theodosian rampart built in the fourth century proved something of an Achilles' heel for the defenders of the great city of Constantinople, since the Crusaders chose to assault the main city gates.

common foe. Initial Byzantine euphoria soon turned sour as the rough 'Franks' (this term was used by both Byzantine Greeks and Muslims) treated fellow Orthodox and other Eastern Christians no better than the Muslim 'infidels'.

On their part, the Crusaders viewed the Byzantines as slippery, unreliable schemers who plotted with the Muslims to prevent them from taking the whole Middle East. By 1203, the Catholic west, as represented by Venice and the French nobility, was ready to wreak terrible vengeance upon the 'apostates' in the east.

SORDID SCHEMES
The whole unsavoury venture began in April 1201 when leaders of a group of French Crusaders made an agreement with the

scheming and ruthless Doge of Venice, Enrico Dandolo. While the 'Franks' were, to begin with, sincerely interested in invading Egypt, Dandolo had far easier fish to fry.

In 1171 the Byzantines – seeing their economy and trade being dominated by the Venetians – had expelled the wily Italians from their realm and Dandolo swore to take vengeance on the Byzantines and re-establish Venetian hegemony in the Aegean and eastern Mediterranean.

The French would-be Crusaders paid the Venetians to supply sufficient tonnage to carry some 34,000 men and 4500 horses to Egypt. Unfortunately, most of the Crusaders paid or organized their own passage across to Palestine, leaving only a paltry 12,000 French knights turned up in Venice. Having already paid out 41,000 marks out of 85,000, the French owed the scheming Venetians a fortune. The Venetians too had invested too much time, money and ships (50 in total) in this venture simply to walk away.

Most fortuitously a candidate to the Byzantine throne, Prince Alexius Angelus, turned up with a tale to tell. His father, Emperor Isaac II, had been blinded and deposed by his brother, the present Emperor Alexius III. Prince Alexius presented himself as the rightful heir to the throne.

Dandolo saw a golden opportunity to give his plans a thin gloss of respectability by 'championing' the young Byzantine pretender who readily agreed to restore all of Venice's trading privileges, pay the Crusaders' debt to Venice and supply their Egyptian venture. Had Alexius known the horrors he was about to unleash upon his unsuspecting countrymen he would, no doubt, have left Venice.

Dandolo now had a specious excuse to invade Byzantine territory using his captive Crusaders. In November 1202, the Crusader fleet set sail from Venice, landed on the Adriatic coast and sacked the Hungarian-protected city state of Zara. Not only was the population reassuringly Catholic but its governor was a fellow Crusader. This did not spare Zara, and the French and Venetians, like the brigands they were, fell out over the division of the loot.

The brutal sack and destruction of Zara proved not only that this was no 'Crusade' in the ordinary sense of the word, but showed also what was in store for Constantinople – as yet only vaguely aware of the threat that loomed over it.

BATTLE OF GALATA

The Franco-Venetian Fleet set sail once more and reached Corfu in April 1203, where the pretender, Alexius Angelus, joined them, little knowing the disaster he was about to wreak upon his still proud and wealthy empire.

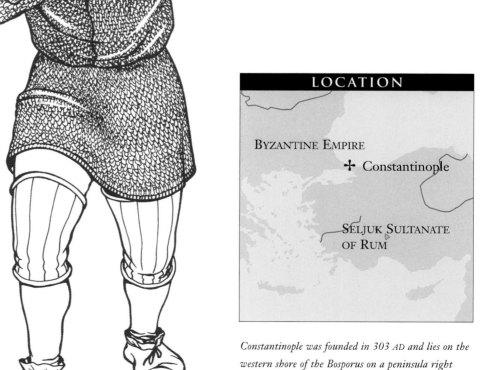

SERGEANT-AT-ARMS
The backbone and unsung heroes of every Medieval army was the 'poor bloody infantry' that was forced to fight hard, dig trenches and siege lines, protect supply lines, occupy ground and (sometimes) get slaughtered on the battle field.

In the case of the Venetians and French who fought at Constantinople the infantry were – as illustrated here by a French 'Sergeant at arms' – disciplined, relatively well cared for in terms of pay, equipment and food, and well equipped.

This man wears a chain mail hauberk and 'kettle' style helmet and is armed with a Anglo-Saxon style two-handed axe favoured by French and Anglo-Norman infantry after 1066.

LOCATION

BYZANTINE EMPIRE

✝ Constantinople

SELJUK SULTANATE OF RUM

Constantinople was founded in 303 AD and lies on the western shore of the Bosporus on a peninsula right between Europe (the Balkan Peninsula) and Asia (Anatolia or present-day Turkey).

This line illustration based on a painting by the Italian Renaissance painter Domenico Tintoretto depicts the Venetian assault upon the walls of Constantinople.

THE OPPOSED FORCES

FRANCO-VENETIAN CRUSADERS

French men-at-arms:	4000
French infantry:	8000
Venetian forces:	8000
Venetian galleys:	50
Venetian sailing ships:	150

Total:	**Men**	**20,000**
	Ships	**200**

BYZANTINES

Infantry, cavalry, Pisan seamen,
Varangian Guards and other
mercenary formations
Navy:
only a handful seaworthy galleys

Total:	**Men 20,000**

The Crusader fleet hove in to sight of Constantinople on 24 June – its massive sea walls, towers and sheer size taking the Franks' breath away. The Venetians who knew of Byzantine weaknesses first hand were not as awe-struck or demoralized by its defences.

On their part, the Byzantines watched from the walls in stunned disbelief as the huge armada sailed slowly but inexorably up the Bosporus. They themselves were led by an Emperor who had usurped the throne, showed no courage, inspired no loyalty and was, like his brother, no leader of men. Characteristically, Alexius had done nothing to strengthen Constantinople's defences and he remained passive in the face of the Crusader attack.

The Franks were as reluctant to fight as the Byzantines and landed, therefore, on the Asiatic shore of the Bosporus, where they easily brushed aside a Byzantine cavalry patrol. Having rejected an Imperial emissary offering to negotiate, the Franco-Venetian armada sailed across the Bosporus just after sunrise on 5 July.

The Venetians, Europe's finest mariners, had constructed their transport ships so that

the French knights could saddle and mount their horses onboard. They had also constructed wooden ramps that could be lowered directly into the water and allow the fully armed knights – again Catholic Europe's finest – to attack as soon as they hit the beaches.

Their landing site was the suburb of Galata, where mainly Italian (Genoese and Pisan) merchants had their homes and warehouses. Galata's only defence was a single, massive, round, tall tower that housed a huge windlass that could raise and lower the gigantic iron chain that strung out across the entrance of the Golden Horn to prevent enemy ships entering it.

For the Byzantines it was vital that Galata and its tower was held at all cost, so Alexius III had taken command of its defenders. It would have been far better had one of his generals been there instead. The sight of 100 sailing ships disgorging horses and heavily armed knights with disconcerting discipline and awe-inspiring precision proved too much for the poorly led and motivated defenders. As the knights lowered their razor-sharp lances and spears in preparation for a massed cavalry assault, the Byzantines' frayed nerves snapped and they fled in panic northwards – with Alexius leading the vanguard.

The following morning, the Byzantines launched a dawn attack that was easily repulsed by the French. Having prevented any relief reaching the garrison of the Galata Tower, they then set out with scaling ladders and panache to storm the tower. The garrison proved tougher than the field troops and repulsed assault after assault. Eventually, the attackers managed to make a breach in the walls, and the Byzantine troops gave up, preferring to surrender alive than be massacred. The Venetians immediately cut the windlass and the great barrier chain crashed into the waters of the Golden Horn. The Crusader armada swept past, defeated whatever Byzantine ships could or were willing to offer resistance and became masters of this vital, strategic stretch of water.

Constantinople's massive, tripled, land wall, built by Emperor Theodosius, was viewed as impregnable; not so, however, the lower sea walls along the Golden Horn. Even with a height of 9m (30ft) and with massive towers at regular intervals, they remained the city's weak spot.

On Friday 11 July, the French army moved north from Galata without any attempt by the poorly led Byzantines to harass or impede their progress. They were also disastrously allowed to repair a partly demolished bridge across the narrower, upper stretch of the Horn – again without the Byzantines launching a counter-attack.

THE FIRST ASSAULT

The attackers chose, quite wisely, to make a combined assault upon the sea wall along the Golden Horn that fronted the Palace and city quarter of Blachernae. This was in the extreme northwestern corner of Constantinople, where the land wall

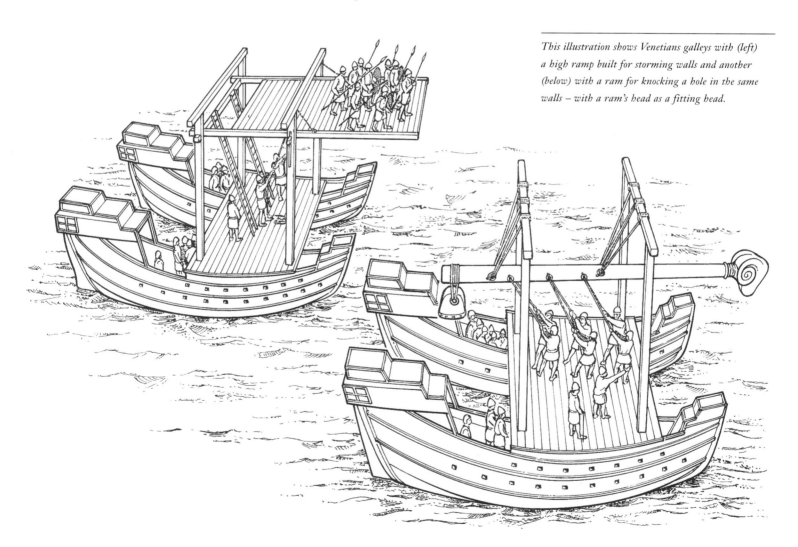

This illustration shows Venetians galleys with (left) a high ramp built for storming walls and another (below) with a ram for knocking a hole in the same walls – with a ram's head as a fitting head.

CONSTANTINOPLE

1203

4 The French Army move north along the eastern shore of the Golden Horn, and capture and cross a bridge at the northern end of the Horn.

5 Assembled north of the Theodosian Wall, the French begin the assault only to be repelled by the Byzantines and an energetic counter-attack spearheaded by the axe-wielding Varangian Guards.

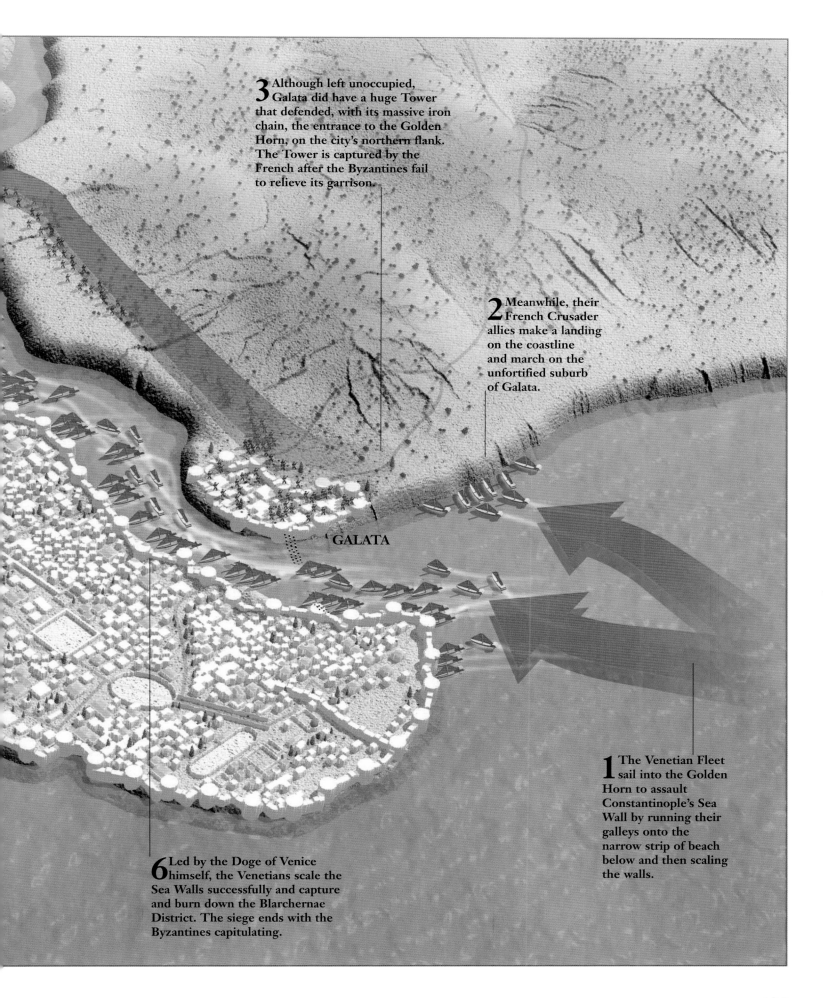

3 Although left unoccupied, Galata did have a huge Tower that defended, with its massive iron chain, the entrance to the Golden Horn, on the city's northern flank. The Tower is captured by the French after the Byzantines fail to relieve its garrison.

2 Meanwhile, their French Crusader allies make a landing on the coastline and march on the unfortified suburb of Galata.

GALATA

1 The Venetian Fleet sail into the Golden Horn to assault Constantinople's Sea Wall by running their galleys onto the narrow strip of beach below and then scaling the walls.

6 Led by the Doge of Venice himself, the Venetians scale the Sea Walls successfully and capture and burn down the Blarchernae District. The siege ends with the Byzantines capitulating.

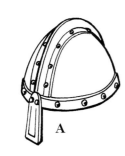
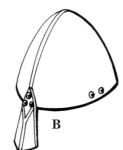
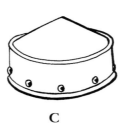

A   B   C

CONSTANTINOPLE

D

E

The strong Norman-French influence can be seen in the design and style of the helmets worn by the crusaders. A, B and C (dating from the eleventh to thirteenth centuries) show the design becoming simpler and more stylized, possibly due to cost or the craftsmanship required to make such an helmet. In designs D and E (thirteenth to fourteenth centuries), the vital nose guard has been restored.

connected with the sea wall and the Blachernae section protruded. It was Constantinople's Achilles' heel.

On the morning of Thursday 17 July, the French attacked here but were met with fierce resistance by axe-wielding English and Danish mercenaries belonging to the Emperor's feared elite Varangian Guards. These northern warriors relished close combat, cutting down both French knights and horse with their massive, razor-sharp battle-axes in great swinging motions.

The Venetians were far more successful. Their ships rode low in the water, weighed down with catapults and mangonels in the forecastles, and covered gangplanks and scaling ladders suspended by rope tackles between the yardarms. The tops of their masts were level with the towers of the sea walls but the crews proved reluctant to move up close or beach their vessels.

Whatever his character flaws, the blind old Doge was no coward or fool. He ordered the crew of his galley to beach the vessel, and one of his squires – once the galley was on the narrow beach below the sea wall – to drive the Banner of St Mark into the soft ground. The Venetians were heartened by their commander's gesture and their other ships began to beach as well. They stormed the walls but were met with fierce resistance from the defenders, who faced the very real prospect – after 900 years of immunity – that these attackers might succeed.

After many long hours of deadly and fierce fighting, the Venetians had seized 24 towers in the wall, breached the ramparts

In this highly romanticized and sanitized painting, the 'upright' Crusaders, led by a 'benign' Baudouin, seem almost like liberators of an oppressed population. The reality was quite different, with the Crusaders actively destroying an existing state for their own ends.

CONSTANTINOPLE

This illustration portrays Baudouin showing brave resolution by scaling the walls of a very Oriental-looking Constantinople, defended by an 'Asian' enemy, when, in fact, the Crusaders were fighting and butchering fellow Christians.

womenfolk and some 4500kg (10,000lb) of gold from the Imperial Treasury. In the hour of her greatest need and darkest peril since her foundation in 303 AD, Constantinople was without a ruler. The Imperial Council met and decided to restore the blinded and deposed Isaac II Angelus – hoping to remove the reason for the Crusaders' presence. Only when Isaac II agreed to make his son, the pretender and Catholic puppet, Alexius, his co-Emperor and honour his obligations, did the French withdraw to a camp outside Galata. Constantinople, at least for the present, was safe.

Isaac II and Alexius IV were crowned on 1 August. They were, however, to prove unpopular rulers, since Alexius III had emptied the Treasury and the 134,000 marks they paid to their enemy had to be squeezed out of the city's population. The Orthodox clergy were furious that Alexius IV had promised to subordinate them to Rome's dictates.

In November 1203, a group of drunken, loutish French knights went amok in the streets and attacked a Mosque used by the city's Muslim population. The Byzantines, no longer willing to accept the behaviour of their unwanted guests, attacked them and during the fighting yet another fire was lit.

On 25–28 January, Constantinople's senators, clergy and prominent citizens met to depose the hated Alexius IV and his crippled father. They were led by Alexis Ducas, known as Murzuphlus for his shaggy eyebrows, who had Alexius and his father arrested, imprisoned and then strangled with bowstrings. The usurper was promptly crowned as Alexius V.

This, finally, was the excuse that Dandolo had been looking for all along. He immediately seized it, storming the walls yet again, sacking Constantinople and then dividing the weak and defenceless Byzantine Empire. In early March, the leaders of this discredited and sordid 'Crusade' met in the Galata camp and agreed that Count Baldwin of Flanders (1172–1205) should be 'crowned Emperor' of this Latin-occupied Empire. All trade would, of course, be under Venetian control.

and poured into the streets of the Blachernae district below. They set fire to the wooden houses in the district with devastating result.

WINTER OF DISCONTENT

These fires were the signal for Alexius III – true to form – to flee the city with his

THE SECOND ASSAULT

Murzuphlus may have been both a murderer and a usurper but he was a capable and energetic leader. He had repaired the sea wall and added height to the towers. When, on Friday 9 April, the Venetians tried to scale and storm the walls using their usual techniques, the assault failed. Using these new, higher towers, the Byzantines poured catapult fire into the massed French troops and Venetian ships below. Three days later, on Monday 12 April, the Venetians latched ships together in pairs and could therefore overwhelm each tower in turn. The French eventually managed to capture and open one of the city's gates, bursting into the streets within like a floodtide.

SACK OF CONSTANTINOPLE

In the words of the Byzantine minister and nobleman, Nicetas Choniates, the Franco-Venetians – 'Devlish Barbarians' – set upon the Imperial capital with a vengeance, killing all Greeks without pity, whether women, children, adults, military or civilian. For three days, between 12 and 15 April, Constantinople burned, while the attackers indiscriminately looted, raped and murdered. The Franks destroyed while the Venetians, more cool headed and logical, looted and sent the booty back to Venice to adorn the Republic's palaces, homes and libraries.

In the chaos, Murzuphlus was able to flee to Adrianople. He later married Eudocia, the daughter of exiled Alexius III, but, in the fine tradition of the Angelus dynasty, was blinded by his father-in-law. The French eventually captured and murdered him in 1206.

What shocked Choniates was not the wanton destruction, murder and mayhem as much as the acts of desecration against the Orthodox Church. A prostitute was installed on the Patriarch's throne and then, to add insult to injury, the Patriarch was named as a Catholic Venetian. Churches were plundered, urinated in and used as stables, brothels and barracks. If a Muslim Arab or Turkish army had taken the city, they could not have behaved worse.

In return for appointing a Venetian as 'Patriarch' of Constantinople, Dandolo agreed that the most prominent of the French Crusaders, Count Baldwin of Flanders would be 'crowned' Emperor of Byzantium on 16 May. Naturally, the remaining Byzantine states of Nicea and Trebizond did not accept this travesty and continued to fight the invaders and occupiers. It was only in 1261 that Constantinople was retaken and the last occupiers expelled, but by then the Empire was in ruins, and unable to stem the floodtide of Ottoman Turks coming from the East. The Ottomans could thank the French Crusaders and the Venetians for much of their success.

A seated Doge gives his and the Franco-Venetians blessing to the enthronement of the usurper Latin 'Emperor' Baldwin (Baudouin) I (1204–05) in this classical-style painting by the Venetian artist Andrea Michieli (1542–1617).

ADRIANOPLE
1205

ADRIANOPLE WAS ANOTHER BATTLE THAT SHOWED THAT WELL-HANDLED LIGHTER TROOPS COULD DEFEAT AN ARMY THAT INCLUDED POWERFUL FORCES OF ARMOURED KNIGHTS. AS USUAL, CRUSADER IMPETUOSITY RESULTED IN A BATTLE ON THE ENEMY'S TERMS, AND BROUGHT THE WHOLE ENTERPRISE TO RUIN.

WHY DID IT HAPPEN?

WHO A Crusader army including 300 knights under Baldwin I, opposed by several thousand Bulgar soldiers under Tsar Kaloyan of Bulgaria.

WHAT The Crusaders were goaded into pursuing lighter troops they could not catch, and once drawn out were attacked from all sides.

WHERE Adrianople, Bulgaria.

WHEN 14 April 1205.

WHY The Crusader army had invaded the Balkans with the intention of capturing Constantinople.

OUTCOME The Crusaders were decisively defeated.

The Crusades were not a simple matter. While a great number of individuals responded 'Deus Vult!' to the idea of taking the Holy Land back from the infidel, they all had their own reasons for going on Crusade, and as subsequent Crusades were organized, so the variety of motivations increased. A desire for glory or plunder, a favour owed or a feudal duty to a lord, or even real religious zeal; there were many reasons for joining.

There were also compromises to be made and necessary 'sideshow' operations required to open the way to the Holy Land and to keep the logistics chain working. Alliances were made with local leaders and with the Byzantine Empire, and allegiances within the Crusader armies could shift as leaders jockeyed for power among their peers.

Thus any given Crusade was in fact a complex matter and prone to changes of plan, some of which could be quite radical. The Fourth Crusade, proposed by Pope Innocent III in 1198, involved a particularly major shift of direction.

The original plan was to capture Jerusalem by landing in Egypt and advancing overland from there. The overall leader was to be Count Thibaud of Champagne, but upon his death in 1200 command passed to Count Boniface of Montferrat (c. 1150–1207), an Italian nobleman. Boniface came to an agreement with the Doge of Venice that Venetian ships would be made available to move the Crusader army to Egypt.

Venice was at the time the foremost maritime power in the Mediterranean,

These city walls in Iznik, Turkey date from the Byzantine period. The cities of the Byzantine Empire came under attack from many directions during their history. A good set of walls was more than a showpiece to impress visitors – it was a necessity for survival.

ADRIANOPLE

CRUSADER INFANTRY

Although infantry was not highly regarded in Europe, the troops deployed by the Crusaders gave good service throughout many campaigns. Their equipment was fairly basic but serviceable, with each man carrying a close-quarters weapon (a short sword, a dagger or a small axe) in addition to his main weapon. Protection took the form of a metal helmet and body armour of quilted cloth, leather or sometimes mail.

The presence of spearmen and crossbowmen made it possible to use elementary combined-arms tactics. The crossbowmen could strike the enemy hard from a considerable distance, but were very vulnerable to fast assault by lightly armed cavalry. They were thus protected by a hedge of spear points and a wall of shields while they loaded and picked their targets.

In this manner the Crusader infantry provided a solid base to cover the knights until they charged and while they rallied for their next attack. The infantry was rarely decisive but could prevent a defeat from being any worse by a stubborn defence.

wielding enormous influence through its fleets, money and those who owed it favours. Thus, in 1201, when it became apparent that Count Boniface could not muster the expected 35,000 men, nor pay the agreed sum for transport, the Venetians decided to offer an alternative solution. They had spent many months preparing for the operation, recruiting sailors and building ships to transport the army. They wanted something in return for their investment.

The port of Zara in Dalmatia had been a Venetian possession, but was now an independent city-state under the protection of King Emeric of Hungary. Venice wanted the city back and proposed that the Crusaders could pay for transit with service against Zara rather than hard cash.

Boniface agreed, and entered into another deal at the same time. This one was with Alexius IV Angelus, whose father, Isaac II Angelus, had been deposed from the throne of the Byzantine Empire. Alexius offered religious, fiscal and military incentives to Boniface to help him regain his throne. Once Alexius was emperor of Byzantium he would reunite the Byzantine church with that of Rome and provide a large force to assist in the Egyptian undertakings. He would also pay a very large amount of cash, and this was especially attractive to the underfunded Crusaders.

So rather than sailing to Egypt to fight the infidel, the Crusade must first assault and capture Zara from the Catholic Hungarians and take Constantinople from the Christians who dwelt there. Despite strong opposition from the Pope, the Crusaders sailed for Zara, where they found the city festooned in banners depicting a cross – a broad hint that the people of Zara were Christians too. The city was besieged anyway and fell soon after.

Pope Innocent III was dismayed and excommunicated the leaders of the Crusade as well as their Venetian allies, but this did not prevent the operation from continuing. After the Crusaders had taken Zara they sailed to Constantinople as planned, arriving in June 1203. The Crusader army was diminished by losses in battle, but far more men were lost through desertion. Crusading for God in the Holy Land was one thing; being mercenaries for Venice was entirely another. Nevertheless, the city fell and Alexius was installed as Byzantine emperor. Finally, the way was open for the Crusaders, reinforced by Byzantine troops, to begin the mission they had set out on.

TROUBLES IN THE CITY

All was not well for those who remained in Constantinople. Alexius was crowned as Emperor but lacked funds to pay the promised sum to the Crusaders, while

LOCATION

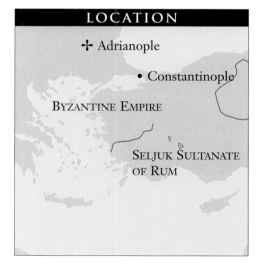

The Crusaders sought to secure their position in Asia Minor by subjugating the surrounding area. However, the massive loss at Adrianople severely limited their ambitions in the region.

Baldwin I (1171–1205), the first Latin Emperor of Constantinople, was crowned at Constantinople in 1205. Although it was in decline, the Byzantine Empire was rich and capable of putting on great demonstrations of power. The coronation of Baldwin was carried out with all due pomp and ceremony.

THE OPPOSED FORCES

CRUSADERS (estimated)

Knights/men-at-arms:	400
Infantry:	5000
Total:	**5400**

BULGARS (estimated)

Total:	**20,000**

public feeling against the 'Latins' was increasing. Alexius had a number of religious icons melted down to provide gold for his debts, which further incensed the population. There was even fighting within the city, and this led to the Great Fire, in which much of the city was destroyed.

Alexius asked the Crusader army to stay on to protect him, but despite their support he was murdered and deposed by a member of his own court, Alexius Ducas. This provoked further fighting, after which Constantinople fell to the Crusaders for a second time and was subjected to a vicious three-day sack. Not only did the Crusaders pillage everything they could, they deliberately defiled holy places, bringing yet another rebuke from the Pope. After dividing the Byzantine Empire between Venice and the leaders of the Crusade, thus creating the Latin Empire, the Crusaders began trying to consolidate their position. This proved to be a difficult undertaking.

LATIN EMPIRE ATTACKED

From the fall of Constantinople to the battle of Adrianople almost exactly a year later, there was extensive fighting in the region. Many minor rulers were deposed or murdered, and the Latin Empire found itself under attack from all directions. The Empire was a prestigious possession and could be used as a base for crusading into the Holy Land, and so its new rulers were disinclined to give it up. However, the pressure was increasing.

In order to secure their position, the Crusaders campaigned against various states of the region, and had been successful in pacifying a large area. Conquered regions were given to the Crusader leaders to rule as princes answering to the Latin Emperor.

The first Latin Emperor was Baldwin I (1172–1205), formerly Count Baldwin of Flanders. He was young, and popular for his courage in battle and genuine religious fervour. He ruled Constantinople itself and some associated territories, and all the princes were under his rule in a loose feudal arrangement. This displeased Count Boniface, who had been a rival for the throne and was to receive a large territory when it was conquered.

Boniface wanted his kingdom to be independent rather than part of the empire, and this led to clashes with Baldwin, who disagreed with some elements of Boniface's strategy. At one point civil war between the Crusaders seemed likely, but matters were resolved and the conquest continued.

Boniface was successful for a time, but early in 1205 the Greek populace of Thrace revolted against the Latin Empire and formed an alliance with Tsar Kaloyan of Bulgaria, who had previously offered to make an alliance with the empire and had been turned down.

Kaloyan's Bulgarian forces and local Greeks ousted the Latin garrison at Adrianople and took control of the city. This could not be tolerated and the Latin Empire gathered its forces to retake the city.

The Latin army was typical of western European forces of the time: a core of mounted, heavily armoured knights and men-at-arms backed up by a few thousand

'Chronicle in Miniature' by David Aubert. This scene depicting the Crusader assault on Constantinople in 1203 is one of utter chaos and violence, which is accurate even if the image is representative rather than a precise depiction of events. The tumbled ladders at left suggest an assault during a siege. This was one of the few situations in which knights would fight dismounted.

infantry armed with spear and shield or a crossbow. The impact of the mounted knights was normally enough to shatter most foes, and allow the Crusaders to win even when outnumbered. The force that set out was confident of victory – perhaps too much so. Such overconfidence may have contributed to the eventual disaster that befell the imperial force.

THE FIRST CLASH

Baldwin arrived outside Adrianople, intending to besiege and recapture the city. He encountered a large force under Kaloyan that included Bulgarian and Wallachian troops loyal to the Tsar and as many as 14,000 more lightly equipped Cuman allies. Both armies encamped about 24km (15 miles) apart, making preparations for the inevitable battle.

CRUSADER MAN-AT-ARMS

Men-at-arms were not knights themselves but were equipped very much like them, and often mounted. Many knights would lead a number of men-at-arms and lighter-equipped infantry. As a rule, men-at-arms fought mounted, like their knightly masters. However, on occasions, both would dismount to fight. This was usually for terrain rather than tactical reasons – tactics were rather primitive and knightly hosts too ill-disciplined to pay much attention to factors that were not obvious and imminent, such as ground too rough or broken for horses. When forced to fight on foot, the crusader men-at-arms gave good account of themselves, fighting with spears and a variety of hand weapons including axes and maces before resorting to their swords.

ADRIANOPLE

1205

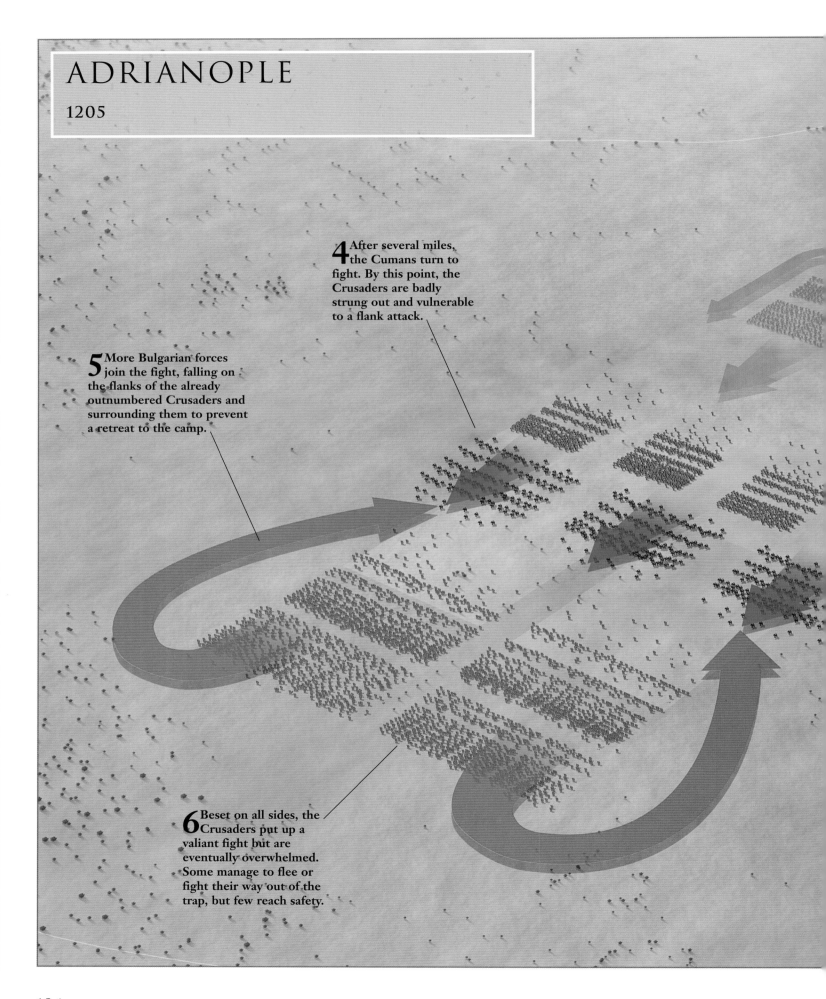

4 After several miles, the Cumans turn to fight. By this point, the Crusaders are badly strung out and vulnerable to a flank attack.

5 More Bulgarian forces join the fight, falling on the flanks of the already outnumbered Crusaders and surrounding them to prevent a retreat to the camp.

6 Beset on all sides, the Crusaders put up a valiant fight but are eventually overwhelmed. Some manage to flee or fight their way out of the trap, but few reach safety.

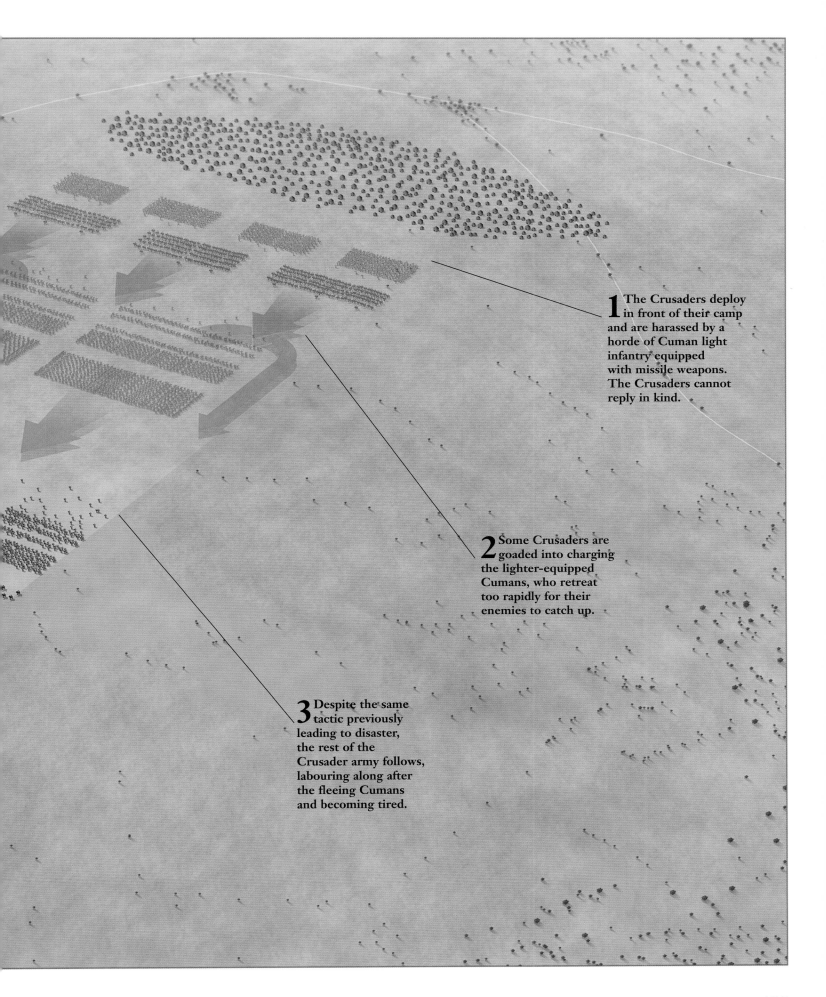

1 The Crusaders deploy in front of their camp and are harassed by a horde of Cuman light infantry equipped with missile weapons. The Crusaders cannot reply in kind.

2 Some Crusaders are goaded into charging the lighter-equipped Cumans, who retreat too rapidly for their enemies to catch up.

3 Despite the same tactic previously leading to disaster, the rest of the Crusader army follows, labouring along after the fleeing Cumans and becoming tired.

The spear or lance is a staple weapon of horsemen the world over, giving the horseman the advantage of reach. Note the rope handgrip and wrist strap on the lance at left, and the secondary point at the rear of the weapon. The two scimitars are excellent weapons for a horseman; ideal for a fast passing cut and handy in the chaotic mêlée of a close-quarters cavalry action.

ADRIANOPLE

Kaloyan knew all about the devastating charges of the Crusader knights, and he knew how that weapon could be blunted. He sent a large force of his Cuman allies to make an attack on the Crusaders, who naturally responded aggressively. The Cumans fled and were pursued for several kilometres. This tired out the more heavily equipped Crusader infantry and especially the knights' horses. The Latin force also lost cohesion and began to straggle badly.

At this point, the Crusaders wisely decided to break off the pursuit and return to their camp. However, as they began to make their weary way back, the Cumans turned and attacked them, shooting arrows into the Crusaders and harassing their retreat all the way back to the camp.

COUNCIL OF WAR

Baldwin was dismayed at the losses his force had taken, and convened a council of war, at which the prevailing opinion was that it had been unwise to chase after enemies that were fleeter of foot and could turn to fight at a time of their choosing. The Latin leaders discussed strategy and decided that they would stand firm and make their enemies come to them. They were determined not to fall for the same trick again.

Thus, the following morning, the Crusader army formed up in front of the camp and awaited the Bulgarians' attack. It was not long in coming. Again the Cumans rushed up close to the Crusaders, showering them with arrows, and then fell back.

LATIN MISTAKES

Despite all that had been discussed and agreed, the Crusaders went after the Cumans. Perhaps they had no choice. The Cumans were armed with missile weapons and the Crusaders were mainly equipped with hand weapons. One of the worst experiences for troops is to have to take fire without being able to reply, and even disciplined soldiers are prone either to retreat or to try to advance and chase their assailants off.

The Crusaders were not all that disciplined; their main striking force was made up of men who believed that the headlong charge was the only right and proper way to make war, and that there was something suspect about a man who did not get stuck in with sword and lance at the first opportunity. This impetuosity may have been the cause, or it could have been fear that the army might break up under the Cumans' galling fire, but in either case the Crusaders once more began to advance.

The force under the command of Count Louis of Blois was first to move forward, and soon the whole army was advancing. Again the Cumans ran away, and the Crusaders had no choice to pursue. Some accounts claim that the pursuit went on for two full leagues – 10 km (6 miles) – before the Crusaders were able to come to handstrokes with their enemies.

CRUSADERS MAKE A STAND

Once more the Latin army was badly strung out and tired, and again the Cumans turned and began shooting once more. They were joined by the rest of Kaloyan's army, and the Crusaders were soon outnumbered. Disorganized and exhausted, they could not unleash the devastating knightly charge, and were soon beset on all sides.

The situation was desperate, and Count Louis was wounded twice as he led his men in the fight. Some of his men urged him to escape, but Louis would not abandon the Emperor, whose own command was heavily engaged. Emperor Baldwin, too, refused to retreat, and ordered his men to stand with him. Emperor Baldwin was a skilful and courageous warrior, and he excelled himself on the battlefield at Adrianople. Some of his men fled and others stood their ground, but eventually the Crusader force was worn down. Count Louis was killed, along with Bishop Peter of Bethlehem and several other notable Crusaders. Baldwin himself was captured alive after a long fight.

The Crusader army was utterly defeated and few of those who fled reached any form of safety. Casualties among the common soldiery numbered in the thousands and many of the knights were killed.

AFTERMATH

Tsar Kaloyan had Emperor Baldwin blinded, and never released him. Baldwin died a prisoner some time after his brother Henry of Flanders had assumed the throne of the Latin Empire. Kaloyan allied with the Nicean Empire, the remnant of the Byzantine Empire that had not been taken by the Latins, and drove the Crusaders out of Thrace and much of the surrounding territory. Count Boniface was also a casualty

in this war: he was killed in battle at Messinpolis in 1207.

The whole purpose of this ill-fated adventure was to get a Crusading army to the Holy Land. After the conquest of Constantinople in 1204, the Crusaders were free of their obligations to Venice and Alexius and finally in a position to head for the Holy Land. Some actually got there, but only a tiny fraction of those that originally set out. Nothing of significance was achieved. Indeed, the Fourth Crusade did more harm than good.

Troubles in the new Latin Empire proved to be a fatal distraction for many years as well as creating the final split between the Catholic (European) and Orthodox (Eastern) Churches. Jerusalem remained in the hands of the Muslims under the Ayyubid dynasty, though a Crusader kingdom clung to the coastal regions under constant pressure.

This image depicts the Latin Emperor leading his men in action. He is charging with lance couched (gripped under the arm for maximum impact), but a skilled man could also thrust to the side with his lance, allowing him to strike an enemy as he passed without inviting a return blow.

BEZIERS
1209

THE CATHOLIC CHURCH CONTINUALLY TRIED TO CRUSH THOSE WHO PROMOTED A DIFFERENT VERSION OF CHRISTIANITY TO THAT COMING FROM THE VATICAN. AND WHEN THE CATHAR SECT SPREAD OVER A WIDE AREA OF THE PYRENEES, THE CHURCH TURNED ITS CRUSADING ZEAL ON THE HERETICS.

WHY DID IT HAPPEN?

WHO The Duke of Burgundy (1166–1218) and the Count of Nevers (d. 1219) aided by the Abbot of Citeaux with about 11,000 soldiers of all sorts, prepared to besiege the city. The opposing leader, Viscount Beziers, Raymond-Roger Trancavel (1185–1209), had already fled to raise a relief force, leaving the unknown town elders to maintain the defence until his return.

WHAT On the first night a scuffle on the bridge outside the city was won by the ribauds from the Crusader army and they forced their way in.

WHERE The city of Beziers by the Mediterranean coast on the Orb river and in the foothills of the Pyrenees.

WHEN 21–22 July 1209.

WHY The Pope insisted on crushing the heretical Cathar sect that had evolved in the region.

OUTCOME Everyone in the city was killed. The ribauds were robbed of their loot by their own knights and the city was burned.

The passes through the Pyrenees are a natural bottleneck between the Iberian Peninsula and the rest of Europe, through which people and ideas flow. By contrast, the mountainous valleys are isolated like land-locked islands. Here, in the middle ages, evolved a different interpretation of Christianity. This local version rated God and the Devil as equal in stature and power, an idea that can be traced to Zoroastrianism, an Iranian religion pre-dating Judaism. Men and women were valued equally and the holiest people, known as 'Perfect Men' or 'Perfect Women' and whom we would call priests, eschewed all property and wealth, and travelled between private houses, living simply on the donations of their flock. Their creed did not allow for holding property or churches. They did, however, revel in the simple joys of music, dancing and storytelling, a characteristic that is the origin of what we now regard as medieval chivalry and courtly manners.

This sect, known as the Cathars, spread from the mountain fastnesses to the plains beyond, though they were content to live side by side with Jews and Catholics. The powerful Catholic Church, however, was in no mood to tolerate such heresy. First, the church sent priests to preach but these were scorned and rejected. Then, it put pressure on the feudal overlord of the area, Raymond V (1134–1194) and his heir Raymond VI

This view from the southern bank of the River Orb shows the town end of the long bridge the Crusaders had to cross to attack the heretics. Much of the medieval street plan has been lost but this bridge follows the footprint of its Roman predecessor.

BEZIERS

(1156–1222), Counts of Toulouse, to eradicate the heresy. Raymond VI prevaricated and paid lip service to the church's doctrine. He was publicly humiliated and forced to renew his vows of religious fealty to the Catholic Church, but in the end he would not turn on his own people. Exasperated, Pope Innocent III (c. 1161–1216) finally declared a Crusade against the Cathars.

THE CRUSADER ARMY

King Philip II of France (1165–1223) and his heir declined to lead such an expedition against their own vassals but they did permit the Duke of Burgundy and the Count of Nevers to lead the Crusader army. The Burgundian aristocracy were distracted by the threat of rebellion in Poitou by King John of England (1166–1216) supported by Count Otto IV of Germany, and only 500 Burgundian knights answered the call.

The army that assembled at Lyons to be blessed by the Pope was a motley crew, with the 500 knights forming the battle-hardened spearhead. In battle, they wore a mail suit that covered them from head to toe, plus a helmet with full facial protection and just slits for the eyes and breathing holes around the mouth. Over this mail they wore a sleeveless surcoat to below the knee, but slit to the waist for ease of riding. Their shield, supported by a shoulder strap, and their lance pennon would have borne some kind of pattern, although true, inheritable, heraldry was only just becoming widespread. The lance was about 3m (10ft) long and if dropped or broken could be replaced by a long sword carried in a scabbard from a belt on the left side.

Similarly armed and mounted, but of lower status and with probably less up-to-date armour, most notably in the style of the helmet, were perhaps double that number of sergeants. A further 4000 sergeants armoured with just a thigh-length mail hauberk followed on foot. They were supported by about 400 crossbowmen. Their crossbows could fire a short thick arrow, known as a quarrel, to a distance of about 300m (330yd). To cock the weapon in this period, the string was hooked to the belt and with a foot in the stirrup the weapon pushed down with the leg. The crossbow was effective against mail and shields, and was widely available on both sides of the conflict despite it being previously banned by the Pope on two separate occasions. It made killing a peasant's social superior all too easy.

Some of these were mercenaries serving for pay, some fulfilling their feudal duties of 40 days' military service.

SUPPORTING FORCES

In addition, there were as many as 5000 ribauds – undisciplined and uninvited infantry armed with a wide assortment of

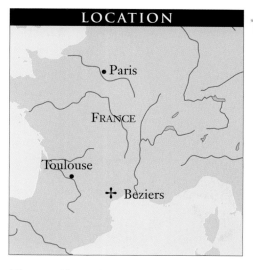

LOCATION

The town of Beziers lies at the lowest crossing point of the River Orb – a true bottleneck on the routes from eastern Spain to France and Italy beyond.

FRENCH KNIGHT
He wears the latest fashion, a surcoat over his mail armour. It is too early for heraldry to appear on the surcoat, so this was probably just plain white. His helmet is an evolution from the conical type with nasal guard to this 'barrel helm'. His primary weapon was the lance, usually made from ash with a leaf-shaped metal point. The knight would hold this couched under his armpit with the aim of transferring the full momentum from horse and rider to the point of impact. Once this had struck an enemy, he would attempt to withdraw the lance intact. Eventually, it would break and he would then resort to a sword long enough to reach a man cowering on the ground.

BEZIERS

This illustration from the fourteenth-century Chroniques de France ou de Saint Denis *shows Pope Innocent III excommunicating the Cathar heretics. It gives a useful indication of the style of civilian dress common at the time.*

THE OPPOSED FORCES

CRUSADERS (estimated)

Knights	500
Mounted Sergeants	1000
Sergeants on foot	4000
Crossbowmen	400
Ribauds	5000
Total:	**10,900**

CATHARS (estimated)

City Guard	3500
Unarmed civilians	30,000
Total:	**33,500**

improvised or cheap weapons. This latter group came from the basic needs of a medieval army on the move. Men and their animals needed to be fed, shod, clothed, healed and entertained, and those who supplied these needs were opportunists who uprooted themselves from sedentary society and followed the army wherever it went.

The normal dangers of the times meant that, in common with every other strata of society, they armed themselves with what weapons they could afford and carry. Daggers and knives were universal, clubs and sundry craft and agricultural tools widespread, swords commonplace. Individually, they might not be very intimidating but their sheer numbers and determination could make them formidable opponents.

The chance of wealth makes a wonderful motivator. Not to be forgotten

were 1000 squires. Most knights had two to serve their needs, but they took no part in the fighting.

Accompanying the host was a siege train of dismantled catapults, stone throwers, cats (a wheeled hut with reinforced roof and a battering ram suspended from the roof beams) and even a siege tower, plus their attendant engineers and carpenters. They were carried by barge down the Rhone and then by ox cart along the old Roman roads. This cross-section of medieval society was watched over by several hundred clerics, who were headed by Arnaud Amaury, Abbot of Citeaux. The whole force comprised some 13,000 men plus at least the same number of horses (for war, riding and draught), oxen and animals for food. They formed a column in excess of 9km (5.6 miles) long.

Among their number was Raymond VI, Count of Toulouse, doubtless under close ecclesiastical supervision. There is no record of what he did when the fighting started, but he later left the Crusade and led an army in defence of the Cathars.

THE CRUSADERS ARRIVE

The host took 30 days to reach Beziers, 250km (156 miles) to the west, the first Cathar town of any size. At Montpellier, about 80km (50 miles) short of the city, the Viscount Beziers, Raymond-Roger Trancavel, came forth and tried to save himself by joining the Crusaders. Abbot Amaury rejected the volunteer, however. Having failed to quell the heresy in his

fiefdom, he now had to suffer the consequences and would be shown no mercy. Returning to his city, Raymond-Roger instructed the citizens to prepare their defences, and set off with the Jews to raise a relief force in Carcassonne. Provisions were gathered in from the surrounding area and the defensive ditches cleaned out and deepened.

The medieval city of Beziers lay on the northern bank of the River Orb close to the Mediterranean Sea. Here, the Romans had built a road, the Via Domitia, from Spain to France and Italy beyond, and a single bridge crossing the river. The bridge is 300m

This illustration was produced more than 100 years after the sack of Beziers. By that time, the surcoats had started to sport heraldry, which had extended to the horses caparison. The simple, hooded, full-length tunic of the Cathars depicted here would have been universally worn by most ordinary civilians at that time.

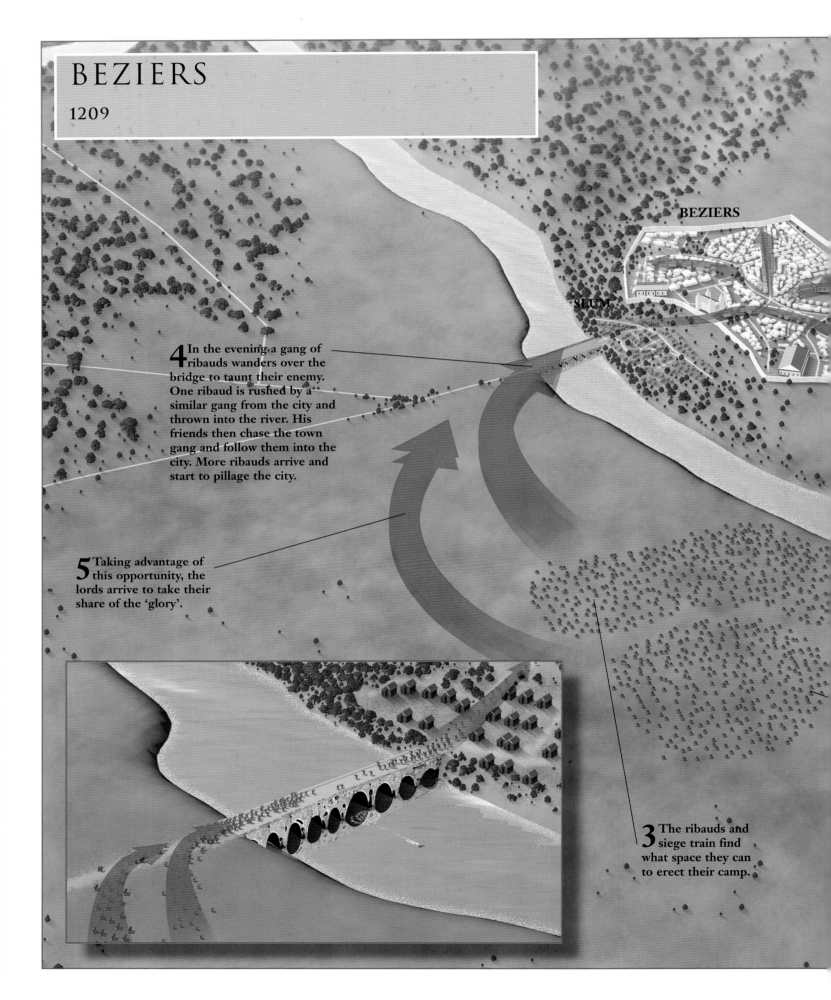

BEZIERS

1209

BEZIERS

SLUM

4 In the evening a gang of ribauds wanders over the bridge to taunt their enemy. One ribaud is rushed by a similar gang from the city and thrown into the river. His friends then chase the town gang and follow them into the city. More ribauds arrive and start to pillage the city.

5 Taking advantage of this opportunity, the lords arrive to take their share of the 'glory'.

3 The ribauds and siege train find what space they can to erect their camp.

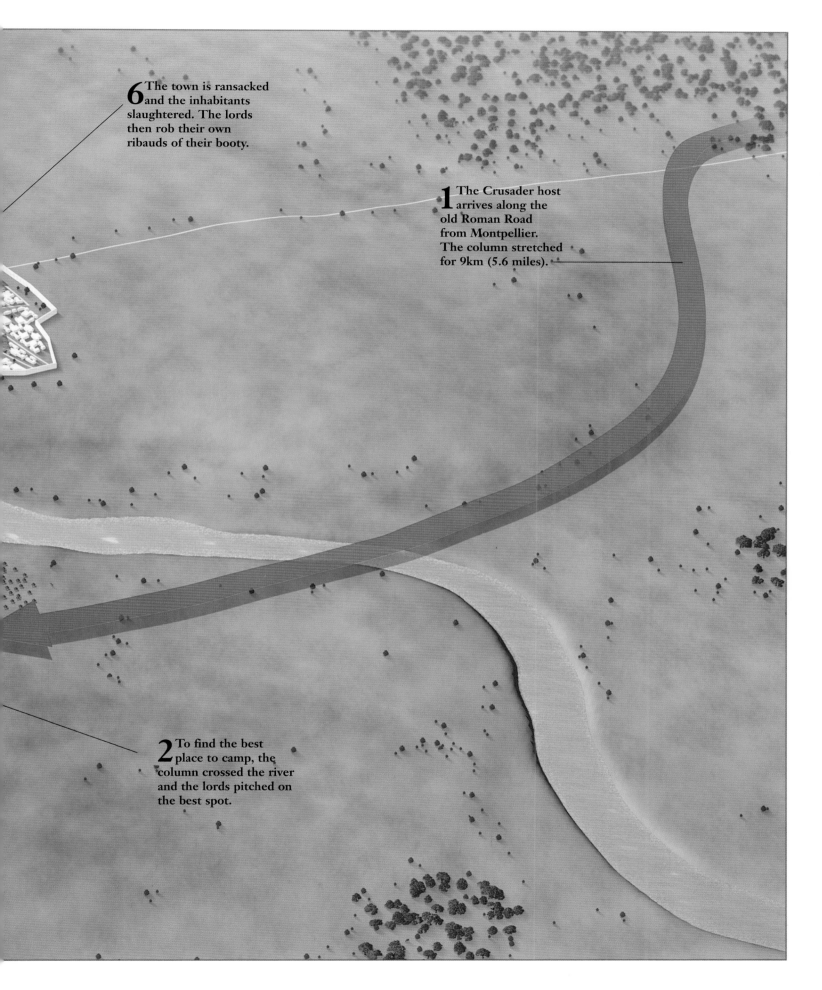

6 The town is ransacked and the inhabitants slaughtered. The lords then rob their own ribauds of their booty.

1 The Crusader host arrives along the old Roman Road from Montpellier. The column stretched for 9km (5.6 miles).

2 To find the best place to camp, the column crossed the river and the lords pitched on the best spot.

BEZIERS

(330yds) long and spans both the deeper, narrow summer channel and the broader winter flood bed of the river. The medieval walls hugged a rocky promontory, raising a defender 20m (66ft) above the bridge, making the near end within crossbow range of walls capable of holding 400–500 bowmen. Nestling below the walls was the Faubourg, an overspill of tenements and huts for which there was no room within the walls. Storming across the bridge would be a bloody business even for armoured knights and sergeants, and the width of the river meant the catapults and stone throwers could only reach the Faubourg, not far enough to suppress the crossbowmen on the walls while the knights attempted to cross.

INITIAL DEPLOYMENTS

The Crusading host arrived before the city on 21 July. The elderly Bishop of Beziers who had travelled with the Crusaders

Portrait of a Carthusian by Petrus Christus. This is a rare gem – a portrait of an unnamed 'Perfect Man'. His tunic is a plain version of the civilian dress depicted on page 141. You might, perhaps, perceive hidden strengths of character behind his eyes.

advised the townsfolk to accept the inevitable. They should deliver 200 named heretics to the army and save their own skins. The demand was refused; the walls were tall and strong, the river wide and the host would whither away when their 40 days was up.

The Crusaders crossed the river, above or below the city we don't know which, and camped on flat, sandy ground to the southwest, a decent distance away to prevent a surprise attack. The makeshift shelters of the ribauds lay closer to the bridge. Inevitably, as darkness gave way to dawn, some brave lad wandered over the bridge, a dagger in his belt and wine in his hand, perhaps showing off to friends or even a girl. Such cheek was too much for the defenders. They too had brave lads on their side. A gang of them threw open the gate and rushed the hero, stabbing him and heaving his body over the parapet and into the river.

The opportunity presenting itself, other ribauds charged the gang of defenders, forcing them back amid much hullabaloo

This thirteenth-century fresco depicts the misnamed Pope Innocent III. Note how much closer together his eyes are than those of the 'Perfect Man' opposite.

145

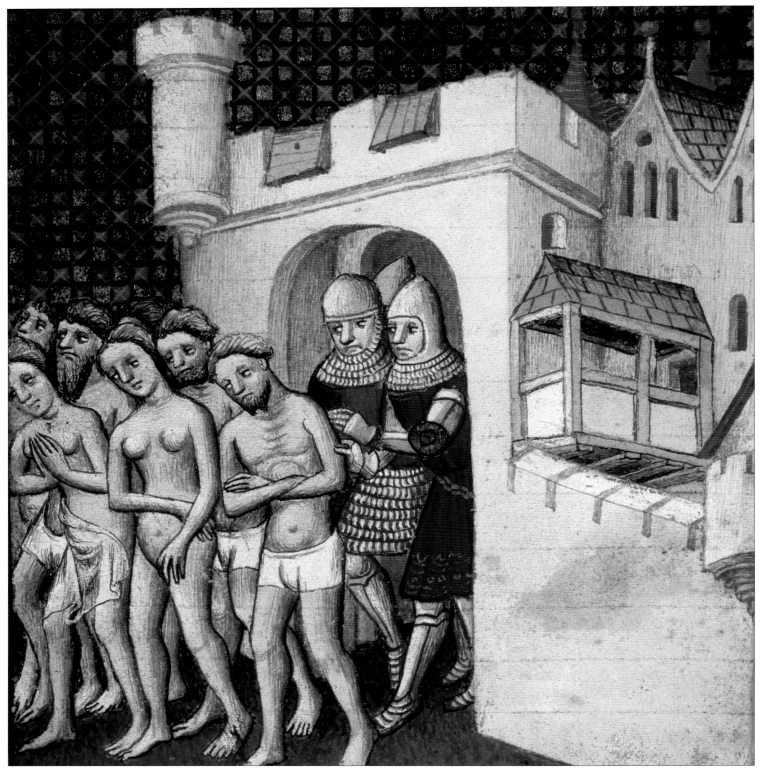

Expulsion of the Cathars from Carcassone shortly after the fall of Beziers. The medieval walls of Carcassone have been restored and well repay a visit. The knights are depicted in fourteenth-century armour.

into the Faubourg and all the way to the gate and into the city. The commotion stirred both sides. The Crusaders rushed to exploit this heaven-sent opportunity, while the townsfolk quickly stirred themselves to retake the gate.

In the close-quarter scrum in the narrow, twisting city streets, the men had to bear the screams of friends, wives and children who were trying to escape as the defenders resisted, but they had no answer to so many unhampered ribauds forcing their way deeper into the city. And thus the butchery started.

MASS SLAUGHTER

For three hours the knights and all the other Crusaders joined in with God's

work. There were Catholics and Cathars in the city, former friends and neighbours, men, women and children. The leading cleric, Arnaud Amaury Abbot of Cîteaux, with the Crusaders was asked: 'How shall we recognize the Cathars?'

His reply showed a sentiment derived from passages in both testaments of The Bible, and has passed into history: 'Kill them all. God will know his own'.

So they did, the entire population, even those Catholics who sought sanctuary at the very altars of their own churches. By noon all were killed. But this was no rash impulse on the part of the Abbot. On 10 March 1208, Pope Innocent III with Abbot Amaury and 12 Cardinals in council had already decided that the Cathars should be 'annihilated… From Montpellier to Bordeaux the Cathars are to be destroyed'. His subsequent letter to the Pope boasted: 'Neither age, nor sex nor status have been spared.' Estimates of the death toll vary between 7000 and 60,000.

The ribauds who had captured the city and slaughtered the inhabitants also looted it, and carried off more wealth than they could have ever dreamt of possessing. This outraged the Crusader knights' sense of their own importance and they turned on their brave lads, wrenching the loot away from them.

In frustration, and by way of retaliation, the ribauds deliberately set fire to the city, completing the destruction.

AFTERMATH

The Crusade wore on, capturing castles and cities and slaughtering heretics where they could. Many tens of thousands were burnt to satisfy the church's thirst for power. It eventually overreached itself, incurring the intervention of the King of Aragon, and military action petered out with the surrender on 15 March 1244 of the castle of Montsegur, where another 200 unrepentant Cathars were burnt alive.

The heraldic arms of Beziers. As a rule the simpler the design, the longer the coat-of-arms had been established. This pattern was thought to be the arms of Beziers' feudal lord Raymond-Roger Trancavel.

The Inquisition continued the work of rooting out pockets of the heresy for another 35 years, but never quite managing it entirely. In 1300 there were still more than a dozen Cathar 'Perfect Men' operating in the area, while others had escaped to Italy.

The French crown eventually took over many of the captured lands, and although the heresy was effectively expunged, the Dominicans eventually took on board many of the Cathar ideals of poverty and humble service – traits that had, until now, been conspicuous by their absence among medieval clergy.

A thirteenth-century crossbowman. This was the missile weapon of choice for the professional soldier. It was so feared by the knights that there were various papal edicts banning its use on certain days. A hook hangs from the soldier's belt, which engages in the string and the bow is then pushed downwards using the leg muscles to make it ready for use. The range was about 240m (262yd) and its missile, the quarrel, could penetrate all forms of armour then in use.

LAS NAVAS
1212

WHEN THE SQUABBLING SPANISH CHRISTIAN KINGS FINALLY UNITED UNDER THE BANNER OF A CRUSADE, THEY WERE ABLE TO INFLICT A CRUSHING DEFEAT ON THE ALMOHAD DYNASTY THAT CONTROLLED SOUTHERN SPAIN AND MUCH OF NORTH AFRICA.

WHY DID IT HAPPEN?

WHO An army of Crusaders from Spain and the rest of Europe under Alfonso VIII of Castile (1155–1214) against a larger Muslim force led by Abu 'Abd Allah al-Nasir (d. 1214).

WHAT Al-Nasir's deployment on open ground allowed Crusader heavy cavalry and infantry to overrun his lighter infantry and destroy a much larger Muslim force.

WHERE Las Navas de Tolosa, in the Sierra Morena mountains, southern Spain.

WHEN 16 July 1212.

WHY Al-Nasir had launched an attack in 1211 to defend and expand Muslim territory in the Iberian Peninsula. This was countered by a united Spanish and European Crusade (or Reconquista) in 1212, led by Alfonso VIII of Castile.

OUTCOME The Crusader victory was one of the most decisive of the time, with some three-quarters of the Muslim force being killed. It heralded the eventual Christian *Reconquista* of the Iberian peninsula.

The Muslim conquest of Spain had been carried out with incredible speed: cities fell rapidly to siege or intimidation, and armies were destroyed quickly in battle, which almost always were decided in favour of the Muslim conquerors. Most historians blame these defeats on the disunity of the various Visigothic kings who seemed unable to come together in a concerted defence of their lands.

The remaining northern Christians never gave up the idea of the *Reconquista*: the reconquering of the Iberian lands that had been lost to the Muslims. Yet, between the eighth and eleventh centuries, there was little fighting between the two parts of Spain other than a few border clashes. The reason for this was simple. The Christian Asturians in the north were divided and not powerful enough to take on the Muslim principalities in Al-Andalus to the south; nor were the Muslims to the south united enough to take the war to the Asturians.

By the middle of the twelfth century the Almohad dynasty had taken control of Muslim southern Spain and much of north

Depicted in a contemporary illumination from the Indice de los Privilegios Reales *King Fernando III of Castile, son of the victor of Las Navas, Alfonso VIII, was able to build on his father's success by making the largest land gains of the* Reconquista, *including the cities of Córdoba, Jaén, Seville, Arcos, Medina-Sidonia, Jerez and Cádiz.*

Africa. They were aiming to make war on the Christian kingdoms to reclaim some of the lands that been lost in the previous two centuries and to expand their territory once more.

Civil wars among the Spanish Christian kingdoms had always been a problem and border squabbles and inheritance questions constantly plagued them. Much of this can be blamed on the familial relationships that tied these kingdoms together – all the rulers descended from the same ancestral Léonese-Castilian kings – leading to more fighting between Christians before the beginning of the thirteenth century than between Christians and Muslims. A king needed to be secure in his realm, not fearing the attacks of his cousins, and at the same time filled with the religious desire for warfare against Muslims to launch a Reconquista Crusade into Al-Andalus. The greatest Crusading king was to come at the end of the twelfth century: Alfonso VIII, King of Castile, who led the Christian forces at the battle of Las Navas de Tolosa in 1212.

THE *RECONQUISTA*

Alfonso VIII was born on 11 November 1155, the eldest son of Sancho III of Castile and Blanca of Navarre. Only two years old when he inherited his throne, Alfonso was protected so well during his minority by his mother and council that he not only survived his youth, but also prospered under their tutelage. They especially taught him what it was to be a Christian king in Spain, and how to watch his enemies (and his friends). Somewhere in his training he also developed a desire for *Reconquista*. Almost immediately after his majority, he started campaigning against the Almohads. His first expedition was the relief of the siege of Huete, under attack by Caliph Abu Ya'qub Yusuf I in 1172. Threatened by weather problems and the arrival of a Castilian relief army, the Andalusians withdrew. For this Alfonso VIII and his army received an indulgence pardoning their sins from the Papal legate, Cardinal Hyacinth. Five years later, Alfonso met with Kings Fernando II of León and

Alfonso II of Aragon to plan a joint Crusade. This resulted in the capture of Cuenca – with a siege lasting nine months – after which Pope Lucius III celebrated by founding an episcopal see in the newly captured city.

For the next few years, warfare between Christians and Muslims in Spain was restricted to the frontiers, with neither side driving too far into the other's lands. The only exception came in 1184 when Caliph Abu Ya'qub Yusuf I invaded Portugal and besieged Santarém, but when Fernando II came to assistance of the Portuguese king, Afonso I, five days into the siege, the Caliph, who had been fatally wounded, retreated to Seville.

The fall of Jerusalem to Saladin in 1187 affected the whole Crusading world. Despite the battle taking place a continent away, word of Muslim success reached Spain quickly. Andalusians celebrated and

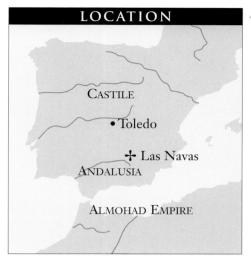

CASTILE
• Toledo
✝ Las Navas
ANDALUSIA
ALMOHAD EMPIRE

Following the Battle of Las Navas, the borders of Andalucian Spain were pushed further to the south than ever before, leaving only the Kingdom of Granada remaining in Muslim hands until conquered by Ferdinand and Isabella in 1492.

ANDALUCIAN HORSE ARCHER

Iberian Muslim forces made great use of mounted archers. Combining excellent mobility with good striking power, horse archers could sweep across an enemy line with speed and lethality. Successive attacks would fatigue their opponents, with many choosing to flee the battlefield rather than sustain further injuries. And, being so mobile, they could also easily evade any enemy counterstrike.

LAS NAVAS

Pope Innocent III was head of the Catholic Church from 1198 to 1216 and thus presided over the disastrous Fourth Crusade, the Reconquista *victories of Alfonso VIII of Castile, and the early Albigensian Crusades. His support of these endeavours never failed, but his rewards were few, and none so great as the Spanish victory at the Battle of Las Navas de Tolosa.*

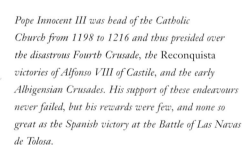

THE OPPOSED FORCES

CRUSADERS (estimated)

Castile:	3000 cavalry
	15,000 infantry
Aragon:	1500 cavalry
	7000 infantry
Navarre:	200 cavalry
Portuguese:	250

Total: 26,950

MUSLIM FORCES (estimated)

Andalusians:	3500 cavalry
	15,000 infantry
Almohads:	3000 cavalry
	30,000 infantry

Total: 51,500

Christians mourned. No doubt, *Reconquistadors* wondered if they should leave their struggle to join the newly called Third Crusade. However, such speculation was soon quelled by Pope Clement III, who reassured the Spanish Christians that they were to continue their fight against the Muslims to the south.

Two years later, Alfonso VIII responded by participating in the Crusade of Silves, which led to his seizure of several towns south of the Guadiana River – but he could go no further. Other Iberian soldiers, joined by Crusaders on their way to the Holy Land from Northern Europe, captured Alvor and Silves in Portugal – the latter site giving the Crusade its more modern name. But success was short-lived, as Abu Ya'qub Yusuf (c.1160 –1199), known more prominently as al-Mansur ('the Victorious') who had followed Abu

Ya'qub Yusuf I as Caliph in 1184, countered these attacks in 1190–91, eventually even regaining Silves.

DEFEAT AT ALARCOS

Alfonso VIII launched a new Crusade in 1195, when he joined knights from the Order of Calatrava and Archbishop Martín of Toledo in attacking the Guadalquivir region. At the same time, Alfonso started constructing a castle at Alarcos on the Muslim side of the Guadiana, thus announcing his intention to stay. It was likely that this concerned al-Mansur almost more than anything else. But he was away, taking care of affairs in Marrakech, and unable to respond very quickly. It was not until 30 June that he reached Cordoba with his Almohad army, and five days later he marched out of that city towards Alarcos. Alfonso learned of al-Mansur's movement shortly thereafter and gathered his army in response. The two forces met outside the unfinished fortress on 18 July, in what resulted as a major defeat for the Castilian Christians. Alfonso quickly withdrew to Toledo, abandoning the border fortifications of Malagón, Benavente, Calatrava, Caracuel and Torre de Guadalferza. But the battle had been also very costly for the Muslims, leaving al-Mansur unable to take further advantage of victory, as he retreated to Seville in order to regroup.

After this defeat, despite constant calls from the Papacy and other churchmen for Alfonso VIII and his royal Spanish co-religionists to restart the *Reconquista*, the Christians seemed unwilling to launch further campaigns into Al-Andalus. In part, this was the result of resentment by Alfonso of the kings of Aragon, León and Navarre for not joining him at Alarcos – although Alfonso IX of León had simply not arrived in time – and blame by these kings of Alfonso for trying to go it alone. Several years of warfare between these Christian kings followed, with a 'Crusade' even being called by Pope Celestine III against Alfonso IX in 1196–97; in part because he had not agreed to go on his own Crusade.

On the other side in the period following the battle at Alarcos, al-Mansur was busy. From 1195 to 1197 he launched assaults into lands to the north. Although these were little more than raids, bringing few permanent gains to the Muslims, they badly irritated those kings whose realms they invaded. Finally, the Christian kings pushed for peace, and al-Mansur agreed to one for ten years. In 1199 al-Mansur died in Marrakech and was succeeded as Almohad Caliph by his son, Abu 'Abd Allah al-Nasir (d.1214). Fortunately for him his father's truce with the Spanish Christians allowed the cleaning up of rebellious factions in Northern Africa without risking his Spanish lands.

A NEW CAMPAIGN

In 1211, al-Nasir, called 'Miramamolín' by the Christians, crossed from Morocco to Spain. He intended not just to protect his realm from Christian attack but also, it seems, to wage war against Castile. Al-Nasir held that Alfonso VIII was the most fearsome of his potential opponents. In July he laid siege to the Calatravan Castle of Salvatierra, protecting the road to Toledo. As Alfonso could not respond, the garrison soon surrendered. But they had held long enough for the weather to change, and al-Nasir could not campaign further that year.

The Spanish kings and the Catholic Church responded quickly to the capture of Salvatierra. Nothing militarily could be done until the following year, although Pope Innocent III did issue an indulgence to anyone who would support a Crusade against the Andalusians, directed not just at the Spaniards but also at the French and

When Seville fell to Fernando III of Castille in 1248 – depicted here in an early modern print by Juan Antonio de Vera y Figeuroa – it was seen as his greatest victory. While he divided his conquests among the Military Orders, Church leaders and nobles who fought with him, he kept Seville for himself, moving his capital there. When he died in 1252, he was buried in the Great Mosque, which he had Christianized and was rebuilding as a Cathedral.

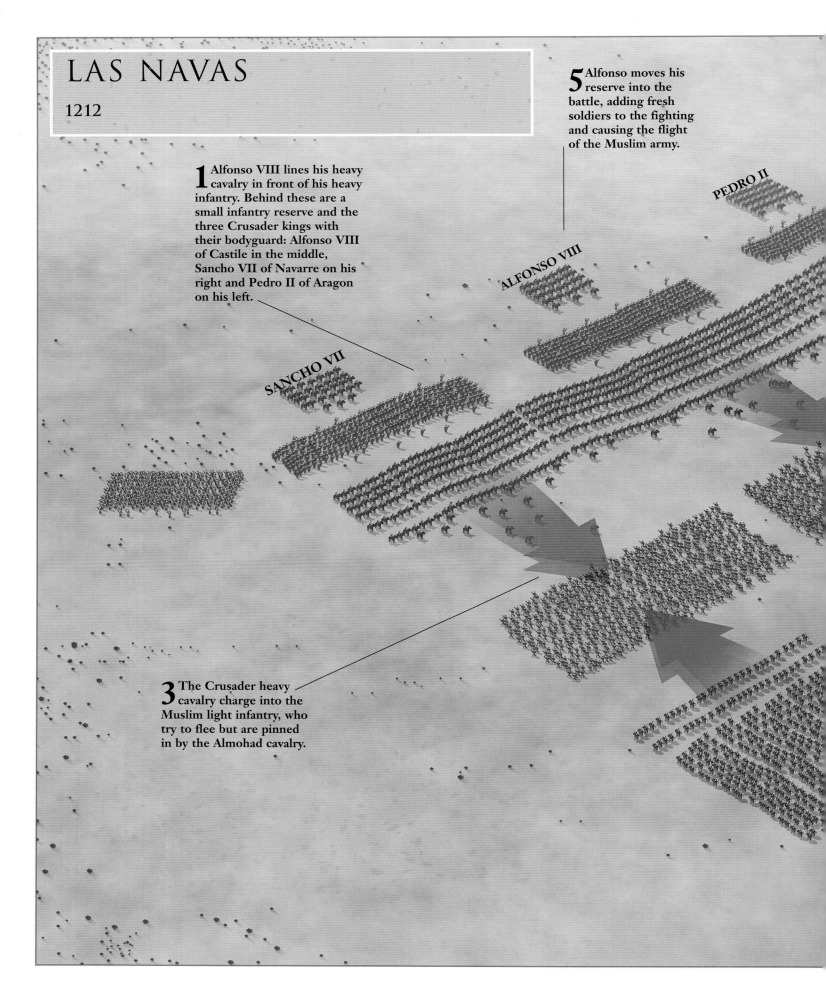

LAS NAVAS

1212

5 Alfonso moves his reserve into the battle, adding fresh soldiers to the fighting and causing the flight of the Muslim army.

1 Alfonso VIII lines his heavy cavalry in front of his heavy infantry. Behind these are a small infantry reserve and the three Crusader kings with their bodyguard: Alfonso VIII of Castile in the middle, Sancho VII of Navarre on his right and Pedro II of Aragon on his left.

PEDRO II

ALFONSO VIII

SANCHO VII

3 The Crusader heavy cavalry charge into the Muslim light infantry, who try to flee but are pinned in by the Almohad cavalry.

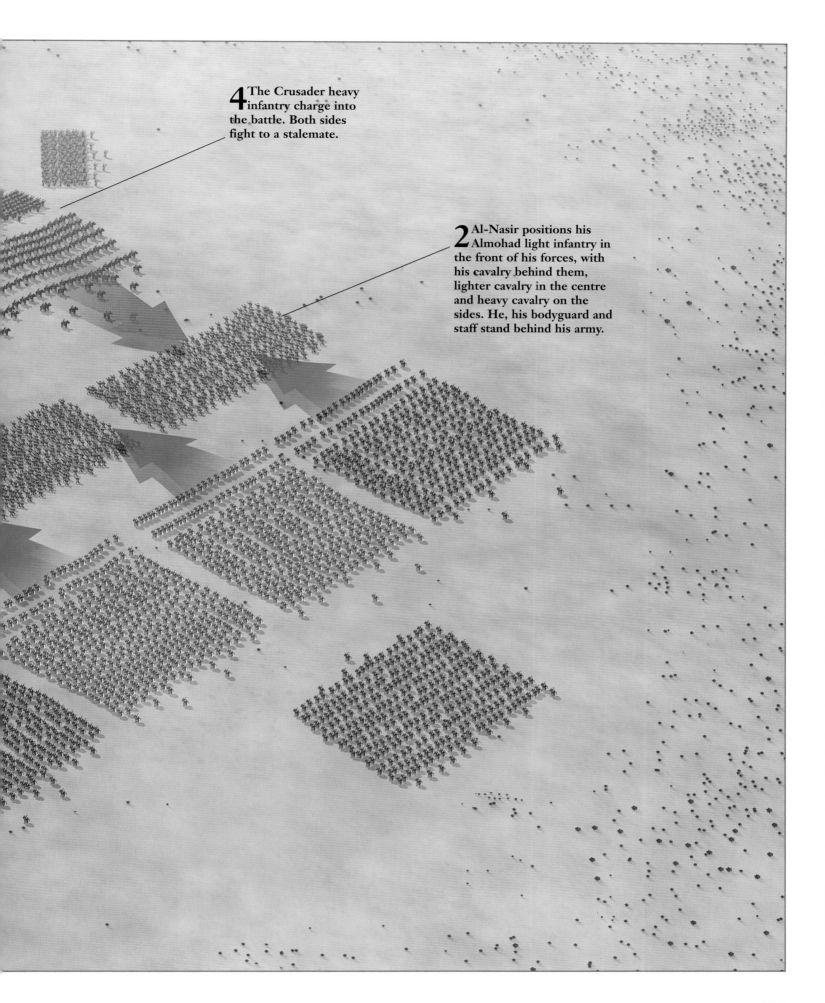

4 The Crusader heavy infantry charge into the battle. Both sides fight to a stalemate.

2 Al-Nasir positions his Almohad light infantry in the front of his forces, with his cavalry behind them, lighter cavalry in the centre and heavy cavalry on the sides. He, his bodyguard and staff stand behind his army.

Provencals. On 20 May, the Crusaders met in Toledo. Several kings were present, not only Alfonso VIII of Castile but Pedro II of Aragon, Sancho VII of Navarre, and Afonso II of Portugal. Participating as well were Archbishop Arnald Amaury of Narbonne, Guillaume of Bordeaux, Roderigo of Toledo, the Bishop of Nantes, along with numerous knights of the Templar, Hospitaller, Santiagan and Calatravan Orders, all led by their Spanish Masters. Although a total

number of Crusaders is not known, some sources give an (almost certainly exaggerated) figure of more than 50,000. Those same sources also place the numbers of Muslim soldiers at more than 150,000.

A month later, on 20 June, having given leadership of the expedition to Alfonso VIII despite his defeat at Alarcos, the Crusaders left Toledo, marching towards Al-Andalus and conquering everything on their route. On 24 June, they captured Malagón, slaughtering the inhabitants. On 1 July Calatrava fell to them.

On 3 July, the Muslims retreated from Ultramontane, abandoning it to the Crusaders, and the next day Alarcos was reclaimed. On 5–6 May, Caracuel and Benevente Castles, fortresses near Calatrava, were captured, and on 7 May Salvatierra. By 11 July, the Crusaders had entered the Fresnedas, camping on 13 July in the Sierra Morena Mountains.

AL-NASIR DEPLOYS

During this time the Almohad army had been moving towards the Crusaders. On 13 July, they had marched to Las Navas de Tolosa, only a few kilometres away from their enemy. For two days there was no action. Al-Nasir had clearly picked the terrain where he wanted to fight, but initially it seemed as if Alfonso did not want to have a battle there. From the sources it is unclear why this is the case: the field chosen was fairly flat and wide, with most historians believing that it gave no clear advantage to the Muslims. If anything, it benefited the Crusaders. Al-Nasir's soldiers were mostly infantry and archers, lightly armoured and carrying swords, spears, maces, axes or bows. His cavalry was similarly armed and armoured, and he also had small numbers of mounted archers.

Consequently, he should not have desired such a wide and flat battlefield. The Crusaders, on the other hand, had a large number of heavy cavalry who operated best in such terrain, as did their heavy infantry. They were all armoured in mail from head to toe, with strong helmets and shields, and carrying lances (or spears) and swords as their chief weapons.

That this was ultimately recognized as a good field for battle can be seen in

KNIGHT OF SANTIAGO
The Templars, Hospitallers, and Teutonic Knights were undoubtedly the most famous Crusading monastic military orders. In Spain they were joined by several others, including the Orders of Santiago, Montesa, Calatrava, Alcántara, San Julián del Pereiro, Trujillo and San Jorge de Alfama. The largest of these, Santiago – named after the important Christian shrine at Santiago de Compostela – was founded in the middle of the twelfth century and given its own rule in 1171 at the behest of Pope Alexander III. Knights of this Order promised to use their military talents to further the Reconquista *and were frequently used to garrison fortifications along the frontiers. They also took part in battles, for example at Las Navas, as heavy cavalry.*

Alfonso's formation at Las Navas on the morning of 16 July. His heavy cavalry were formed in a long line in front of an equally long line of heavy infantry. Behind these stood a small infantry reserve and the three kings with their bodyguards: Alfonso VIII of Castile in the middle, Sancho VII of Navarre to his right and Pedro II of Aragon to his left. On their flanks were archers whose responsibility it was to keep the more numerous Muslim forces from attempting to encircle or outflank the Christians.

Al-Nasir had ordered his light infantry directly to oppose the Crusader heavy cavalry. Behind them he placed his Muslim cavalry: lighter cavalry in the middle and heavy cavalry on the sides. Al-Nasir, his bodyguard and his general staff were positioned behind this formation.

The tactics planned by both sides were not new. As was almost customary in European armies by the mid-thirteenth century, Alfonso VIII planned to take the offensive by charging his heavy cavalry forward and to follow almost immediately with a charge from his heavy infantry. If the cavalry did not rout their opponents by

intimidation alone – something that they managed often – or were unable to sweep them off by the shock of their assault, the infantry would join in the attack. Even the strongest troops had difficulty withstanding the ferocity of this attack, and weak troops, especially those whose participation was based on obligation rather than occupation, generally fled at the first sign of combat. But the Muslim formation countered this potential flight fairly well by penning the light infantry in with elite infantry and disciplined cavalry troops.

Indeed, Muslim military leaders seem to have anticipated the failure of their light infantry in the face of a heavy cavalry charge. As these formations collapsed with the impact of the Crusaders, the Christian cavalry would carry on through until they themselves would be attacked and enveloped from three sides by the Muslim cavalry. The Crusader infantry charge was designed to thwart this by adding their strength to the cavalry.

However, there is no doubt that the greater numbers put on the field by al-Nasir made him confident of victory, against both the Christian cavalry and infantry.

Muslim cavalry in Spain from the eighth to the fifteenth century were generally less heavily armoured than their Christian counterparts and relied more on skirmishing than the frontal charge.

His victory at the Battle of Las Navas de Tolosa vaulted Alfonso VIII into a legendary status unequalled by any in Spain save El Cid. Blessed by the Church for his Reconquista *endeavours, Alfonso is depicted in this later portrayal wearing a cross on his surcoat and a crown on his head. One of his generals, perhaps an ecclesiastic of high rank or the Master of one of the military orders, rides behind him, receiving his battlefield commands.*

THE CRUSADERS CHARGE

Alfonso and the other Crusader kings did not fear these greater numbers, though. They believed that God was on their side and they could not lose. Before the battle they had all taken an oath, 'Victory or Death', and this had bred confidence in them and their soldiers. Using this as impetus, the cavalry began their charge.

Within seconds they had slammed into the Andalusian defensive lines; minutes later, they were joined by their infantry. True to previous form, the Muslim infantry folded but their cavalry swept onto the charging Crusader forces. Bloody hand-to-hand fighting ensued.

After a while, the Crusaders started to falter, and it looked as if a similar defeat to that suffered at Alarcos would follow. All of al-Nasir's soldiers were now fighting – but

Alfonso had not yet sent all of his troops into the battle. Alfonso drew this reserve into a smaller unit and moved it into the conflict.

By this time the Andalusians were becoming fatigued – the stress of combat had, no doubt, exhausted all of the soldiers within the actual fray – so the entrance of fresh troops by the Crusaders quickly turned the tide of battle. Only a short time later, Muslims began fleeing from the battlefield, and soon the combat was over.

AFTERMATH

The Crusaders had won their greatest *Reconquista* victory. Fleeing Muslims, mostly on foot, were ridden down and killed, and very few escaped. By nightfall the Almohad army had been annihilated, with chroniclers of the time tallying a loss of 100,000, which is certainly an exaggeration. However, it is not out of question that as many as three-quarters of the Muslim force had been destroyed. Al-Nasir was wounded, although he did make it to Marrakech before he died on 25 December 1213.

The battle was also costly for the Crusaders, however. Several thousand of them were killed at Las Navas – chronicles count 2000, many from the knights and leaders of the Military Orders, including: Pedro Gomez de Acevedo, bannerman of the Order of Calatrava; Alfonso Fernandez de Valladares, commander of the Order of Santiago; Pedro Arias, Master of the Order de Santiago, who died of wounds on 3 August; and Gomez Ramirez, Master of the Templars. Ruy Diaz, Master of the Order of Calatrava, was so badly wounded that he was forced to resign his command.

The battle of Las Navas de Tolosa was as close to a decisive battle as any during the Crusades. The military manpower of Southern Spain had been almost completely depleted, while there were thousands of Crusaders still in arms and newly flushed with victory. They followed Las Navas by the conquest of numerous Muslim cities: Baños, Tolosa and Vilches (18 July); Baeza (20 July); and Úbeda (3 August). The following year even more gains were made.

There was now no stopping the *Reconquista*, although Alfonso VIII would die on 5 October 1214, leaving his son, Fernando III, to make the greatest acquisitions: Córdoba, Jaén, Seville, Arcos, Medina-Sidonia, Jerez, and Cádiz. By the time Fernando died, on May 30, 1252, the Almohad Empire had disappeared, replaced in Al-Andalus by the Nazhari Kingdom of Granada, until its conquest by Ferdinand and Isabella in 1492 entirely restored Christian rulership to Iberia.

One of the other Crusader leaders at the Battle of Las Navas was Afonso II, King of Portugal (who reigned 1212–1223). Normally, the King of Portugal stayed out of Reconquista *efforts elsewhere in Spain – especially as other Christian kings often claimed his throne. Afonso, however, chose to unite his army with those of the Kings of Castille, Aragon and Navarre to defeat the Almohads.*

ALPHONSVS SECVNDVS LVSITANIÆ REX III.

LAKE PEIPUS
1242

THE BATTLE OF LAKE PEIPUS, IN WHICH CHRISTIAN CONFRONTED CHRISTIAN, EXPOSES THE AMBIGUITY OF THE BALTIC CRUSADES. ALTHOUGH A MINOR ENCOUNTER, THE BATTLE EFFECTIVELY ENDED WESTERN CRUSADING AGAINST RUSSIA, AND SECURED PRINCE ALEXANDER NEVSKII OF NOVGOROD'S FAME AS THE HERO WHO HALTED WESTERN AGGRESSION.

WHY DID IT HAPPEN?

WHO A Russian force, largely from Novgorod and led by the city's prince, Alexander Nevskii (1219–1263), defeated a small western army composed of Danish knights, militia from the diocese of Dorpat, Estonian tribal levies and a small number of Teutonic Knights, under the overall command of Bishop Hermann of Dorpat.

WHAT A Novgorodian victory over a mixed Crusader and western colonial army.

WHERE On the shore of Lake Peipus, near the modern Russian–Estonian border.

WHEN 5 April 1242.

WHY Papal desire to force the Orthodox Christians of Russia to acknowledge papal supremacy combined with Scandinavian and German desire to claim Novgorodian resources and trade networks to launch a crusade against Novgorod.

OUTCOME With the Crusader defeat, effective western aggression against Novgorod came to an end. Novgorod's position as the leading Russian state was confirmed, leading in time to the creation of a Russian empire under the Tsars.

The Baltic was the home of Europe's last non-Christian peoples. Twelfth-century Baltic Crusades were largely ineffective, especially because of the difficulty of holding conquered land. Thus a new policy emerged in the thirteenth century. The papacy made a determined effort to create a 'church state' in the Baltic, a state ruled by bishops and papal legates under the supervisory leadership of the popes. Two elements, however, stood in the way of making this dream a reality. First, there was the strong influence of Orthodox Christianity in the region. Second, there were the widely varying motives of the western

This engraving presents the venerable Alexander Nevskii, the subject of later hagiography. In reality, he was only about 22 years old at the time of his victory on Lake Peipus, and died aged 44.

Crusaders, who were willing to accept papal indulgences but did not share in the papacy's goals. The Orthodox Christians of Russia refused to accept papal authority, and to western eyes appeared to be schismatics who were hindering the conversion of the Baltic region. To western merchants and warlords, the Russians, perhaps more importantly, also appeared to be dangerous rivals for the resources of the region. These two factors reached a height by c. 1240, culminating in the Crusaders' defeat at Lake Peipus in 1242.

In the late 1230s, the papal legate William of Modena preached a Crusade and organized a western coalition against Novgorod. Novgorod was the greatest Russian state at the time, a trading centre so impressive by northern European standards that it was often called 'Lord Novgorod the Great'. If any state could contest western control of the Baltic region, it was Novgorod. In the 1230s, however, Russia was reeling under Mongol invasions. Most Russian states had been conquered, and Novgorod, while maintaining technical independence, had accepted Mongol overlordship in 1237. Thus, the time seemed right for a western attack that would defeat Novgorod and finally force its rich and influential townsmen into a reunion of eastern and western Christianity.

William of Modena's efforts to launch a crusade had considerable success, in large part because the kings of Sweden and Denmark were attempting an eastward expansion that they were very happy to label a 'Crusade', thus winning a measure of financial assistance, and of course spiritual rewards, while attracting volunteers from elsewhere in Europe.

Similarly, the Teutonic Knights, members of a military religious order that had begun to carve out a state in the Baltic, were willing to attack their powerful and schismatic neighbour to further their own interests. By 1240, William himself returned to Italy, content that his efforts would lead to a western triumph.

THE CAMPAIGN

The western coalition that William had brought into being had little cohesion, and various elements of the Crusader force set out with no serious thought having been given to a master strategy. The Swedes, led by their king, Eric IX (1222–1250), thrust into Finland in the spring of 1240. The alarmed burghers of Novgorod responded to the threat by recalling their prince, Alexander, who had been driven out of the city shortly before. Alexander assumed leadership in the fight against the Swedes, greatly assisted by the highly trained troops of archers he had taken into exile with him.

LOCATION

Lake Peipus lies on the boundary between Catholic and Orthodox Christianity in the Baltic. In 1242, Estonia was being colonized by Germans, who wanted to expand into Russia.

TEUTONIC KNIGHT

The Teutonic Knights were members of a military religious order that established a state in Prussia and Latvia in the thirteenth century. Although few in number, they were highly successful at recruiting crusaders to aid their conquest of the pagan Slavic lands of the north.

LAKE PEIPUS

He defeated the Swedes at a site on the Neva River on 15 July 1240; the delighted Novgorodians commemorated the event by bestowing on Alexander the honorary title 'Nevskii'.

Despite Alexander's great victory over the Swedes, the threat to Novgorod remained. A second western force had already taken the field against them. This second army consisted of former members of the disbanded military Order of Swordbrothers, western knights who had become feudal overlords in Estonia, Danes, the German bishop of Dorpat, a Russian force led by Prince Jaroslav, and a few Teutonic Knights. This second invasion enjoyed considerable success, capturing Isborg in September 1240. The westerners then defeated a relief force sent from the Russian city of Pskov and went on to besiege Pskov itself, which surrendered on terms.

By April 1241, this mixed army occupied lands east of the Neva River, and had constructed a fortress at Kopore. From that base, the westerners launched devastating raids that penetrated to within 32km

Opposite: The Battle on Ice (1942; oil on canvas) by Vladimir Aleksandrovich Serov (1910–68). In Soviet Russia, Alexandre Nevskii was a popular hero, and his victories were exploited to the full in World War II propaganda. This is in part because he came from a pre-Tsarist era, but also because he repelled German invaders from the West.

(20 miles) of Novgorod. These Crusaders were so certain of victory that they despatched one of the border bishops, Heinrich of Oesel-Wiek, to petition the Pope for authority over the conquered regions.

Although Alexander Nevskii had already abandoned Novgorod again, after another quarrel with the merchant leadership of the city, he was recalled once more. The Novgorodians agreed to his demands, in

This Russian druznik *cavalryman is typical of Alexander Nevskii's cavalry at Lake Peipus. More lightly armed than their western counterparts, such troops were especially effective in attacks on disorganized enemies.*

THE OPPOSED FORCES

WESTERN ARMY (estimated)

Teutonic:	
Knights:	20
Order men-at-arms:	c. 200
Danish & Estonian knights	c. 200
Dorpat militia	c. 600
Estonian tribal levies	1000
Total:	**2000**

NOVGOROD ARMY (estimated)
Mixed force, perhaps half cavalry and half infantry

Total:	**c. 6000**

LAKE PEIPUS

1242

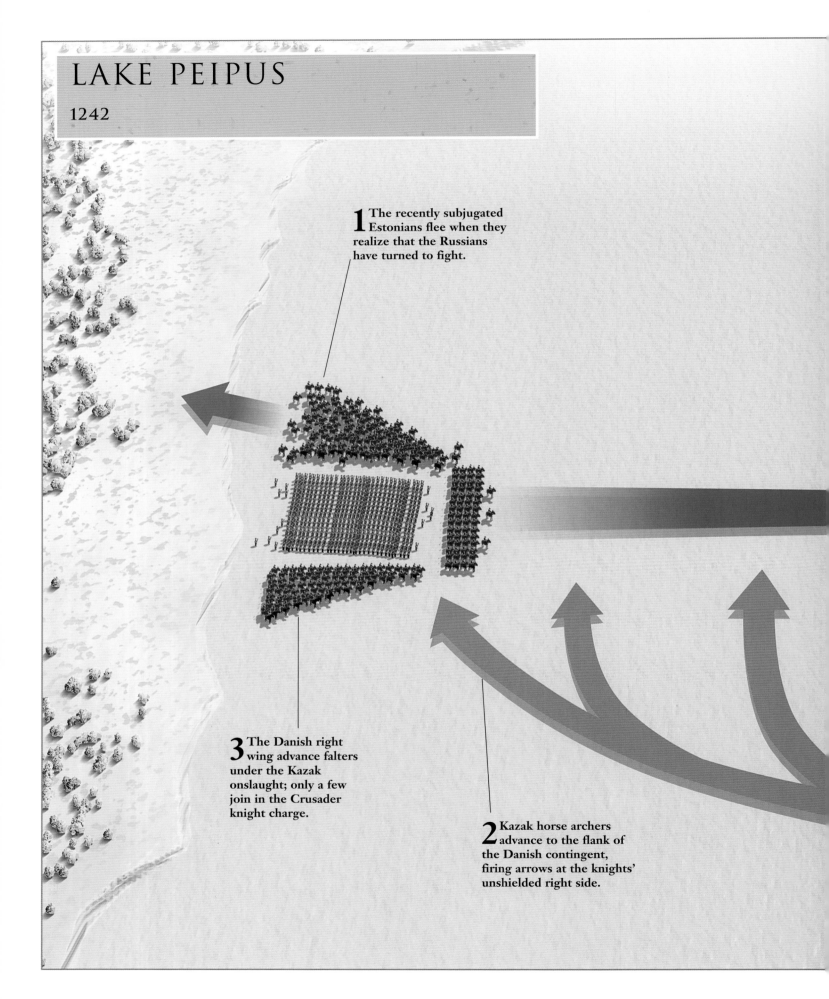

1 The recently subjugated Estonians flee when they realize that the Russians have turned to fight.

3 The Danish right wing advance falters under the Kazak onslaught; only a few join in the Crusader knight charge.

2 Kazak horse archers advance to the flank of the Danish contingent, firing arrows at the knights' unshielded right side.

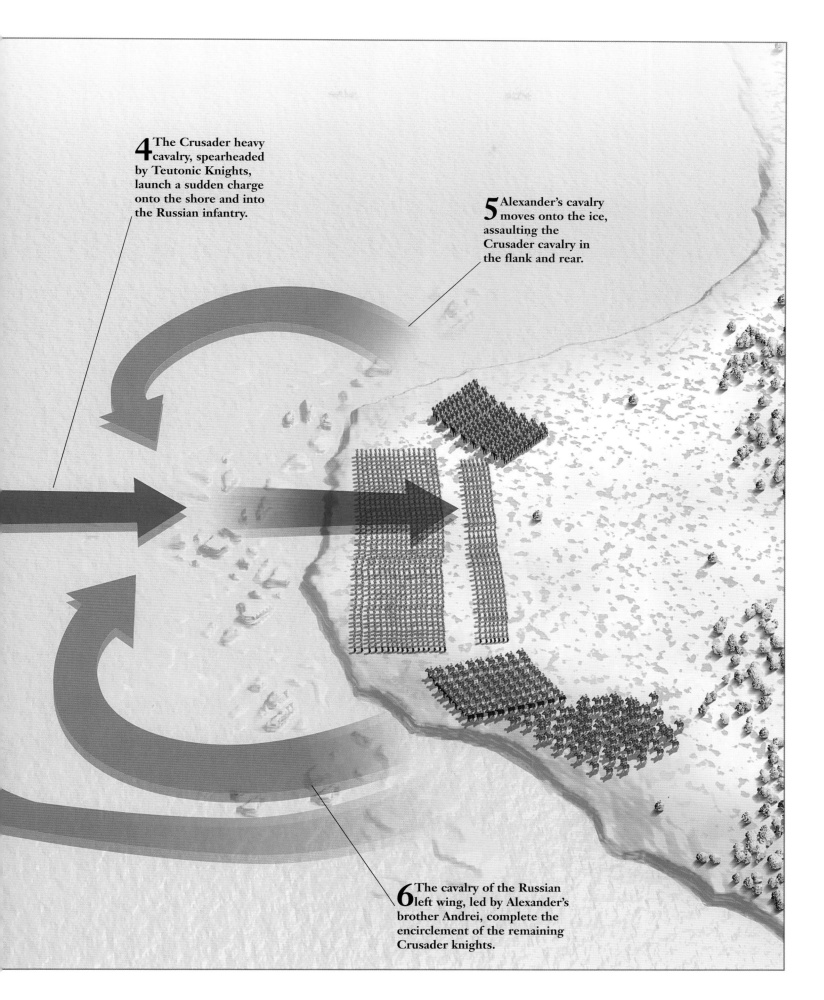

4 The Crusader heavy cavalry, spearheaded by Teutonic Knights, launch a sudden charge onto the shore and into the Russian infantry.

5 Alexander's cavalry moves onto the ice, assaulting the Crusader cavalry in the flank and rear.

6 The cavalry of the Russian left wing, led by Alexander's brother Andrei, complete the encirclement of the remaining Crusader knights.

In this Soviet propaganda image, Alexander Nevskii appears as a staunch defender of Russia against foreign aggression. He was also a practical man who later accepted Mongol overlordship and ruled Novogorod in their name.

return for his agreement to fight the German–Pskov coalition. Alexander proved worthy of their trust.

He regained the territory east of the Neva late in 1241, and in March 1242 re-took the town of Pskov. Alexander and his force then proceeded to raid deep into the German border diocese of Dorpat, apparently hoping to give the westerners a taste of their own medicine. It is clear that his intention was a major raid and he had no serious plan to expand Novgorod's territory. Apparently content with his success, Alexander and his 6000-man army turned for home after his advance force was driven back from a bridge.

THE BATTLE ON THE ICE

It seems likely that Bishop Hermann of Dorpat misunderstood Alexander's move, interpreting the Novgorodian withdrawal as a flight. It is also possible that Alexander had seriously underestimated the number of troops that the Bishop of Dorpat had at his disposal. Whatever the case, Bishop Hermann appears to have been exhilarated, thinking he had caught his formidable enemy at a considerable disadvantage. Most of the Crusader force from the preceding autumn had disbanded, but some were still present in Hermann's diocese, comprising a force that he clearly thought sufficient for the purpose.

Hermann set out in pursuit of Alexander's army with these troops; a force consisting of somewhere between 1000 and 2000 fighting men (the number given in extant sources varies widely), which seems somewhat foolhardy against an enemy 6000 strong. One must, however, take into account that the westerners were much better armed and armoured than most of the Russians – and probably intended merely to harry the retreating force rather than meet them in pitched battle.

Alexander's army retreated across the frozen waters of Lake Peipus; the Crusader army, close behind, also took to the ice, north of where the Russians were crossing. The Russians won the race to the shore and Alexander Nevskii had time to organize his force before the westerners arrived. He drew up the Russian army at a place on the eastern shore called Raven Rock, where the broken ground would cause difficulty for a manoeuvring and mounted attacker. The ground was made even more awkward by the build-up of ice ridges on the shore, caused by Lake Peipus freezing and refreezing during the course of the winter.

The site was well chosen for a defensive battle, especially since the terrain limited the effectiveness of the western heavy cavalry. Alexander placed his infantry, armed with spears, bows and axes, in the centre. It should be noted that, despite Sergei Eisenstein's magnificent portrayal of

the battle of Lake Peipus in his celebrated 1938 film *Alexander Nevsky*, the Russian force consisted largely of professional soldiers – not peasant militia desperately struggling to save Holy Mother Russia, as the highly propagandistic film portrays. Alexander also had some light cavalry, which he placed on his flanks. Some of these cavalrymen were mounted archers, probably Kazaks or Cumans.

The fact that the Russians had drawn up their army and offered battle apparently caused some consternation among the outnumbered Crusaders. This is suggested by the behaviour of their native Estonian levies, who were probably not very willing to fight in the first place; they are reported to have fled immediately when they caught sight of the enemy. Nevertheless, despite the fact that the western force was

This scene from Eisenstein's film Alexander Nevsky *(1938) presents the Russians as a peasant militia defending their homeland. In reality, they were a highly professional force.*

A Novgorod Polk infantryman (c. 1240). Russia was first settled by the Vikings travelling along its rivers. They met the nomadic tribes who roamed the steppes. So Russian arms and armour reflect both Western (Norse) and Eastern influences. This infantryman wears chain mail armour with a sleeveless, waist-length quilted tunic and a round, Turkic-style breastplate. He has a simple, Norse-style conical helmet with a nose guard, and is armed with a long-handled axe.

charge against the Russian position. Clearly, they were hoping to force the Russian centre to flee in disorder, allowing the escaping foot soldiers to be picked off at leisure. The Crusaders thus formed their heavy cavalry in a wedge, with the Teutonic Knights and their men-at-arms – the best troops – at the forefront.

With very little preliminary manoeuvring, this wedge charged deep into the massed infantry that formed the centre of the Russian line. The line, however, did not break. It is probable that the Crusader charge was fatally slowed by a combination of the large number of Novgorodian archers (whose weapons would have been particularly effective against Crusader horses) and the broken terrain they had to cross.

FLANKING ATTACK

The charge might still have won the day if the Russian cavalry, posted on either wing, had not engaged at about the same time. These lighter horsemen hit the flanks of the western army, the horse archers on the Russian left flank causing particularly serious damage to the Danish knights on the Crusader right. The Russians outnumbered the Crusaders by such a large margin that they were able to surround the westerners completely.

Many of the Danish knights turned back and tried to re-cross Lake Peipus, only to be pursued by the Russian cavalry. This is the only point at which fighting is likely to have taken place upon the frozen lake itself. Even if some of the heavier western horses broke through the ice with their riders, it is unlikely that anyone drowned, since the lake is extremely shallow (in areas as little as 30cm [12in] deep). Nonetheless, this manoeuvring on the frozen lake was enough

outnumbered at least three to one, the Crusaders still had a reasonable chance of success. The core of their army was heavy cavalry, both knights and men-at-arms. Wearing heavy mail, reinforced with plate, and being mounted on large warhorses, each knight would literally have far outweighed any opponent he faced. More importantly, the knights were trained in western chivalry's signature close-order cavalry charge, which in the thirteenth century achieved victory in battle after battle, especially when launched against unsupported infantry.

The Crusader leaders (we have no information on who commanded during the actual battle; it may have been Bishop Hermann himself) decided on a sudden to win the battle of Lake Peipus the nickname 'Battle on the Ice'.

About 400 Crusaders were killed, close to half the force that actually engaged the enemy; six Teutonic Knights and 44 others were captured. The casualties might have been higher but Alexander Nevskii permitted the pursuit of the defeated westerners to continue only to the far shore of the lake.

AFTERMATH

Lake Peipus was, in reality, an unimportant battle that was made into a centrepiece of Russian anti-western ideology by later legend, most notably Eisenstein's compelling theatrical spectacle *Alexander Nevsky*, with its blood-stirring soundtrack by Sergei Prokofiev. After winning his victory, Alexander offered favourable peace terms, again confirming that Novgorod intended no westward expansion. The bishop of Dorpat and his allies promptly accepted. Novgorod withdrew from the border territories it had seized and Alexander freed his prisoners, while the westerners released their hostages.

The battle did, however, have an effect on western prestige and may have encouraged several of the conquered Baltic peoples to rebel against their western masters. Shortly after Lake Peipus, the Prussians rebelled against the Teutonic Order that had subjugated them, although such a revolt may have been inevitable anyway. It is certain that the Order was not seriously weakened in the Battle on the Ice. Very few Teutonic Knights participated in the battle, and neither the order's grand master, master for Livonia, or the latter's acting master was even present on the occasion. The next year, the Estonians rebelled against Denmark, a revolt that was also doomed to failure.

This failed Crusade against Novgorod also revealed the weakness of the papacy's grandiose schemes for the region, as the Pope proved unable to channel the divergent interests of the north into a single master plan that might have had some effect. Perhaps the most important impact of the battle, though, was to enhance the prestige of the Russian prince Alexander Nevskii. The legend of the

battle on the Neva and the battle of Lake Peipus grew over time, leading to Alexander's eventual veneration as a saint for his role in protecting Russian orthodoxy. He also emerged as the clear victor in political terms, allowing him to begin the consolidation of power in Russia that would culminate several centuries later in the union of Russia under the Tsars.

This Soviet propaganda poster, likening the Crusader invasion of Russia in 1242 to the German invasion in World War II, helps explain the exaggerated importance given to the Battle of Lake Peipus.

LA FORBIE
1244

LA FORBIE WAS THE WORST DEFEAT SUFFERED BY THE CRUSADERS AND CAUSED A SHARP DECLINE IN THEIR POWER IN THE HOLY LAND. CASUALTIES AMONG THE KNIGHTLY ORDERS WERE ESPECIALLY SERIOUS. IT ALSO MARKED THE BEGINNING OF MAMLUK DOMINANCE IN EGYPT.

WHY DID IT HAPPEN?

WHO A Crusader army containing about 6000 western soldiers plus 4000 local allies, opposed by around 11,000 Muslim troops.

WHAT After their allied troops were broken by a sudden attack, the westerners launched their own assault, driving deep into the enemy army.

WHERE Near La Forbie, northwest of Gaza.

WHEN 17–18 October 1244.

WHY Jerusalem had fallen to Muslim forces, prompting a campaign to defeat them in the field and restore the situation.

OUTCOME Surrounded in the middle of the enemy army, the Crusaders were defeated with massive casualties.

For 250 years the cities of the Holy Land had been changing hands as the balance of power shifted between the Crusaders and their Muslim opponents. Possession of Jerusalem was the greatest prize of all, and was the ultimate object of the Crusaders. The Fifth Crusade had completely failed to achieve anything, let alone the recapture of Jerusalem from the Muslims.

After the Fifth Crusade, the lands of the Ayyubid dynasty were divided into two major areas. Al-Kamil, Sultan of Egypt, granted rulership of the Syrian territories to his brother

while retaining control of the Egyptian lands himself. He also agreed a truce with the defeated Crusaders that lasted for eight years.

The truce ended when Frederick II (1194–1250), the Holy Roman Emperor, tried to reclaim Jerusalem. He had married into the dynasty that ruled what remained of the Kingdom of Jerusalem and thus had a claim of sorts to all of it. The Crusaders were deeply divided, mainly along the lines of support for Frederick as Holy Roman Emperor on one side, and the Pope on the other.

Pope Gregory IX, wearing the papal crown. He had a troubled reign characterized by revolts and conflict with the Holy Roman Emperor. The Crusade he had pushed for took place only after his death.

MAMLUK ARMOURED CAVALRYMAN

The Egyptian Mamluks (or Mamelukes) demonstrated the danger of creating a class of elite warriors who were also slaves. Recruited from non-Muslim boys from Anatolia and Syria, they were thoroughly indoctrinated to serve Islam. They were trained to be fierce warriors and from the early thirteenth century the Egyptian Ayyubid dynasty came to rely on the Mamelukes as the backbone of the their powerful cavalry arm.

The Mamluks lived by a strict code comparable to that of the European knightly orders. Their world was closed, isolated from the society they served, and while this produced highly capable soldiers, it denied the Mamluks a stake in the society they served. Once they became involved in politics, it was only a matter of time before the Mamluks seized power for themselves.

LOCATION

PRINCIPALITY
OF ANTIOCH

OUTREMER

La Forbie • Jerusalem
Gaza

AYYUBID
DYNASTY

The massive Crusader defeat at La Forbie led to calls for a fresh Crusade to re-establish Christian power in the Holy Land. French king Louis IX took up the cross shortly after, launching the Sixth Crusade.

Frederick and the Pope were not friends. As Holy Roman Emperor, Frederick was trying to increase imperial power at the expense of the Pope's influence, and this was resented both by Pope Honorius III (1148–1227) and his successor Gregory IX (c. 1143–1241). Frederick had sworn to lead a crusade when he was crowned in 1220 but by 1227, when he finally set out,

the Pope's patience had worn thin. A setback due to plague caused Frederick to be excommunicated, and after some back-and-forth diplomacy between Pope and Emperor, Frederick decided to go his own way, widening an already deep rift.

Frederick finally began his Crusade, largely without papal support, in 1228. The campaign ended not with battle, but with a

LA FORBIE

Frederick II held a number of royal titles as Holy Roman Emperor in addition to his own, King of Sicily. His attempt to consolidate his power as Emperor brought him into conflict with the Pope, who excommunicated him twice and even referred to him as the Antichrist.

THE OPPOSED FORCES

CRUSADERS (estimated)

Knights	1000
Infantry	6000
Allied Syrian cavalry	4000
Allied Bedouin cavalry	1000
Total:	**12,000**

EGYPTIANS/KHWAREZMIDS (estimated)

Mamluks	6000
Khwarezmids	10,000
Total:	**16,000**

deal whereby he ceded territory to the Muslim Ayyubid dynasty in return for an alliance and permission to be crowned as King of Jerusalem. Frederick was not allowed to rebuild they city's defences, however, which had been in ruin since 1217. The two rulers agreed another truce, this one to last for a full decade.

Frederick's acts were significant in that he demonstrated that a crusade was possible without the Pope's support and could be successful through diplomacy rather than bloodshed. He left the Holy Land to attend

to other matters, and the truce eventually expired in 1239.

JERUSALEM FALLS

Little changed for five years, but in August 1244 Jerusalem fell to a large force of Khwarezmids allied to the Sultanate of Egypt. These tribesmen had been displaced from their traditional homelands by the growing power of the Mongols and moved into the Holy Land in force. Their capture of Jerusalem alarmed both the Christian and Muslim states of the region.

The Crusaders could not accept the idea of Jerusalem in Khwarezmid or Ayyubid hands and began to gather their armies. Western forces in the Holy Land were never very large, and, as always, were divided by internal politics. So, too, were the Muslims. The westerners had been a factor in local politics for centuries, and many Muslim leaders were willing to make common cause with them in order to gain an advantage over their rivals. In this case, the Ayyubids of Syria were also unwilling to allow their Egyptian cousins to rule Jerusalem.

Thus the Christians of the Kingdom of Jerusalem made common cause with the Muslim Kingdom of Transjordan and set out to retake the city. The Crusader army had at its heart the usual contingent of Frankish knights, heavily armoured and mounted on large horses. These included contingents from the Templar, Hospitaller and Teutonic orders.

There were about 1000 western horsemen in all, and the heavy cavalry was backed up by about 6000 infantry. As always, these men were supports rather than the main striking force; it was the knights who would decide the outcome of a battle. Overall command of the Christian force was exercised by Walter IV of Brienne (1205–1246), Count of Jaffa and Ascalon, with Philip of Montfort (d. 1270), the Constable of Jerusalem, supporting him.

The Syrians provided a large force of their own, numbering about 4000 cavalry

A Knight Hospitaller charges with sword raised. Founded in Jerusalem, the Hospitallers were a very powerful military and religious order that received papal recognition in 1113. By 1142, the order had eight substantial castles across the Holy Land.

An aerial view of the Crusader castle Krak des Chevaliers in Syria, a fortified hilltop citadel used by the Knights Hospitaller during the Crusades. The Templar and Hospitaller Orders built many impressive fortifications to allow their small numbers to dominate the largest possible area.

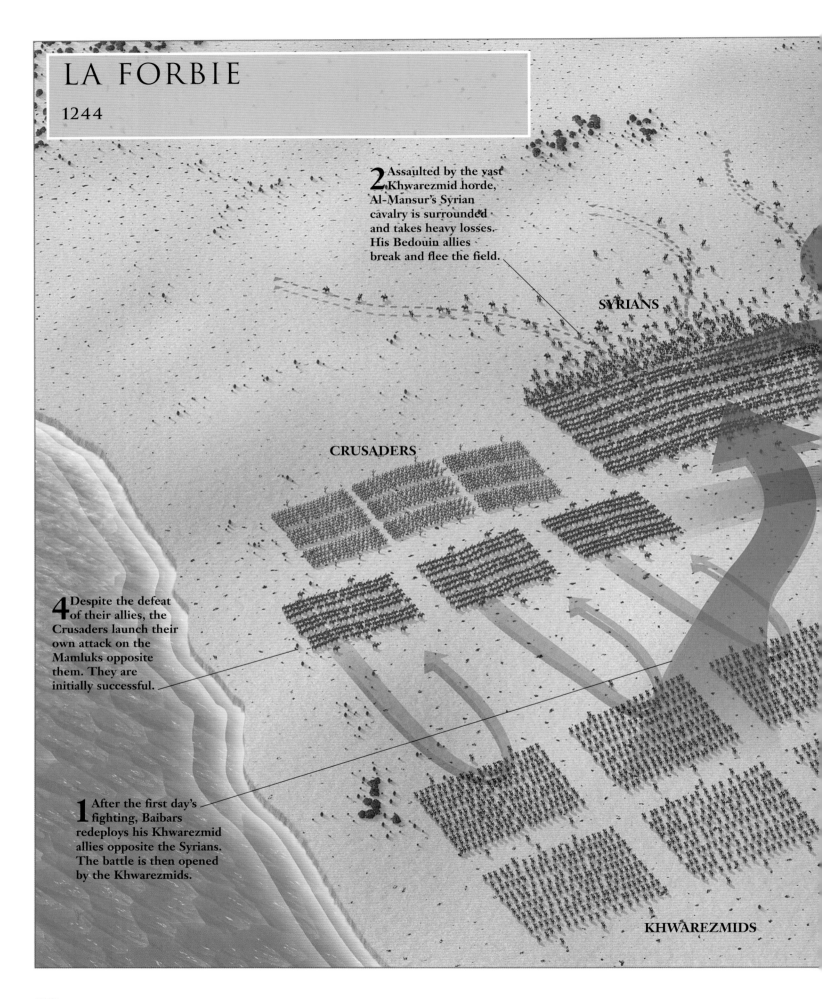

LA FORBIE

1244

2 Assaulted by the vast Khwarezmid horde, Al-Mansur's Syrian cavalry is surrounded and takes heavy losses. His Bedouin allies break and flee the field.

SYRIANS

CRUSADERS

4 Despite the defeat of their allies, the Crusaders launch their own attack on the Mamluks opposite them. They are initially successful.

1 After the first day's fighting, Baibars redeploys his Khwarezmid allies opposite the Syrians. The battle is then opened by the Khwarezmids.

KHWAREZMIDS

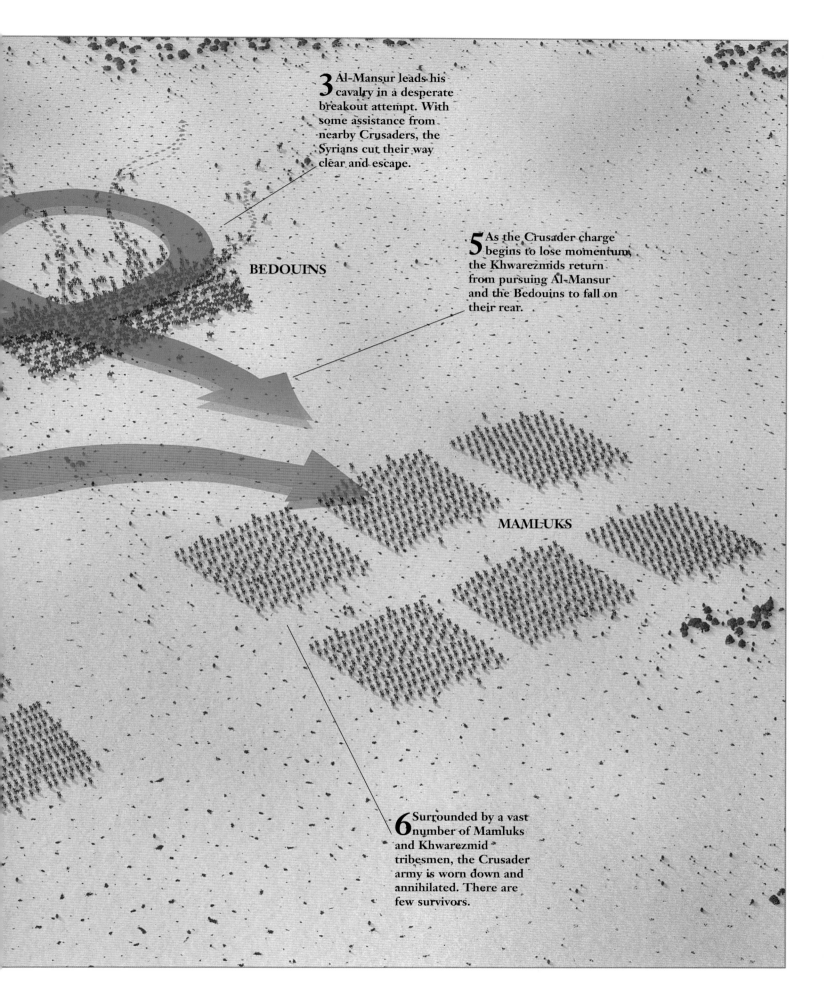

3 Al-Mansur leads his cavalry in a desperate breakout attempt. With some assistance from nearby Crusaders, the Syrians cut their way clear and escape.

BEDOUINS

5 As the Crusader charge begins to lose momentum, the Khwarezmids return from pursuing Al-Mansur and the Bedouins to fall on their rear.

MAMLUKS

6 Surrounded by a vast number of Mamluks and Khwarezmid tribesmen, the Crusader army is worn down and annihilated. There are few survivors.

LA FORBIE

supported by a smaller number of Bedouin tribesmen who formed an irregular light horse contingent, a force commanded by Al-Mansur, Emir of Homs, and an-Nasr Dawud, ruler of Transjordan.

They were opposed by a large force including 10,000 Khwarezmid tribesmen, supporting a full 6000 Mamluks. The Mamluks were elite heavy cavalry employed by the Sultanate of Egypt. They were recruited as slaves from Turkey, usually from non-Muslim areas, and began training when they were children. The boys were thoroughly indoctrinated in the tenets of Islam and their role as elite fighting men of the Sultanate. They became fiercely loyal to their own warrior society – to be a Mamluk was a cultural matter as well as a military one. The Mamluks were well armoured and equipped with good horses. They were extremely well trained and skilled with their weapons, and above all they had faith in Allah and in one another. Six thousand of them were a formidable force even without any allies on the field.

In overall command of the Egyptian force was a Mamluk officer named Baibars (1223–1277). Raised as a soldier from childhood, he was a skilled and courageous leader who knew what the Mamluks under his command were capable of. They would demonstrate those capabilities in the coming battle .

PREPARATIONS FOR BATTLE

The two armies approached one another and it became apparent that the Egyptian army was slightly outnumbered by the Crusaders and their allies. This was something of a novelty for the Crusaders, who were used to being outnumbered. This may have been a factor in deciding to press the attack against the advice of Al-Mansur.

Al-Mansur was of the opinion that the allies should create a fortified camp and wait for a while. Irregular forces are not known for their tolerance of delays, and there was a very real chance that the Khwarezmid tribesmen would disperse if battle was not joined soon. This would leave the Mamluks dangerously outnumbered and hand a massive advantage to the allies.

However, Walter of Brienne wanted to attack straight away. This may have been because of the numerical advantage he already possessed or concern for the fact that his enemies were mounted and thus mobile, while he had a large infantry contingent. It was possible for the Mamluks and their allies to move off and strike elsewhere, preventing his army from coming to grips. However, the most likely explanation is that Walter was confident of victory and impatient to get on with it. This sort of rashness was a common failing in Frankish military leaders at the time.

THE FIRST DAY: 17 OCTOBER

The allies began to advance. The Christian contingent formed the right wing, with the Syrian cavalry in the centre and the lightly

This nineteenth-century depiction of Crusader orders shows the knights wearing the traditional red cross on a white background on their tunics. This pattern was originally used by French Crusaders, but was soon adopted by the English knights, and later became associated with the English flag of St George.

With Sainte Anne in the foreground, this fourteenth century fresco depicts a rebellion against Walter VI (1304–56), the grandson of Walter of Brienne. By the time of Walter VI, the Brienne family were a powerful clan who held lands and property throughout the Mediterranean.

equipped Bedouins on the left. The right of the line is the traditional 'position of honour' and there may have been some argument about who would occupy it, but as the Christian infantry would have its flank protected by the coastline if it took the right, this deployment made tactical sense.

Baibars formed his army with his elite Mamluks facing the Syrians, and his allied tribesmen positioned to meet the Crusader charge. It was not long in coming, and throughout the first day Baibars fought a defensive battle. The Crusaders were as aggressive as ever, launching repeated charges which were largely absorbed by the Khwarezmid tribesmen, whose vast numbers allowed them to soak up casualties.

The first day ended inconclusively, with both armies intact and willing to continue the following day.

A CHANGE OF TACTICS

The Crusaders and their allies began the day with the same dispositions and much the same plan as before – to keep on slugging away until the enemy gave way. However, Baibars, determined to fight on his own terms, threw his horde of Khwarezmids against the Syrians in the centre. A wild charge in overwhelming numbers was something irregular cavalry did well.

The Syrians were caught by surprise and badly mauled. On their flank, Walter of Brienne ordered his knights to support their allies, but it was too late. The Syrian formation had been broken up and Al-Mansur's force was lost in a sea of tribesmen. Many were cut down, but Al-Mansur rallied the 2000 horsemen he had personally brought from Damascus and led a breakout. He was able to get a portion of his force out of the deathtrap, but they numbered just 280.

The Syrians fled the field in disorder, and many of their Bedouin allies, who were not yet under attack, also routed. Those that did not were set upon by the victorious Khwarezmids and slaughtered.

THE CRUSADERS ATTACK

With the centre and left of their army swept away, it might have been wise for the Crusaders to make a tactical retreat. Instead, they went on the offensive and charged into the Mamluks facing them. The charge was initially a success, with infantry following the knights forward and gradually pushing the Mamluks back. The assault drove deep into Baibars' army and caused him some concern.

The Crusader assault gradually lost momentum, and the charges became less and less successful. Meanwhile, the Khwarezmid tribesmen fell on the flanks and rear of the Christians, which were defended by the disorganized infantry. The battle degenerated into a static hand-to-hand fight, with the Crusaders surrounded on all sides by large numbers of enemies.

A mosaic depicting the rule of the sultans of Baibars. Baibars was a talented man backed by a competent and loyal army that believed in him – a winning combination. When he decided to seize power in Egypt, he already held all the cards. His successors ruled Egypt for centuries.

Despite the desperate plight of the Christians, it took several hours to reduce the Crusader army. The well-armoured knights fought on doggedly against an endless succession of opponents, their numbers dwindling gradually until little was left. Finally, resistance collapsed and the battle was over.

Something like 5000 Christians were killed, with several hundred more taken prisoner. The Crusader army was virtually wiped out. The Hospitaller, Templar and Teutonic orders suffered massive casualties, including some of their most important figures. Walter de Brienne himself was taken prisoner. Most of those who escaped were knights who were able to cut their way clear of the mêlée and retreat to Ascalon. Among them was Philip of Montfort.

AFTERMATH

The battle of La Forbie broke the power of the Crusaders in the Holy Land. They had not been able to put such a large force into the field since the disaster at Hattin, and after La Forbie it was no longer possible to assemble an army of any real size.

Although the smashing of the Crusaders had long-term significance, La Forbie did not result in much of an improved strategic situation for the Egyptian Ayyubids. Al-Mansur had survived and was able to put a new army together to defeat the Khwarezmids the following year. By that time, the tribesmen were no longer allied to the Ayyubids and were operating alone.

Baibars, who had risen through the ranks of the Mamluks, became Sultan of Egypt in 1250, when some of his brethren rebelled against the state they served as slave-soldiers, demonstrating the danger of placing military capability in the hands of slaves. Baibars campaigned against the Kingdom of Jerusalem for some years, and reduced it to a small rump along the coast. The Mamluks ruled Egypt for centuries to come.

A Renaissance-period portrait of Almanzor, the westernized version of the name Al-Mansur, leader of the Syrian contingent at La Forbie. The portrait is also heavily westernized; it is unlikely that the Sultan of Homs, a member of the Ayyubid dynasty, actually looked like this.

MANSURA
1250

KING LOUIS OF FRANCE LAUNCHED THIS ATTEMPT TO TAKE THE NILE DELTA AND CAIRO. YET AGAIN, HOWEVER, AN IMPETUOUS COMMANDER CAUSED THE CRUSADER ARMY TO RUN INTO A WELL-PLANNED AMBUSH AND CRUSHING DEFEAT.

WHY DID IT HAPPEN?

WHO King Louis IX of France (1226–70) led an army of 25,000 men against the Ayybid Sultanate of Egypt.

WHAT Having captured Damietta, he was defeated in an ambush at Mansura.

WHERE The Nile Delta city of Mansura (Mansûrah) in Egypt.

WHEN 10 February 1250.

WHY Louis hoped to cripple the Ayybid dynasty and wrench back Jerusalem from Muslim control

OUTCOME It was a massive defeat and brought the Outremer Christians' worst enemy into power.

Egypt was the richest, most densely populated and powerful Muslim country in the Middle East and the core of the Islamic resistance to the Crusaders. It had been ruled firstly by the Fatimid (Shia) Caliphs of Cairo, who had made Egypt the only powerful Muslim sea-power. They, in time, had given way to the Ayybid Sultans (descendents of Saladin bin Ayybid).

In May 1218, a massive Crusader army led by the Kings of Hungary and Cyprus, with the Duke of Austria, had landed in the Nile Delta on a small island west of the fortified port city of Damietta. The Crusaders of this Fifth Crusade intended to use the island as a base to take the port, but before they had been able to act, Sultan al-Kamil Ayybid offered to surrender Jerusalem in return for the Crusaders evacuating the Delta. Instead of accepting this sensible diplomatic solution the Crusader commanders fell out among themselves and the offer was, foolishly, ignored. They chose instead to lay siege to the Damietta, which only fell in November 1219. But Damietta was only the beginning, since the ultimate Crusader goal was Cairo.

After several delays the Crusaders began the general advance in July 1221, but it was halted before it had even begun at the heavily fortified city of Mansura. Forced to give up the siege, the Crusaders sailed home the following month without having achieved anything.

This eighteenth-century illustration portrays the siege of Damietta. Strategically situated on the Nile Delta, Damietta was an important commercial centre for the Arab textile trade. Its capture was a military objective of the Crusaders on several occasions, and it was briefly in their hands in 1219–1221 and 1249–1250. A chain is stretched across the harbour entrance to prevent invading vessels passing (centre left), while defenders fight off troops attacking a tower, using scaling ladders mounted on ships (centre).

JERUSALEM FALLS

Half a world away in Central Asia, the feared Mongol ruler, Genghiz (Djingis) Khan, had invaded the vast and wealthy empire of the Khwarezmid Turks in 1219. Two years later, that empire lay in ruins and the Shah, Muhammed II, was dead, although his son, Prince Jelal ad-Din, continued the resistance against the Mongols. In 1244 that same prince, now a wandering refugee with a mercenary army, took Jerusalem and massacred the Christian population. As if that was not bad enough, a Crusader army was annihilated at the battle of La Forbie on 17 October that same year.

MOBILIZATION

In December 1244 the beleaguered Christian states in the Holy Land gained a formidable champion, when King Louis IX of France took his crusading vows. Louis had taken his vows despite the loud objections of his formidable and domineering mother, Queen Blanche. Louis pointed out that, with the Emperor of Germany and the Pope at each other's throats and England in turmoil, only France could champion the Christian cause in the Holy Land.

The expedition was expected to cost over a million and a half *livres tournois*, but despite being the absolute ruler of western Europe's richest and most populous realm, Louis only had an annual income of a quarter of a million *livres*. Pope Innocent IV (c. 1195-1254) proved to be a generous backer, the Church paying two-thirds of the cost of the Crusade. The rest was raised by taxing France's cities.

Louis built from scratch an entirely new port at Aigues-Mortes in Provence, gathered 15,000–25,000 men (including 2500 knights and 5000 crossbowmen) almost all of them French. The only foreign contingent of note were some 200 knights led by the Earl of Salisbury, and the most noteworthy French force were the Templar knights commanded by their Grand Master, Seigneur Guillaume de Sonnac (William of Sonnac).

Louis had also recruited his brothers, Robert of Artois, Charles Anjou and Alphonse of Poitiers, to accompany him, along with his faithful wife Queen

TEMPLAR KNIGHT

Originally set up as a small, elite force of armed monks to defend the site of the Holy Temple in Jerusalem, the Templars had grown into a State within the State by the time of the Battle of Mansura. Wealthy, influential and politicized, they were envied and disliked by Christians and Muslims alike.

This Templar wears, characteristically, the Order's simple white tunic with a sash across his waist like a monk would in an Holy Order. Yet his round helmet with the perforated face guard for breathing, the heavy broadsword and the heavy metal-framed and coated shield belies this monkish exterior.

The Order's emblem – the Red Cross with forked ends – was both feared and revered by friend and foe alike of this most formidable and controversial of the Crusader Orders. The Templars were bloodily repressed in 1314.

Margaret. He rented 36 sturdy vessels from Marseilles and Genoa and set sail from Provence on 25 August 1248. The French Crusader fleet landed safely three weeks later, on 17 September, at Limassol in Cyprus. During the following winter the troops were left in Cyprus to acclimatize and it was, therefore, only in late May 1249 that the Crusading fleet once more set sail. They were aiming for the swampy coast of the rich, oozing Nile Delta and the coveted prize of Damietta.

DAMIETTA CAPTURED

The Crusaders were in sight of the coast by 6 June, while the Egyptian defenders had ranged themselves along the shore, their armour glittering with gold and brass in the strong sunlight. The Crusaders could be splendid too and the Count of Jaffa had an extravagantly decorated galley powered by 300 oarsmen. Less decoratively, the Crusaders had built, while on Cyprus, a flotilla of flat-bottomed boats that could penetrate up the Damietta arm of the Nile.

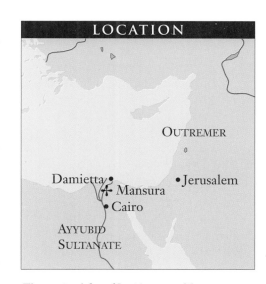

LOCATION

The massive defeat of Louis' army at Mansura brought to a close the French king's ambitions to capture Cairo and secure the Nile Delta.

King Louis IX (1215–70), the perfect Crusader King, emerges from the surf at Damietta with his arms outstretched to thank God for delivering him safely to the shores of the Nile Delta.

THE OPPOSED FORCES

LOUIS IX'S ARMY
Men-at-arms (total):   2500
  (includes 200 English knights
  under Lord Salisbury and 300
  Templar knights under Grand
  Master William of Sonnac)
Crossbowmen   5000
Infantry   10,000–15,000

Total: **17,500–22,500**

AYYBID EGYPTIANS (estimated)
Cavalry and Infantry: 25–30,000

Total: **25–30,000**

The assault began. A French knight waded ashore to plant the sacred French *Oriflamme* pennant on land, and was followed by wave upon wave of Crusader knights and infantry, who plunged into the waist-deep water, bearing shields and arms above their heads. They stuck their lances and spears into the soft sand in order to repel, along with their archers, the expected Egyptian counter-attack. The Egyptians did make a massed cavalry attack against the wall of spears but failed to make any headway and simply broke and fled.

This time, the fleeing troops did not stop to defend Damietta. The city's garrison had no intention of suffering a long siege as did their predecessors in 1218, and they too fled towards the Sultan's camp at Mansura. They were followed in short order by the civilian population.

Deserted, the city of Damietta fell to the perplexed and then jubilant Crusaders, who could not believe their luck. Surely God was on their side? Some believed that it was time to march on Cairo by taking Mansura

Opposite: A medieval book illustration showing Louis IX being met outside Damietta's walls by an Egyptian delegation with drums beating, horns blowing and harp twanging; in reality, Damietta was empty, as the garrison and population alike fled for their lives.

Come il fut prme au Retour auec son oft. E

Pres aucune sorre passez le su
du sondan vint des parties co
zient ala matonbre et ala benie

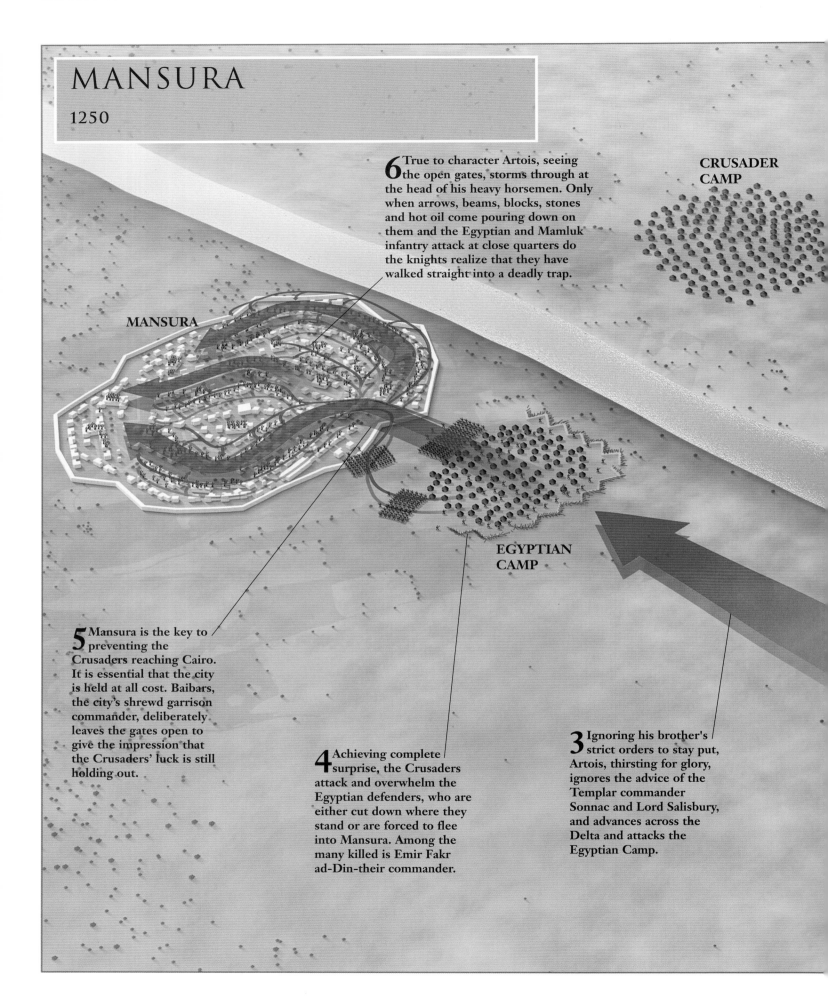

MANSURA

1250

6 True to character Artois, seeing the open gates, storms through at the head of his heavy horsemen. Only when arrows, beams, blocks, stones and hot oil come pouring down on them and the Egyptian and Mamluk infantry attack at close quarters do the knights realize that they have walked straight into a deadly trap.

CRUSADER CAMP

MANSURA

EGYPTIAN CAMP

5 Mansura is the key to preventing the Crusaders reaching Cairo. It is essential that the city is held at all cost. Baibars, the city's shrewd garrison commander, deliberately leaves the gates open to give the impression that the Crusaders' luck is still holding out.

4 Achieving complete surprise, the Crusaders attack and overwhelm the Egyptian defenders, who are either cut down where they stand or are forced to flee into Mansura. Among the many killed is Emir Fakr ad-Din-their commander.

3 Ignoring his brother's strict orders to stay put, Artois, thirsting for glory, ignores the advice of the Templar commander Sonnac and Lord Salisbury, and advances across the Delta and attacks the Egyptian Camp.

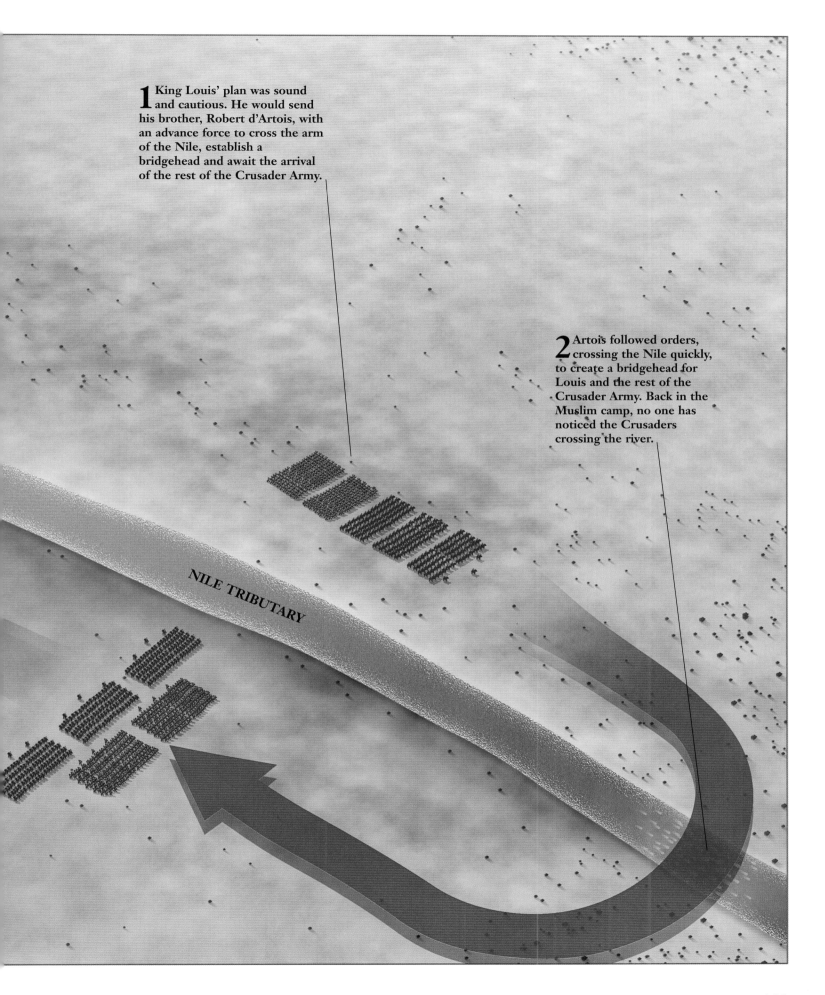

1 King Louis' plan was sound and cautious. He would send his brother, Robert d'Artois, with an advance force to cross the arm of the Nile, establish a bridgehead and await the arrival of the rest of the Crusader Army.

2 Artois followed orders, crossing the Nile quickly, to create a bridgehead for Louis and the rest of the Crusader Army. Back in the Muslim camp, no one has noticed the Crusaders crossing the river.

NILE TRIBUTARY

Crusader William Longsword wielding his two-handed sword at the Battle of Mansura, where he met his own bloody and heroic death.

as quickly as possible but more sensible councils prevailed. Louis IX had remembered that back in 1219 the Crusaders had become bogged down in the black silt and mud of the Delta during the summer flood. He was determined not to advance until conditions had improved.

THE MARCH ON MANSURA

Louis also wanted to wait until his brother, Alphonse of Poitiers, arrived with reinforcements from Cyprus (on 24 October) before he called a council of war. The Outremer lords advised the King to sail to Alexandria and hold this vital seaport and Ayybid naval base instead of marching overland against Cairo. The overland approach would be both time consuming and very dangerous, as had been shown clearly three decades earlier.

Artois, reflecting the King's views, rose up to object, pointing out that one only killed a serpent by cutting off its head. His critics, including his other brothers, pointed out that this was a very risky proposition, and if the objective of this Crusade was to retake Jerusalem, they should capture Alexandria and exchange it, and Damietta, for Jerusalem.

The issue was never in doubt. Trusting in God's good graces, Louis ordered his army to begin, on 20 November, a month-long advance on Mansura.

Disaster struck the Egyptians two days later when Sultan al-Salih died while his heir, Turan Shah, was in Syria. Emir Fakhr ad-Din now had to take command of the Ayybid army against the Crusaders.

Louis' army made camp on the same site on the northern bank of the Nile that had been used by the Crusaders in 1220–21. It was an ill omen. Fakhr's men kept a close eye on the enemy from their fortified base and battle lines on the south bank of the river branch.

They repelled several landing attempts by the Crusaders, and a huge effort to build a causeway across the Nile ended in catastrophe as the Egyptians unleashed their ballistas and used incendiary Greek Fire to great effect. The Crusaders could only watch in chagrin as their enormous effort went up in smoke.

Using his ample field chest, Louis found an Egyptian peasant who was ready to betray the site of a fording point and lead the Crusaders there. Louis laid plans for a surprise crossing at this point but Artois, the chosen commander of the spearhead of the Crusader advance, would undo his brother's master plan through his arrogant imprudence.

THE BATTLE

Louis planned to strike across the Nile without warning, leaving Hugh, Duke of Burgundy, to hold the Crusader camp on the north bank while he sent Artois with the vanguard across the river. Artois was ordered to cross the river, consolidate and, if attacked, defend the bridgehead. These instructions he chose to ignore.

The crossing early in the morning of 7 February 1250 went without a hitch and remained undetected. Instead of staying put Artois placed his own corps at the helm, ordered an advance and attacked Fakhr's camp. The Egyptians were caught off-guard by the unexpected attack and Fakhr – who was taking a bath – was cut down by the Templars before he had a chance to use his scimitar.

So far, so good. Now, however, Artois committed another fatal blunder: he wanted to continue the attack without the main army. Sonnac, already fuming from Artois taking the vanguard in the assault, told the

Prince that this was the height of folly. Artois dismissed the criticism with the wounding insult that the Templars had no wish to secure an outright victory against the infidels since they benefited from the wars. Salisbury intervened by pointing out that Sonnac knew, from his long service fighting the Muslims, what he was talking about. Artois brushed aside this wholly justified criticism by dismissing Salisbury as a coward before ordering his men to advance on Mansura.

A DEADLY TRAP

What Artois did not know was that Mansura's garrison commander, a Mamluk Turk by the name of Baibars Bundukdari (1223–1277), had set a deadly trap for the Crusaders. Baibars – that name would be uttered later by all Crusaders with justified

The Ayyubid Sultans' Mamluk Guards consisted of light cavalry as shown in this illustration. This Mamluk Turcoman horseman wears no armour since his entire tactical raison d'être is speed and mobility. Mounted on his fine Egyptian-bred steed, he is armed with bow, quill of arrows, whip and a deadly sharp scimitar.

MANSURA

Romanticized portrait of Comte Robert d'Artois –
Louis IX's brother – whose tempestuousness robbed
the Crusaders of a possible victory at Mansura.

Louis cried when he heard news of his favourite brother's death. But he was now hard pushed to keep the main army intact as Baibars launched incessant attacks and raids against it. The following day, Baibars launched an all-out assault that was repelled and defeated by Sonnac, who lost his remaining eye and promptly died. That sacrifice was not in vain, however, as his defence had saved the main army and the King from annihilation.

RETREAT AND DEFEAT

The new Ayybid Sultan, Turan Shah, arrived on 28 February and quickly realized that if he moved his galley fleet to land beyond the Crusader position, he would trap them. His orders were promptly carried out, cutting communications between Louis' army camp and their supply base at Damietta. By early March, the trapped Crusaders were already running out of food as Louis dithered, unable to accept that he had been defeated and should retreat, with all haste, to Damietta.

Finally, on 5 April, a demoralized Louis gave the order for his army to retreat northwards, but only about two weeks later and half way to Damietta, the King was forced to accept the unpalatable fact that the army would not reach the port in time. There was little choice but to negotiate with the Egyptian Sultan. At the end of April the two sovereigns struck a gentleman's agreement that in return for paying the Sultan some 800,000 gold bezants, the knights, nobles and higher-ranked members of the Crusader army would be spared.

terror – had left the city gates deliberately open to lure the 'infidels' into the city's narrow, winding lanes. Artois swallowed the bait, hook, line and sinker, and rushed forward. Only when the stones, arrows, beams and scalding hot oil poured down on them from the flat roof tops did the Crusaders realize that they were doomed.

Baibars gave a signal for his infantry to attack and slaughter the trapped knights. Hundreds of knights, including Artois, Salisbury, most of the English and 280 Templars, perished in the bloody streets of Mansura. Only two knights escaped, one of them, Sonnac, minus an eye.

AFTERMATH

Turan Shah did honour the agreement but slaughtered the rank and file of the Crusader army without pity. He also proved to be the last Ayybid Sultan of Egypt, as the Mamluk Guards revolted, murdered him and on 30 July acclaimed one of their own, Aybak, as the first Mamluk Sultan of Egypt.

Fortunately, Aybak stuck to Turan Shah's agreement. On 6 May, Louis, his brothers and the other high ranking Crusaders were released, and half of the ransom was paid two days later. As agreed, Damietta was surrendered, in return for more hostages, on 16 May and Louis and his entourage sailed

off to the Holy Land. He arrived in recaptured Jerusalem on 13 May 1251 and, by early 1252, having signed a temporary truce with the Mamluks, finally released his army from its 'Egyptian bondage'.

Louis remained in the Holy Land fortifying the remaining Crusader strongholds, which did much to prevent them falling into Muslim hands. He returned to France but, in 1267, Louis once again made his vows as a Crusader and sailed off for Tunis, where he died on 25 August 1270. Louis was universally admired for his honesty, piety and devotion to the rule of law. Such qualities, rare in ordinary men, were rarer still for a ruler, and Louis was therefore canonized shortly after his death.

His brother Artois' nemesis at Mansura, Baibars, murdered his way to the post of Mamluk Sultan in 1260. That same year, he marched a Mamluk army against the

Mongols, whom he defeated at Ain Jalut, and during the following years Baibars reduced the Christian forts in Palestine one by one. If Louis was a champion of his faith, so Baibars was a ghazi (Holy Warrior) of Islam.

A manuscript illustration showing the capture of Louis IX during the retreat from 'Mansourah'. From the fifteenth-century chronicle by David Aubert.

The Muslim victor of Mansura, Baibars, was the nemesis of the Christian states of Outremer. In this illustration, Christians captives who have refused to convert are swiftly beheaded.

NICOPOLIS
1396

SINCE THE MASSACRE OF CRUSADERS AT THE HORNS OF HATTIN IN 1187 AND THE SUBSEQUENT EXPULSION OF THE CRUSADERS FROM THE HOLY LAND, THE ARMIES OF ISLAM MOVED WITH THE INEXORABLE FORCE OF THE INCOMING TIDE. NEARLY THREE HUNDRED YEARS LATER THEY HAD SLOWLY FLOODED NORTHWARDS THROUGH THE BYZANTINE EMPIRE, LEAVING THE CITY OF CONSTANTINOPLE STRANDED LIKE A ROCK UPON THE SHORE, AND WERE NOW LAPPING AT THE BORDERS OF HUNGARY.

WHY DID IT HAPPEN?

WHO John of Nevers (c.1371–1419), heir to the Dukedom of Burgundy, and Sigismund of Hungary (1368–1437) raised a 16,000-strong crusade to relieve Ottoman pressure on the crumbling Byzantine Empire.
They were opposed by 'Bayazid the Thunderbolt', Emir of the Ottoman Empire (1354–1402), with 15,000 Ottoman and subject soldiers.

WHAT A wild charge by the western crusader knights was destroyed by the Ottomans. The Hungarians could not prevent their rout becoming general and many Crusaders died in the Danube. Only a few, including the leaders, managed to return home.

WHERE Just south of Nicopolis on the Danube in modern Bulgaria.

WHEN 25 September 1396.

WHY John of Nevers needed to establish his reputation on the medieval world stage by a glorious military expedition.

OUTCOME The Ottoman army returned to continue the siege of Constantinople but failed to take the city.

Of course, Islam was not a single, homogenous society. Those now encroaching on Christian territory were the Ottoman Turks and very different from the Seljuk Turks from the time of Hattin.

The Byzantine Emperor appealed for help from the west, and on 3 June 1394, Pope Boniface IX (1356–1404) proclaimed a Crusade against the Ottomans and, incidentally, also against the other Pope, Clement, in Avignon (in completely the opposite direction to the Ottomans). Nothing like squeezing out a competitor when you have a Crusade at your disposal. Unfortunately, this plan was completely undermined when Clement also supported the Crusade. While the Ottomans maintained their siege of Constantinople and continued raiding in the Balkans, supporting one puppet ruler against another, the Christian princes sent diplomats scurrying hither and thither, recruiting leaders and men, and collecting ships and money. A lot of money was raised as well as large numbers of men and many ships. There were plenty of leaders, but many of those dropped out and it ended as a Burgundy-dominated expedition. The Duke of Burgundy raised 700,000 gold francs and appointed his son, John of Nevers, to lead, though the more experienced Count d'Eu was to wield the true authority.

This near-contemporary illustration of King Sigismund in conference with his French allies at Buda is interesting for its depiction of the dress and armour of the figures, and as an early attempt at perspective in the hedge and wall in the upper-right corner.

It is perhaps in the lavish clothing, harness, 16 flags and green satin tents of Nevers' contingent that we find the real motive for Crusade. John, at 25 years old, still had to establish his reputation and status at home and abroad through extravagant efforts on the field of war. Nevertheless the Crusade was an international expedition with contingents from Spain, Italy, Germany and England.

THE CRUSADE BEGINS

The western part of the army assembled at Dijon, where the laws of the campaign, intended to maintain order and discipline, were proclaimed by the heralds. They commenced their march across Hungary and were joined at Budapest by more contingents: Teutonic Knights, Poles, Hungarians, Transylvanians and some Wallachians, bringing their force to around 16,000. From here on in, they were supplied by a substantial fleet of 70 river craft following the army along the Danube. While this made excellent logistical sense, it also limited their strategic options to the course of the river.

Emerging from the Carpathian Mountains on the southern bank at the Iron Gates Pass, less some of the larger craft, the Crusaders crossed into Bulgaria and started capturing the border towns on the river as well as raiding south to other nearby targets. Not all their targets fell: the Crusaders had not brought any siege equipment with them, and at least one castle held out until the army had passed. The local ruler opened the gates of the town of Vidin, allowing the Crusaders in to massacre the Ottoman garrison, along with John of Never and 300 of his household to be knighted 'on the field of honour'.

The next town resisted a raid but surrendered when the main army arrived. They too were massacred, Muslims and Orthodox Christians alike, except those deemed wealthy enough to be ransomed. The latter were co-religionists to the Hungarian contingent, a cause of deep discontent between the two factions. The army arrived at Nicopolis on 12 September to find that another supply fleet of 44 Hospitaller, Genoese and Venetian ships from Rhodes had sailed through the Black Sea and had been waiting two days for them. This showed a remarkable degree of forethought and timing on behalf of someone in the Crusader army.

NICOPOLIS BESIEGED

Nicopolis sits at the confluence of three rivers: the kilometre-wide Danube runs west to east, the Olt flows down from the

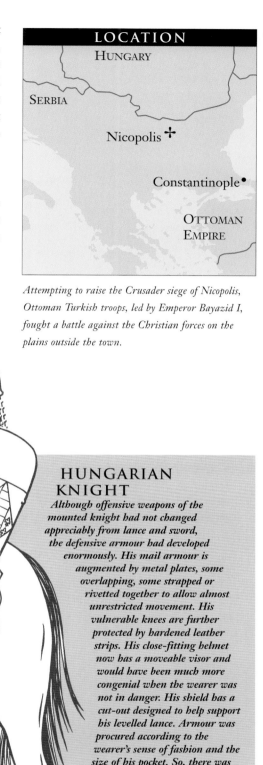

Attempting to raise the Crusader siege of Nicopolis, Ottoman Turkish troops, led by Emperor Bayazid I, fought a battle against the Christian forces on the plains outside the town.

HUNGARIAN KNIGHT

Although offensive weapons of the mounted knight had not changed appreciably from lance and sword, the defensive armour had developed enormously. His mail armour is augmented by metal plates, some overlapping, some strapped or rivetted together to allow almost unrestricted movement. His vulnerable knees are further protected by hardened leather strips. His close-fitting helmet now has a moveable visor and would have been much more congenial when the wearer was not in danger. His shield has a cut-out designed to help support his levelled lance. Armour was procured according to the wearer's sense of fashion and the size of his pocket. So, there was considerable variation, and the armour was so expensive that older pieces were modified and recycled by less wealthy knights. The knight is still vulnerable to the powerful crossbows and longbows of European foot soldiers. But the archery of his Ottoman opponents was largely ineffective against most of this armour. Their greatest hope lay in weight of numbers.

BAIAZETES I.

Bayazid I – 'The Thunderbolt'. Ottoman Sultans of Turkey did not simply inherit from their fathers. Multiple wives meant multiple potential heirs who had to struggle with each other to succeed. The ensuing bloodbath usually ensured that the most ruthless and able inherited the throne.

THE OPPOSED FORCES

OTTOMANS (estimated)

Cavalry:	10,000
Infantry:	5000
Total:	**15,000**

CRUSADERS (estimated)

Mounted men-at-arms:	6000
Infantry:	10,000
Total:	**16,000**

belligerent presence of the Crusader army on their northern frontier succeeded.

'Bayazid the Thunderbolt' and Emir of the Ottoman Empire had already begun to move his best troops northwards, leaving a loose blockade around Constantinople. After gathering reinforcements at Edirne in August, he collected further troops en route, bringing his force to around 15,000 men. At Tarnovo he sent a reconnaissance party ahead to confirm the Crusaders' location. By contrast, the Crusaders had cut off the ears of anyone who suggested the Turks were coming, and only discovered the proximity of the enemy when they reached Tarnovo.

THE OTTOMANS ARRIVE

The Ottomans moved closer and set up camp just a few kilometres south of Nicopolis on 24 September. The ground here is of rolling hills, running roughly northeast to southwest. Bayazid chose his ground and began erecting a field of stakes 5m (16ft) deep across the front where his infantry would fight – a considerable task given the proximity of the enemy.

While this was going and while he was setting up camp, the Crusaders sent out one, or possibly two, raids. Some 1000 men drawn from a cross-section of the army rode south' and skirmished with the enemy cavalry screen. Casualties were suffered on both sides, though it is not recorded whether or not the Crusaders discovered the field of stakes.

Faced with enemy both in the city and to the south, the Crusaders massacred the prisoners from their earlier successes, releasing their guards to join the imminent battle. Apparently, they did not even have time to deal with the corpses, which suggests a degree of panic. Overnight, men on both sides would have looked to the sharpness of their weapons and firmness of the straps on their armour – if they had any. Most of the Ottomans were unarmoured though the best equipped had mail suits reinforced with metal plates on the arms and calves. Many had helmets but these had no face protection. By contrast, the Crusader knight of this period sported a helmet with a full-face visor, fully encased arms, hands, legs and feet, plus a coat of

north and the Osam flows up from the south. It occupies a well-fortified rocky promontory and its garrison had been reinforced. They had after all had plenty of warning of the invasion, and such a river-tied force was bound to end up at Nicopolis sooner or later. The weakest part of the defences lay to the southeast, where the ground was on a level with the fortifications, albeit dissected by gullies.

The Crusaders established two camps, separating the Hungarian and western components of the force. The great differences in language, religion and culture, as well as the nature of the ground and the need to cover as much of the walls as possible made this a prudent idea. The Hungarians started to dig mines; these were in the form of tunnels under the walls, shored up with wooden props to be later burnt, thus causing the wall to collapse. The Burgundian division started building scaling ladders. Neither effort came to anything, but then, they probably were not intended to. The real aim of the siege was to draw out the Ottoman field army, last known to be besieging Constantinople, and in this the plates covering the body. Vital areas such as the neck and groin were further reinforced by mail.

There was also considerable difference in the effectiveness of their missile weapons. Being accustomed to less heavily armoured opposition, the Ottomans do not appear to have had specialized armour-piercing arrowheads such as those available to English longbow men. The quarrels of the crossbowmen in the Crusader army would have been highly effective against even the best-armoured man in the Ottoman force, catching in the mail links and forcing their way into the yielding flesh behind. If they didn't glance off, they could even penetrate solid armour plate.

The leaders of the Crusaders met in conference. The western knights counselled an immediate headlong charge at the enemy, while the Hungarian leader, who had plenty of experience fighting Turks, advocated a more cautious approach. He wanted to send out skirmishers first to deal with the enemy's light cavalry. Hot words were exchanged that night and again the following morning. The knights demanded the right to lead the charge; they were not going to allow any 'peasants' to advance in front, even to clear the enemy's skirmishers from their path, and they set off before the Hungarians were even fully drawn up for battle.

THE CRUSADERS CHARGE

At the bottom of the first hill they crossed there was a small stream running though a line of trees. Beyond that and up the next hill were the first enemy they met: skirmishing horse archers or 'Akinji'. These Ottoman skirmishers loosed what arrows they could, shooting over their horse's rumps and staying ahead of the advancing knights, before riding away to right and left to clear the front of the field of stakes. Behind the stakes stood rank upon rank of mainly unarmoured Ottoman infantry equipped with bow, spear and shield.

The Crusader knights swept forward but the upward slope took some of the impetus out of their charge. The absolute torrent of arrows took more. There should have been many casualties but the

Ottoman arrows lacked momentum and the ability to penetrate western armour in any great quantity. Despite some casualties to men and horses, the knights forced their way through the stakes, losing more men on the way, and finally got amongst the infantry, where they slaughtered a great many.

Bayazid had held back three reserves of his best cavalry: one on each wing and his own household troops in the centre. As the Crusader knights broke through his infantry they had to summon the will to continue into this third line, which was at an even higher elevation. They made the attempt but as they tried, they were charged from behind and both flanks. Desperate fighting ensued but it was the Ottoman cavalry who withdrew and, briefly, the Crusaders thought they had won. It was not, however, to be.

Ottoman camel-mounted musicians. The Turks came from the vast steppes of Asia. There, two things mattered in battle: mobility, and command and control. Commands were transmitted via drums and trumpets and to keep up with the army, they were mounted on camels.

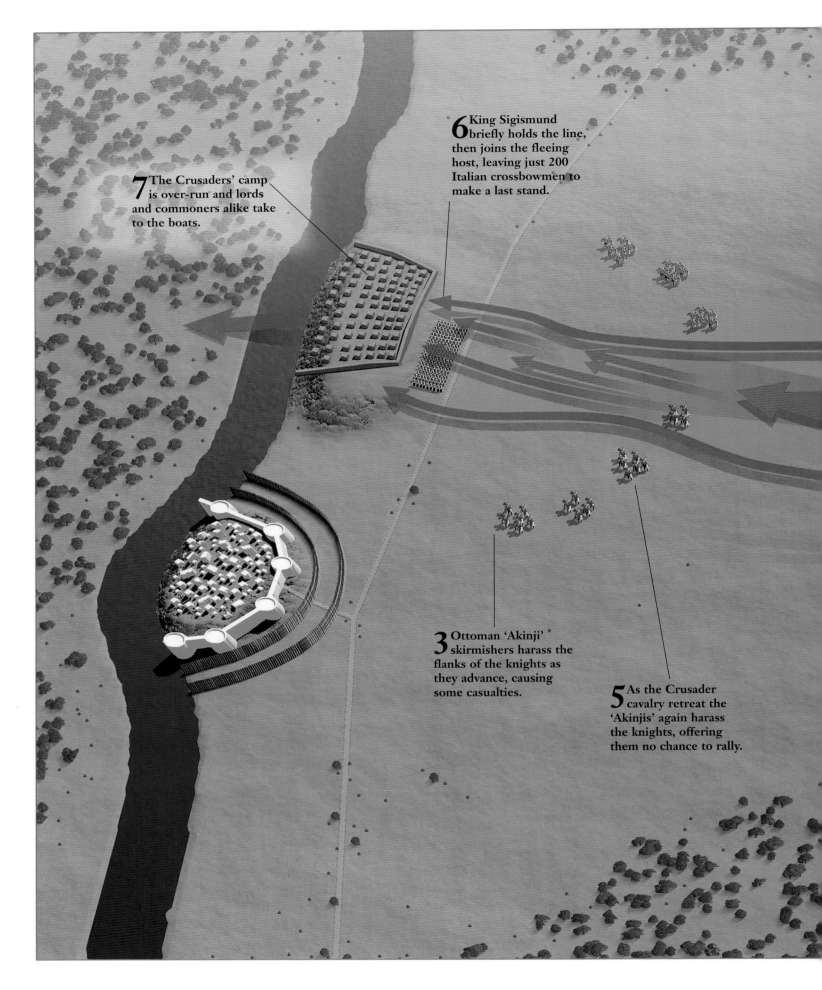

6 King Sigismund briefly holds the line, then joins the fleeing host, leaving just 200 Italian crossbowmen to make a last stand.

7 The Crusaders' camp is over-run and lords and commoners alike take to the boats.

3 Ottoman 'Akinji' skirmishers harass the flanks of the knights as they advance, causing some casualties.

5 As the Crusader cavalry retreat the 'Akinjis' again harass the knights, offering them no chance to rally.

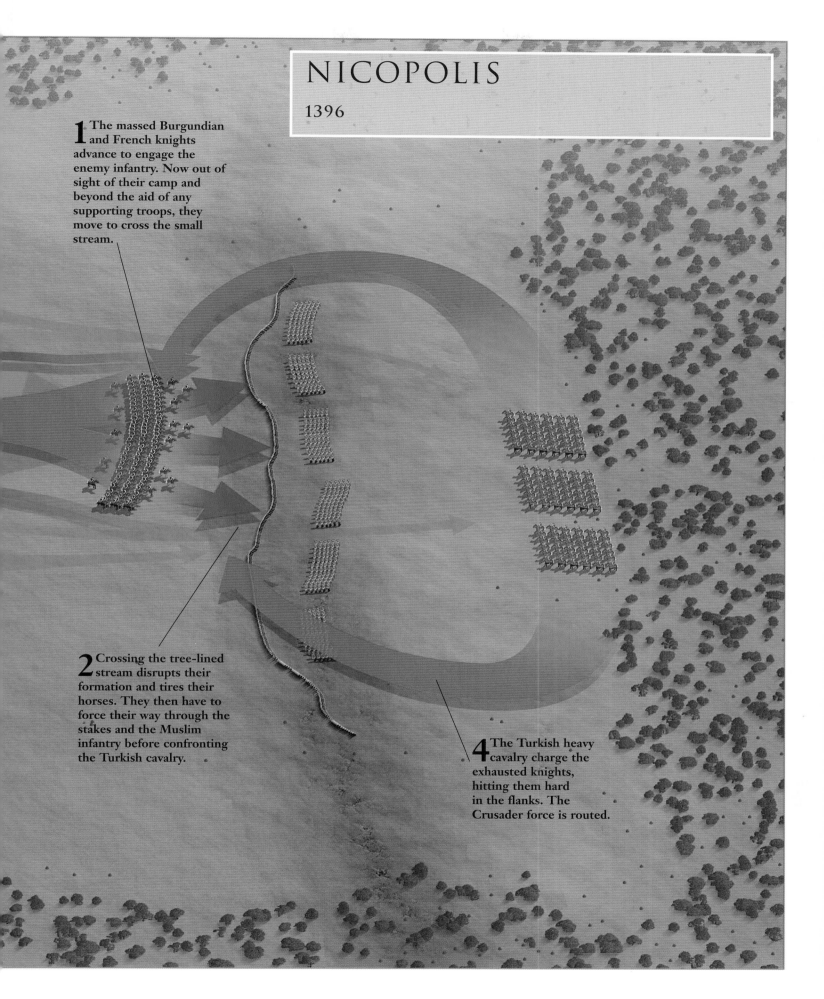

NICOPOLIS

1396

1 The massed Burgundian and French knights advance to engage the enemy infantry. Now out of sight of their camp and beyond the aid of any supporting troops, they move to cross the small stream.

2 Crossing the tree-lined stream disrupts their formation and tires their horses. They then have to force their way through the stakes and the Muslim infantry before confronting the Turkish cavalry.

4 The Turkish heavy cavalry charge the exhausted knights, hitting them hard in the flanks. The Crusader force is routed.

NICOPOLIS

OTTOMAN LANCER
(c.1390)

Ottoman cavalry were less heavily armoured than their European counterparts but were also equipped with bows as their primary weapon. Traditionally, unarmoured, bow-armed cavalry would skirmish with the advancing enemy. A mass of infantry, many again armed with bow, would absorb the impetus of the enemy's charge; then, a counter-strike force of cavalry, as illustrated here, would charge and deliver the coup de grâce. A reserve of armoured cavalry was normally maintained in the rear. At Nicopolis, these tactics worked almost perfectly.

Trumpets blasted, drums thundered, the earth shook, and over the hill came Bayazid's household troops. They crashed down onto the bloodied, disorganized and very weary Crusaders. It was too much. Worn down by the effort of charging and fighting, men broke and fled. Others tried to make a stand where they stood and were either surrendered or were cut down.

AFTERMATH

As those who could fled back towards the Danube and the hoped-for safety of the boats, the Wallachian and Transylvanian light cavalry on either flanks also turned and retired. They had felt the disdain with which they had been treated by these western knights and witnessed the wanton butchery of their fellow Orthodox Christians. Now they chose not to put themselves at risk to save the fleeing westerners.

Sigismund, the King of Hungary, who had been left behind at the start of the charge, still had command of a small body of Hungarian knights behind the westerners. He first tried to stem the fleeing tide of men, then retired steadily, fighting his way past some rallied Ottoman infantry to the shore, where 200 Italian crossbowmen held off the pursuit, indicating the effectiveness of this weapon over the Ottoman armour, until the King got aboard his ship and made good his escape. The Italians were left to their fate. Some of the overcrowded ships sank but others got away, although a dangerous passage through Wallachian lands in the early winter ensured not all survivors made it home.

Those captured also suffered further. In revenge for the earlier slaughter of Moslem captives Bayazid ordered the execution of the more than 2000 prisoners taken during the battle. But, in the end, only about 300–400 were killed before he relented. The survivors of this revenge were either sold into slavery or held for ransom. Many, of course, died from their wounds. John of Nevers finally reached home after a year of incarceration plus another year travelling, and only after an enormous ransom had been paid.

After the battle was over, Bayazid returned to Constantinople to continue the siege. But the great city was too strong and he eventually had to give up. From Bayazid's point of view, indeed from the viewpoint of all rulers of the Islamic empire, these unthinking few Crusaders were a mere annoyance, scratching away like mice at their western borders. The real threat now was from the vast steppes to the East.

Opposite: In this illustration from Froissart's Chronicles, *Sultan Bayazid I accepts ransom money for the Comte de Nevers and other French knights captured during the Battle of Nicopolis.*

GRUNWALD
1410

GRUNWALD WAS A PIVOTAL BATTLE IN THE HISTORY OF EASTERN EUROPE, THOUGH ONE LARGELY IGNORED BY WESTERN HISTORIANS. THE TEUTONIC ORDER ATTEMPTED TO EXTEND THEIR POWER IN POLAND AND LITHUANIA, BUT DEFEAT BEGAN THEIR DECLINE AND THEY WERE EVENTUALLY COMPELLED TO PAY HOMAGE TO THE KING OF POLAND.

WHY DID IT HAPPEN?

WHO Jagiello, King of Poland and Grand Duke of Lithuania (1351–1454), with 44,000 men opposed Ulrich von Jungingen, Grand Master of the Teutonic Order (1360–1410) with 25,000 men.

WHAT The Lithuanian right of the Allied army was driven off but later returned and overwhelmed the last reserves of the Order.

WHERE Grunwald, near Tannenberg in modern Poland.

WHEN 15 July 1410.

WHY To curb the expansion of the Teutonic Order.

OUTCOME The Teutonic Order was defeated and had to surrender many fortresses and their claim to Lithuania.

The Teutonic Order of the Knights of the Cross was founded in 1198 in Palestine and, less than 30 years later, had been granted largely pagan Prussia by the Holy Roman Emperor to conquer for its own. For nearly 200 years the Order attempted to impose this edict themselves and forcibly convert the tribes of northeastern Europe to the Catholic version of Christianity. At one stage they even

A bronze statue of Polish Duke Wladyslaw II Jagiello. This modern statue in heroic pose demonstrates the significance to Polish history of this unifying and victorious leader.

POLISH KNIGHT

This figure bears the arms of Jan Mezyke of Dabrowa, who led one of the divisions at Grunwald. His armour is virtually identical to that of his German counterpart. Indeed, it was probably made by German artisans enticed to Poland by the promise of lower taxes. To limit incidents of mistaken identity in the confusion of battle, the Poles adopted a knot of straw around the upper arm as a field mark, as well as a password. This was a practice that continued into the eighteenth century. Polish heraldry differed significantly from western European heraldry; the Poles ignored the rules of differentiating between members of the same family and the rules limiting adjacent colours. They also added extra colours and made more use of runic symbols.

attacked the Orthodox Christians of Russia.

But it was not always a one-sided fight: they suffered defeats in open battle and from what we would now describe as guerrilla attacks whittling away at their manpower. This was never enough to complete the work. They started building their first castle two years after their establishment at Riga, and moved their headquarters from Venice to the new fortified monastery at Marienburg in 1309. But their residual strength, when not reinforced by foreign contingents for a particular campaign, was in the low hundreds of knights and low thousands of sergeants. It was never enough to conquer and hold the vast wildernesses and sparse population from the River Vistula to the Gulf of Finland, especially after the depopulation following the battle of

Liegnitz in 1241. The normally disunited tribes that made up their opposition compensated for their initial lack of military science through their local knowledge, numbers and fierceness.

When a charismatic leader emerged to unite the tribes, the Order was in trouble. After the marriage of the Queen of Poland, Jadwiga (1374–1399), to the baptized Grand Duke of Lithuania, Wladyslaw-Jagiello, in 1386, the army of their combined countries and constituent tribes would potentially make a formidable force. Not that it altered the course of the Teutonic Order. In 1392, they captured the Polish Duchy of Dobrzyn and in 1398 they took over the Lithuanian province of Samogitia. The province revolted in 1401 with financial support from Poland, but was re-conquered by 1405.

LOCATION

TEUTONIC ORDER

Grunwald ✝

LITHUANIA

POLAND

The Battle of Grünwald (also known as Tannenberg) was fought north of the Vistula River, in the forested areas of southern East Prussia (Mazuria) ruled by the Teutonic Order. This region is today part of Poland.

This later woodcut depicts Duke Wladyslaw II Jagiello in the midst of the battle. The other figures show Polish Winged Hussars of a later period.

THE OPPOSED FORCES

POLES/LITHUANIANS (estimated)
Cavalry:	40,000
Infantry:	10–20,000
Total:	**50–60,000**

TEUTONIC KNIGHTS (estimated)
Cavalry:	21,000
Infantry:	6000
Total:	**27,000**

PREPARATIONS

In August 1409, the Grand Master of the Order became aware of Poland's support for the revolt in Samogitia and declared war on Poland. Then, he declared a year-long truce so that both sides could prepare properly, which seems unusually generous. It is easy for historians to be deceived by this delay. The perception of the Grand Master at the time was that if he could bring the Poles to battle, no matter how many of them there might be, he would defeat them with the superior armour, discipline and courage of his knights. Plus, he believed that he had God on his side. It follows, then, that the more he could allow or persuade to congregate the more he would kill, the greater would be his victory, and the less often he would have to fight them in the future.

THE ALLIED ARMY FORMS

Jagiello met with his nephew and Grand Duke of Lithuania, Witold (d. 1430), at Brzesli-Litewski in the following December and agreed upon a straightforward plan. In addition to calling out their own warriors, they also called on contingents from Mazovia and Ruthenia, plus the Lithuanian army, Tartars from the Crimea and 1500 mercenary knights from Silesia, Bohemia and Moravia. The whole was to assemble at Czerwinsk.

The composition of this Allied force was quite varied. The Polish and Lithuanian nobility fought as mounted lancers like their western equivalent, but their armour was heavily influenced by eastern styles. They were supported by less well-armoured but similarly armed retainers. Polish infantry, principally from the towns, wore a mail jerkin underneath a thick felt coat and carried a fearsome two-handed axe. They were vulnerable to a frontal charge from cavalry and to missiles, but they could wreak havoc on stationary cavalry.

The considerable numbers of Lithuanian light cavalry fought in the style of the steppes; they wore little or no armour and were equipped with bow, possibly with javelin or light lance and shield, but with an axe or mace instead of a sword. Similar Tartar cavalry carried a long, curved sabre instead of the axe or mace.

Lithuanian boyar warrior. Boyars are perhaps best thought of as village elders. They certainly represented the wealthier classes but this man is not rich enough to afford a horse. His equipment portrays his heritage betwixt east and west. His mail suit and sword have western origins. His jerkin of small plates sewn onto a leather backing has eastern influences while his pavise-like shield and conical helmet are distinctly local in origin. He would have formed the front rank of Lithuanian infantry units.

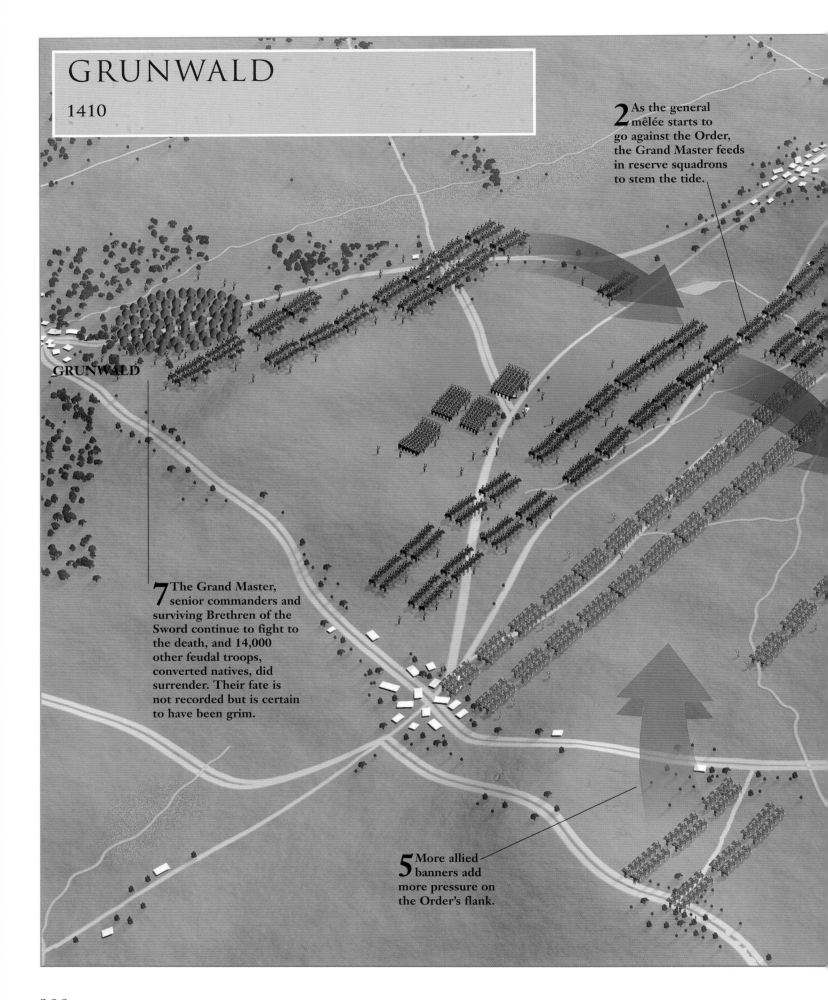

GRUNWALD

1410

2 As the general mêlée starts to go against the Order, the Grand Master feeds in reserve squadrons to stem the tide.

GRUNWALD

7 The Grand Master, senior commanders and surviving Brethren of the Sword continue to fight to the death, and 14,000 other feudal troops, converted natives, did surrender. Their fate is not recorded but is certain to have been grim.

5 More allied banners add more pressure on the Order's flank.

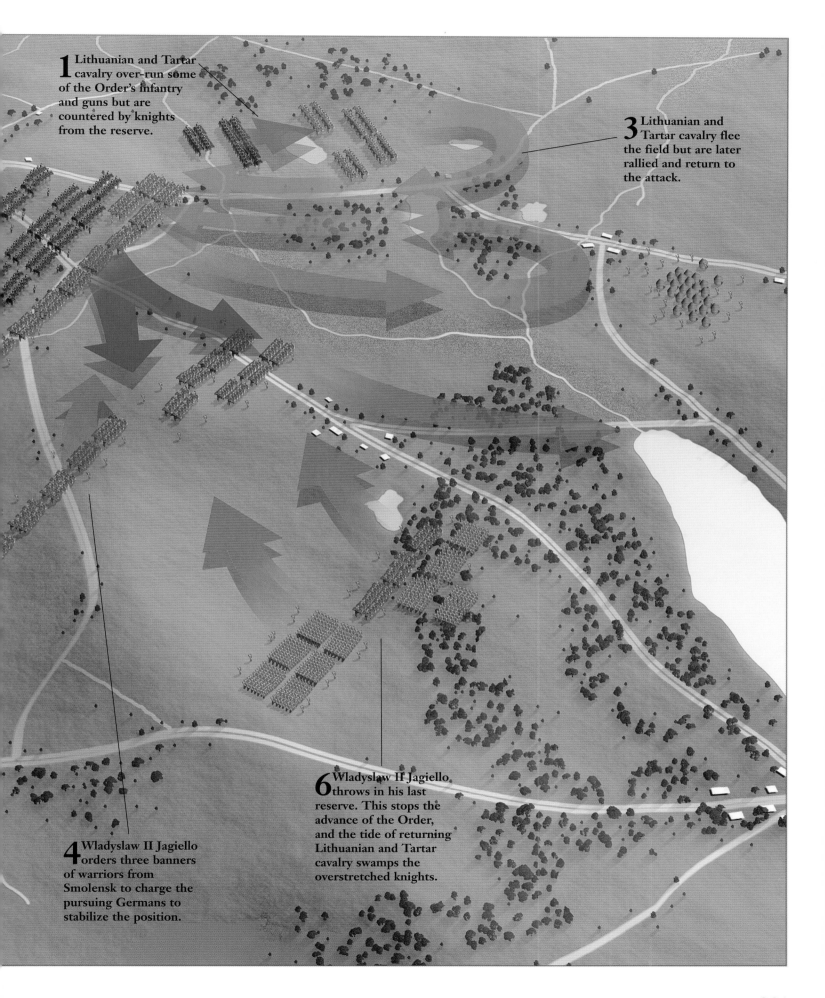

1 Lithuanian and Tartar cavalry over-run some of the Order's infantry and guns but are countered by knights from the reserve.

3 Lithuanian and Tartar cavalry flee the field but are later rallied and return to the attack.

4 Wladyslaw II Jagiello orders three banners of warriors from Smolensk to charge the pursuing Germans to stabilize the position.

6 Wladyslaw II Jagiello throws in his last reserve. This stops the advance of the Order, and the tide of returning Lithuanian and Tartar cavalry swamps the overstretched knights.

GRUNWALD

This is an artist's impression of the battle by Polish painter Wojciech von Kosak (1824–99). He has tried to capture the moment the Grand Master's banner falls (white with yellow cross, centre). The other white flag, to the left, with a red lion is possibly the banner of Konigsberg, commandery of the Grand Marshall but here led by his deputy. The red shield with a double arrow symbol in white (right of centre) is Polish and possibly Gniewosz of Dalewice near Krakow, who hired and led a group of mercenary knights. The fearsome bearded axe was used by infantry of both sides.

In total they had about 6000 knights, 19,000 light cavalry and 19,000 infantry from the tribes and cities.

THE ARMOURED KNIGHTS GATHER

Grand Master Jungingen too was not idle. He needed a massive injection of men and arms to match his more numerous foe. It would take time for the news to travel and even longer for the aid to arrive. His appeal to Bohemia brought forth aid, and Hungary, on Poland's southern border, also declared war. Altogether, there were significant contingents from Germany and Switzerland, plus knights from England, France, Italy and Spain fighting together under a combined banner of St George.

The army of the Teutonic Order was organized in 'banners' or squadrons. The knights wore plate armour from head to foot, with hands, neck and groin areas protected by more flexible mail and a shield carried in the left hand. They were armed with a lance about 4m (13ft) long, carried couched under the right armpit and intended to deliver the full impact of man

and charging horse at its tip. Their foot soldiers could be armoured with helmet, leg armour and shield; weapons being either spear or crossbow and sword. Crossbowmen dispensed with the shield as their weapon needed both hands to load and operate. Instead, they sometimes used a pavise – a large free-standing shield behind which they could shelter. In addition, the Order also pressed large numbers of unreliable, local tribesmen into service. There were about 4000 knights, 11,000 tribal infantry, 5000 spearmen, 4000 crossbow men and perhaps 1000 tribal archers.

It is worth noting that the road network was poor to non-existent and the terrain was heavily wooded with rocky outcrops, and scored with many tributaries leading into the bigger rivers and lakes. The Order therefore made extensive use of water transport for supply, which may have encouraged them to choose Kurzetnik as their first position.

INITIAL DEPLOYMENTS

The Allied plan was to march on Marienburg, 240km (150 miles) to the north, about two weeks' march. This may not have been a serious attempt to capture the place but rather a goad to make the Order come to them. It certainly worked in this instance. To cover this plan, or perhaps simply to occupy the Crim Tartars who had turned up at the assembly area four months early, a number of diversionary raids were mounted in the far north to Memel and northwest into Pomerania.

The Grand Master's spies reported the main assemblage and its initial movements. Although he was somewhat wrong footed, he had assembled his army in Pomerania, 320km (200 miles) to the east of Marienburg. He then ordered his army to Kurzetnik on the River Drweca to block the Allied advance, leaving 3000 men behind to guard against further raids. The Allied army advanced to the river and found it was too strong a position to attack. After two days' stalemate they withdrew to the southeast before turning north again on an alternative route to the Order's capital. Jungingen headed them off before they could get very far and came up with them near the village of Grunwald. To do this the Order had to break camp at 3.00 a.m., dawn in these latitudes in June and July, and march for five hours to approach the Allied army who, by contrast, had marched for just two hours that morning before pausing by Lake Tubien.

THE BATTLE

Both sides deployed for battle while skirmishes took place between opposing light cavalry. Jungingen placed his infantry, including 16 primitive cannon, in the front line, with two lines of cavalry behind and 16 banners, about 3000 men, in reserve. There was also a detachment of infantry in two lines on his far right. On the other side, the more numerous Poles took the centre and left, and the Lithuanians and Tartars the right wing. In between the Lithuanians and the Poles were the mercenary contingents. The Poles retained seven banners behind the lines plus a further four banners hidden in the wood to their rear. Behind the wood was a lake and beyond the lake the three camps, Tartar, Lithuanian and Polish. Separating the two armies at the bottom of the valley was the great stream, probably very low at this time of

year, with marshy areas to both north and south. The high ground on either side of the battlefield gave both commanders a good view of the action, which was a feature they used to good effect.

The Allied army advanced first. On their right, the Lithuanians and Tartars swept over the infantry and artillery before

A re-enactor dressed as a Teutonic Knight. The metal headpiece on the horse's armour is called a Chamfron. In Western Europe, these were passing out of fashion as it became more prevalent for knights to fight on foot due to the dominance of the longbow and crossbow. He makes a good aperitif for the imagination. Multiply by several thousand to imagine the Brethren of the Sword at Grunwald.

GRUNWALD

them as the Order's cannon only managed two ineffective shots. This charge was countered by three banners of the Order and both sides became bogged down in a mounted scrum. In the Allied centre and left a general mêlée ensued between the Allies and the Teutonic Order. While the Allied army slowly started to turn the Order's right flank and push back against the centre, the Grand Master moved extra men to his left to force the issue against the wilting Lithuanians.

The ploy worked and the Allied right wing broke with the Order in pursuit. The crucial area of the battlefield now became the exposed right flank of the Allied army. Could it be turned before the Teutonic right flank crumbled? The Polish King ordered three banners to support the soldiers from Smolensk and managed to stabilize their position.

Meanwhile, on the Allied left, four reserve banners were added to the pressure on the Order's flank and it started to crack. Now, the knights who had pursued the Lithuanians returned to add their weight against the Polish right, and the King had to throw in his last four squadrons from the wood. He had no more reserves left but again the position was maintained. The Grand Master did have reserves, however, and now was the time to use them. Bellowing the war cry of the Order 'Gott mit uns' he led their charge into the centre of the battle line.

This was the critical moment and he could well have reversed the fortunes of the battle, but sometimes even Kings cannot turn tides, and it was not to be. Instead some of the routed Lithuanians

It is a sad fact that many horses died on campaign from cold and the arduous conditions. So, inevitably, troops who set off mounted ending fighting on foot. The emblem of the Order was a black cross on a white shield, which appeared on the shield. His well-fitted mail jump suit is reinforced with carefully crafted metal plates held in place by leather straps or rivets. The armour is so well made that it weighs less than the normal load of an infantryman in WWI and barely restricts movement. Since he is now dismounted he has abandoned his lance and relies on his sword, with a dagger in his belt as a last resort.

had been rallied by Witold, their Grand Duke, and, outflanking the Order's left wing, started to attack their rear, particularly the reserve squadrons most recently committed.

DEFEAT AND AFTERMATH

With all their reserves committed and both flanks compromised, the Teutonic Order was in very serious trouble. To their everlasting credit, they did not break and flee. Instead, virtually the whole senior command of the Order, plus many knights, fought to the death. The 3000 men they had left in Pomerania might have made all the difference – but hindsight is a wonderful thing.

The Grand Master had brought 51 banners to the battle, each with its own following of knights or infantry. Fifty-one banners were captured by the Allied army, preserved in the Krakow Cathedral and

faithfully recorded by Jan Dlugsz perhaps 40 years later. The power of the Order was broken and their recently captured territory had to be returned immediately.

Within 50 years they had to sell their spiritual home, Marienburg, to the King of Poland and within 70 years the Grand Master also had to pay homage to the King. Poland, on the other hand, became a significant European nation for the next 300 years before succumbing to its geographical position between two larger belligerent powers.

Opposite: Re-enactments, such as this one in Poland, give an idea of the colour and drama of the events at Grunwald, as well as allowing serious students to see the weapons in use at first hand – hopefully without too much bloodshed.

VARNA
1444

THE CRUSADE THAT ENDED IN THE TURKISH VICTORY AT VARNA WAS WESTERN EUROPE'S LAST SERIOUS ATTEMPT TO SAVE CONSTANTINOPLE FROM THE OTTOMAN TURKS. IT WAS THE WORST CRUSADE DEFEAT OF THE FIFTEENTH CENTURY.

WHY DID IT HAPPEN?

WHO A Crusader army largely composed of Hungarians under their king Ulászló I (Vladyslav III of Poland), but including Germans, Transylvanians, Poles and Wallachians, confronted an Ottoman Turkish army led by Sultan Murad II.

WHAT The Crusader army, outnumbered at least 2:1, fought a day-long battle with the Ottomans.

WHERE Just outside the Bulgarian port of Varna, located on the west coast of the Black Sea, north of Constantinople.

WHEN 10 November 1444.

WHY The Crusaders were engaged in an ambitious plan to drive the Turks from the territories they had conquered in the Balkans.

OUTCOME The Crusaders were defeated in a major battle that cost them nearly half of their army.

By 1440, the last remnant of the Byzantine Empire was close to defeat at the hands of the expanding Ottoman Turkish sultanate. The Byzantine emperor, John VIII, undertook a journey to Italy in 1438–39 to make a personal appeal for western assistance, even agreeing to a reunion of Orthodox Christianity with western Catholicism at the Council of Florence in July 1439. In response to the emperor's plea for help, Pope Eugenius IV organized a crusade, appointing Cardinal

EVGENIVS · PP · IIII · VENE ·

212

Pope Eugenius IV (r. 1431–1447) was born to Venetian merchants, who were particularly affected by Ottoman expansion into Europe. He relied on Venetian connections for a fleet for the Varna campaign.

VARNA

Julian Cesarini as legate to coordinate action against the Turks in eastern Europe. Crusader plans took on a greater urgency when the Ottoman Turks besieged Constantinople in 1442.

While many westerners were concerned about the plight of Constantinople, the Christian kingdoms of eastern Europe were much more worried about the Turks on their own doorsteps. Sultan Murad II (1421–1451) had seized Thessalonica in 1430, annexed Serbia in 1439, and by 1440 the Turks were encroaching on Hungary with an attack on Belgrade. Fortunately, the Hungarians had a great military leader, the heroic Janos Hunyadi (c. 1407–1456), governor (*voivode*) of Transylvania. Under Hunyadi's inspired leadership, the Hungarians won major victories over the Turks in 1441 and 1442. The danger was far from past, however, especially as the Turks had responded to the Hungarian victories by arming their elite infantrymen (the Janissaries) with firearms, and by organizing a cannon corps.

It was this disagreement and confusion about the new Crusade's goals – whether it was intended to protect Constantinople or Hungary – that helped assure its failure.

In 1443, the so-called 'Crusade of Varna' got under way. Pope Eugenius planned to send galleys to the Dardanelles to prevent the Turks from reinforcing their eastern European provinces from Anatolia. The effort failed because Venice, the greatest

sea power of Europe, refused to cooperate.

Notwithstanding this naval failure, a land army of some 25,000 men set out in September. The core of this force was Hunyadi's Transylvanians, but the army also included units from every Balkan country, plus Czech and Moldavian mercenaries, as well as volunteers from Italy, France, and Germany. The campaign went on for four months, earning it the contemporary nickname 'the long campaign'. The expedition was successful, taking the cities of Nish and Sofia, but the Crusaders had set out so late in the year that poor supply and cold weather caused great hardship and eventually forced them to retreat.

After the successes of 1443, the Pope pushed eagerly for another campaign in 1444. The timing seemed propitious. The Ottoman position had weakened in the

LOCATION

Varna on the shore of the Black Sea was a useful base from which to campaign against the Ottoman Turks, who by the 1440s had penetrated deep into Europe.

ARABIAN CAMEL CAVALRY

According to one account, the Ottoman force at Varna included a contingent of Arabian camel cavalry, mounted archers riding swift-paced dromedaries. Such a force could easily have created chaos in the Crusader ranks.

Dromedaries are hardy and fast, able to travel up to 220km (150 miles) per day. Their lightly armed riders, armed with compound bows, could easily skirt the flanks of the Crusader force, peppering both infantry and cavalry with arrows.

More devastating, though, was the very presence of the camels. Horses cannot bear the smell of camels; circus horses have to be specially hardened to tolerate being near them. Thus the proximity of camels on the field would have caused panic among the Crusader horses.

summer, when Sultan Murad II, discouraged by his failures and internal difficulties, abdicated in favour of his 12-year-old son Mehmed II.

DIPLOMATIC EFFORTS

Ottoman diplomatic efforts had some success in undermining the western alliance. They made a separate treaty with the exiled ruler of Serbia, who had fought as a Crusader in 1443, and thus they reduced the Crusader ranks by about 5000 men. The Ottomans also negotiated a truce with King Ulászló of Hungary.

Ulászló vowed to keep the peace for ten years, but in August he reversed himself and vowed to renew the war against the Turks, apparently under pressure from the papal legate. Although the legate argued that vows made to non-Christians were not binding, many contemporaries believed that it was Ulászló's perjury that led directly to the Crusaders' defeat at Varna. There is even a Hungarian legend that Ulászló survived the battle and spent the last years of his life as a wandering penitent to atone for his oath-breaking.

OPENING MOVES

All of these negotiations and counter-negotiations took time, ruining the delicate coordination of the Crusade. In 1444, the papacy eventually succeeded in providing seapower. A papal fleet, consisting of 22–24 galleys (mostly manned by Venetians) reached Gallipoli in July, but the Hungarians only crossed the Danube on 20 September.

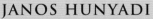

JANOS HUNYADI

Janos Hunyadi (c. 1407–1456) led the Crusade forces at Varna, surviving the battle to continue the fight against the Ottomans. He was a noble whose military career began in the service of the Holy Roman Emperor Sigismund, who rewarded him with lands and titles. Hunyadi supported the young Polish King Ulászló's (Vladyslav III) bid to become king of Hungary, and was rewarded with the governorship of Transylvania. He proved to be Europe's most successful general against the Ottoman Turks, who were expanding into Europe, winning several impressive victories before his defeat at Varna. After the battle, Hunyadi became regent of Hungary. He died of plague in 1456, shortly after driving off the Turks besieging Belgrade and destroying the Ottoman fleet. His death was regarded as a catastrophe in the West. Hunyadi's son Matthias Corvinus later became king of Hungary.

Thus the fleet had ample time to grow discontented, while the Turks had ample warning of the new Crusade. The young Sultan Mehmed II's advisers, alarmed by the growing crisis, convinced Sultan Murad to return to power. He raised a force 40,000–45,000 strong and set out for the threatened Ottoman provinces in Europe, crossing the Bosphorus north of Constantinople late in October 1444. The papal fleet made no attempt to stop them; contemporary sources do not tell us why.

Meanwhile, the Crusader army marched towards the Black Sea, expecting to meet the papal fleet there. When they reached Varna on 9 November, they discovered that the fleet had not arrived. We don't know why they were absent, but one possible reason is that the fleet's commanders had grown tired of waiting in the increasingly dangerous weather of late autumn. Of far more immediate concern to the Crusaders was the discovery, made late in the evening 9 November, that a large Turkish army was camped nearby, a little to the southwest of the city.

The Crusade leaders held a council that night. The papal legate Julian proposed a

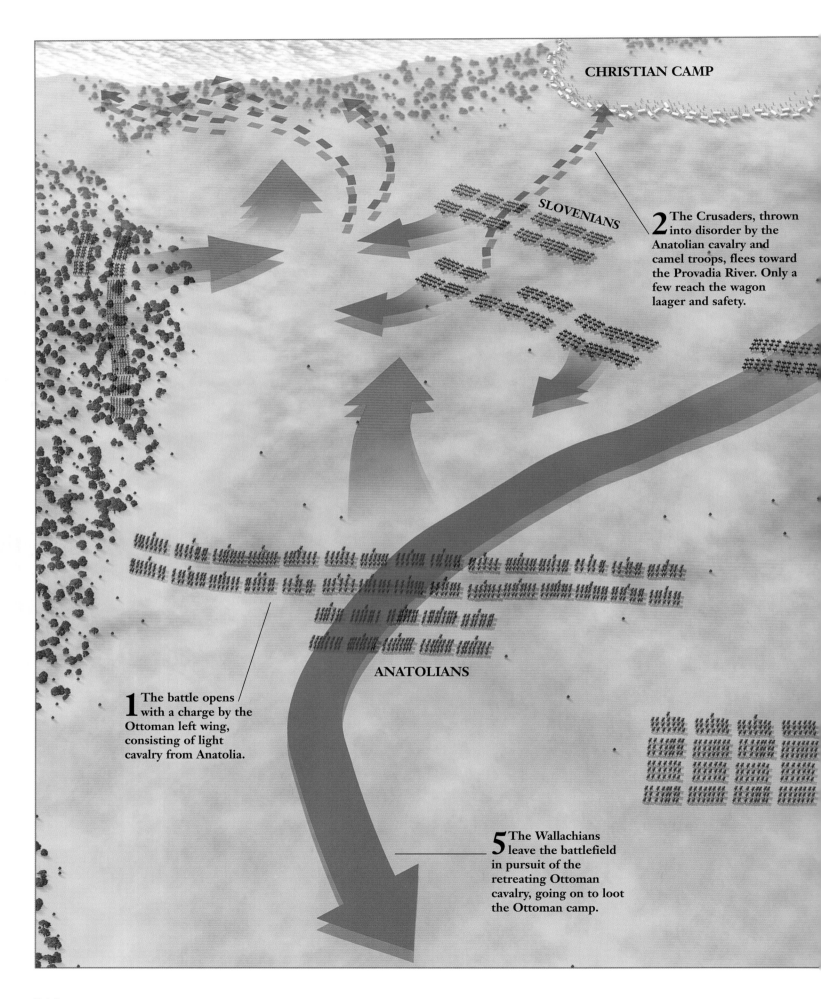

CHRISTIAN CAMP

SLOVENIANS

2 The Crusaders, thrown into disorder by the Anatolian cavalry and camel troops, flees toward the Provadia River. Only a few reach the wagon laager and safety.

1 The battle opens with a charge by the Ottoman left wing, consisting of light cavalry from Anatolia.

ANATOLIANS

5 The Wallachians leave the battlefield in pursuit of the retreating Ottoman cavalry, going on to loot the Ottoman camp.

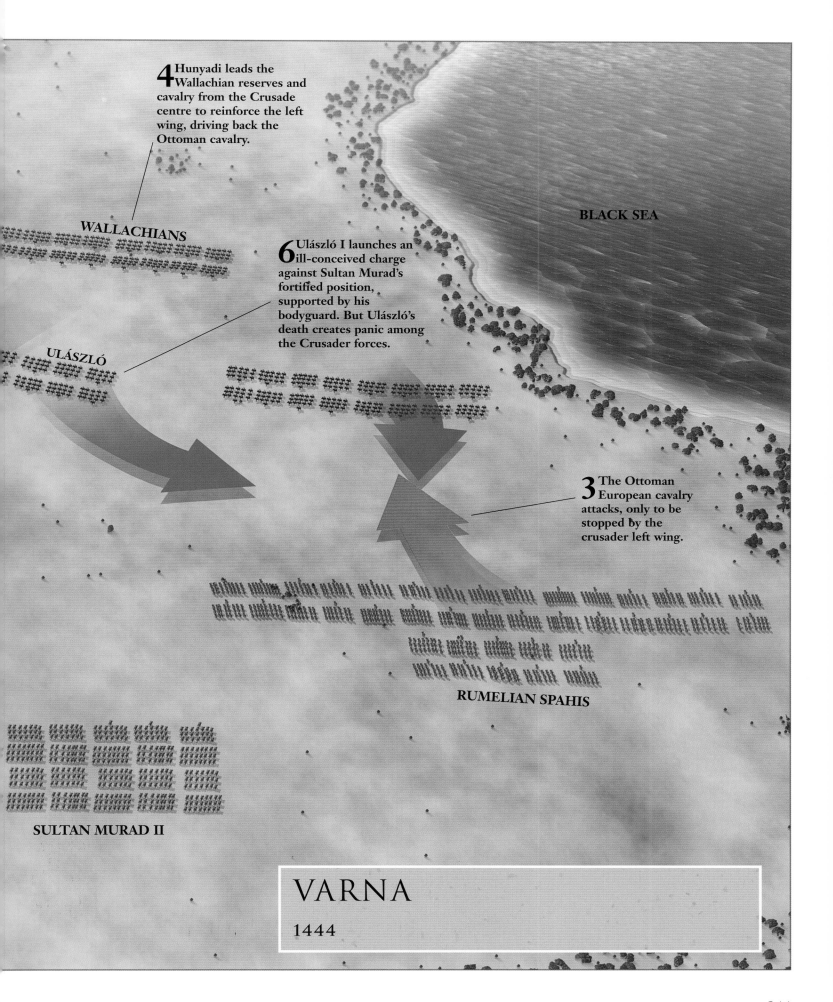

4 Hunyadi leads the Wallachian reserves and cavalry from the Crusade centre to reinforce the left wing, driving back the Ottoman cavalry.

WALLACHIANS

BLACK SEA

6 Ulászló I launches an ill-conceived charge against Sultan Murad's fortified position, supported by his bodyguard. But Ulászló's death creates panic among the Crusader forces.

ULÁSZLÓ

3 The Ottoman European cavalry attacks, only to be stopped by the crusader left wing.

RUMELIAN SPAHIS

SULTAN MURAD II

VARNA

1444

VARNA

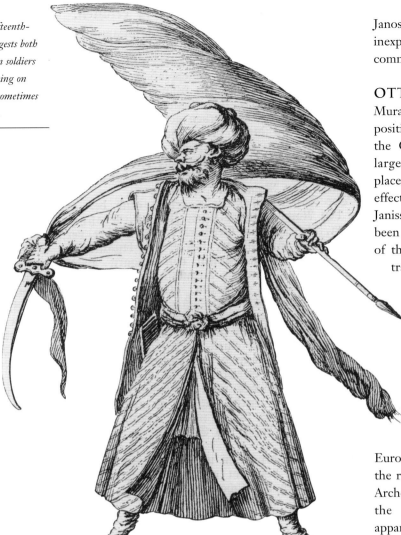

This romantic image of a fifteenth-century Ottoman officer suggests both daring and display. Ottoman soldiers wore little body armour, relying on quilted coats for protection, sometimes reinforced with metal layers.

Janos Hunyadi (rather than the young and inexperienced Hungarian king) in overall command.

OTTOMAN FORCES

Murad II drew up his army in a strong position, apparently wary of the power of the Christians' heavy cavalry against his large numbers of Turkish infantry. He placed his infantry in the centre. The most effective part of this force was the sultan's Janissaries, the elite slave soldiers who had been taken as boys from the Christian parts of the sultanate, converted to Islam then trained into a highly effective force. They had recently been equipped with handguns.

Supplementing them were levies from the sultan's European possessions. This infantry force, about 10,000 strong, dug in behind the line of the Turkish cavalry wings, fortifying their position with ditches and two palisades. Murad placed his cavalry on the wings, European Spahis (lightly armed cavalry) on the right and Anatolian Spahis on the left. Archers and light cavalry were deployed in the Frangen Hills at some distance, apparently to prevent a possible Christian encirclement.

CRUSADER DEPLOYMENT

Facing the Turks, the Crusader force, almost entirely composed of cavalry, was divided into national units. King Ulászló held the centre with a force of about 3500 men comprised of the Polish and Hungarian royal guard, Hungarian mercenaries and Hungarian nobles. The left wing, 5000 men strong, also included some Hungarian nobles with their retainers, as well as Transylvanians and Germans, all under the command of Hunyadi's brother-in-law Michael Szilagyi.

The right wing, led by Bishop Jan Deminek of Varadin and the papal legate, provided the largest number of Christian warriors at the battle, a mixed force of about 6500 German mercenaries and Crusaders from several countries. The right wing, unlike the rest of the Crusader force, was deployed in depth. A reserve of some 4000 Wallachians (commanded by a son of the

withdrawal, since the Crusaders were heavily outnumbered, and the lie of the land favored the Turks. Such a move was impractical. There was no clear escape route for the Crusaders, especially in the absence of the papal fleet. The Black Sea and a lake hemmed them in on two sides, with difficult mountain roads and swampland making a speedy retreat impossible.

When the council rejected his first scheme, Cardinal Julian then suggested that the Crusader army dig in, using wagon laagers as field fortifications, and wait for the Christian fleet to arrive. This plan, too, was rejected; it is likely that provisions were too short for the Crusaders to hold out long, and their leaders had no idea when or if the fleet would arrive.

And so the Crusade leaders decided on a rapid attack against the Turkish army, with

THE OPPOSED FORCES

CRUSADERS
Cavalry	
(mixed light and heavy):	c. 20,000
Handgunners:	c.300
Total:	**c. 20,300**

OTTOMAN TURKS
Infantry (Janissaries & local levies):	c. 15,000
Cavalry (Rumelian & Anatolian Spahis):	c. 30,000
Total:	**c. 40,000**

infamous Vlad Drakul) was drawn up behind the Crusader centre, and the small contingent of mercenary gunners were left behind to guard the camp. The Christian army deployed in a broad crescent, anchored at each side by Lake Varna and the Frangen Hills.

THE BATTLE OPENS

The battle opened with a charge by the Ottoman left wing. The Christian right wing withstood their attack, driving the Spahis back in apparent disorder. Two Christian units, led by the bishops of Erlau and Varadin, then broke ranks and pursued the retreating Muslims. Some historians have suggested that the Turkish retreat was merely a ploy to disrupt the Crusader ranks. Whether caused intentionally or not, the Crusader pursuit exposed the whole Christian right wing to attack.

As the two pursuing units advanced, an Anatolian cavalry force (which included some Arabs on camels) hit them on the flank. Some of the Christians, trapped in mid-charge, tried to escape to the nearby fortress of Galata. Most were killed or drowned in the Provadia River.

The rest of the Christian right wing went quickly to their comrades' aid, but were soon surrounded. One unit made it safely back to the wagon laager at the rear; few others survived. Among those who fell in this part of the battle was the papal legate Julian Cesarini.

While the Christian right wing was being mauled, the cavalry of the Ottoman right wing also attacked. This was the crux of the battle. The Christian left wing held up under the Ottoman charge, but soon found itself in difficult straits. Janos Hunyadi, however, again proved his ability as a general. He took the Wallachian reserves as well as a cavalry unit from the Christian centre and led them personally to reinforce the beleaguered left wing.

With Hunyadi's assistance, the Ottoman cavalry were driven back after a long fight in which the Ottoman commander was killed. At least some Hungarians pursued them some 5–6km (3–4 miles); the Wallachians made it all the way to the Ottoman camp, looting it and then departing, instead of returning to the battlefield.

At this stage in the battle the Crusaders seemed to be winning, and a powerful and effective Christian force still remained under Hunyadi's command.

THE KING ACTS

When Hunyadi rode to relieve the left wing, he firmly adjured the 20-year-old King Ulászló to stay put, leaving him in nominal command of the Christian centre. This did not suit Ulászló's notions of heroic kingship. So instead of waiting, he led his

HUNGARIAN HANDGUNNER

Almost the only infantrymen in the Crusade army were a small contingent of Hungarian handgunners, left to defend the wagon laager. The arquebuses they used were painfully slow to load and fire by means of a match that was laid against the touchhole. They were also notoriously inaccurate, since the soldiers propped the guns on their shoulders instead of controlling the recoil, and the guns' smooth bores did not spin the bullets as modern rifles do. Handgunners could not easily advance in battle, and they were not effective at all in bad weather. Fifteenth-century handguns could, however, be effective when used to defend a fixed position, especially if the gunners were equipped with large shields to protect them against enemy arrows, as in this illustration.

VARNA

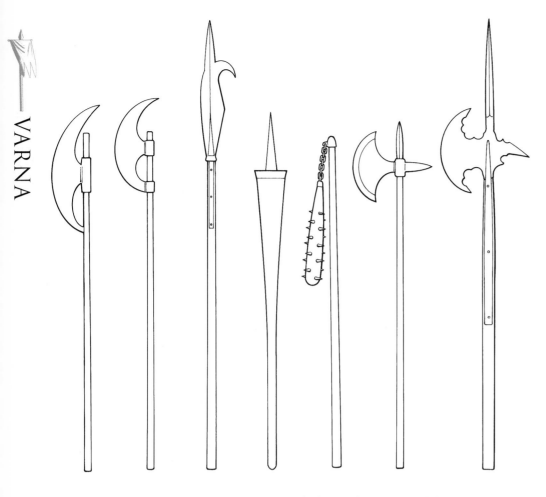

The illustrations below above various pole-arms popular among foot soldiers in the fifteenth century. From left to right: two 'bearded' axes; a glaive with a hook to pull horsemen to the ground; a Flemish goedendag, combining a spear point with an iron-rimmed club; a flail, based on an agricultural instrument, but turned into a deadly spiked club that could be swung at a distance; and two weapons that are an early and later form of the halberd.

bodyguard of 500 Polish and Hungarian knights against the Janissaries in the Ottoman centre. He appears to have been attempting a personal duel with Murad II, for whose banner he was aiming. The Ottoman defences and their guns fatally slowed the Christian charge, so much so that Ulászló himself was killed and his cavalry panicked. Many were killed as they fled, and the slaughtered king's head was taken as a prize.

At the end of the day, the two armies disengaged with no clear victory on either side. The Christian losses were so heavy, however, that the Crusader camp disintegrated and the army began to retreat – along narrow, dangerous roads and through swampland, where the Turks could pursue them at leisure. It is estimated that of the c. 13,000 Christians killed in the battle of Varna, only half fell in the battle itself, while the other half were brought down during the retreat, despite the fact that the Ottomans did not even pursue them for the first day. The Ottoman army, too, suffered extremely heavy losses, to the point that

Sultan Murad is reported to have said afterwards: 'May God never grant me another such victory.'

AFTERMATH

The battle of Varna did not have a significant impact on Hungary's ability to defend itself, despite the loss of their king and the three-year succession dispute that followed. Janos Hunyadi survived the battle and became regent of Hungary, which he continued to defend until he was defeated at Kosovo in 1448. The majority of Christians killed in the battle were mercenaries, which also limited the battle's impact.

The battle of Varna cannot be taken as an indictment of 'old-fashioned' western heavy cavalry either. The battle was closely contested, and in particular the Crusader right wing showed how effective a close-order charge of knights could still be. However, by fifteenth-century standards, the Crusader force was horribly unbalanced, with almost no infantry. A more balanced force of supported cavalry might well have won the day, even against the odds they faced at Varna.

The battle's greatest impact was on a group who weren't even there: the Greek Christians of Constantinople. They had refused to join forces with the Crusaders, officially because of King Ulászló's broken oath to the Turks and the likelihood of divine vengeance, but doubtless also because they did not want to leave Constantinople undefended with the Turks so close.

Quite simply, the Crusade was in the wrong place to be useful to the Orthodox Christians, but their failure to appear at Varna made them appear unworthy of western support. The fact, too, that the Crusaders had failed to break the Turkish army at Varna made it certain that a final Turkish attack on Constantinople would come soon – as indeed it did only nine years later.

John Hunyadi's last great victory was in 1456 when, using a largely peasant force that had been raised with the help of the Franciscan friar Giovanni of Capistrano, he forced the Turks to abandon Belgrade.

BIBLIOGRAPHY

Asbridge, Thomas S. *The First Crusade: A New History*. New York: Oxford University Press, 2004.

Aubrey, Burl. *God's Heretics*. Stroud: Sutton Publishing Ltd, 2002.

Bennett, Matthew & Nicholas Hooper. *Cambridge Illustrated Atlas*. 'Warfare: The Middle Ages 768–1487'. Cambridge: Cambridge University Press, 1996.

Black, Bob. 'Leignitz' in *Miniature Wargames* magazine No 238. Bournemouth: Pireme Publishing, 2003.

Bradbury, Jim. *The Routledge Companion to Medieval Warfare*. London: Routledge, Taylor and Francis Group, 2004.

Cowper, Marcus. *Cathar Castles*. Oxford: Osprey Publishing Ltd, 2006.

DeVries, Kelly. *Infantry Warfare in the Early Fourteenth Century: Discipline, Tactics, and Technology*. Woodbridge, Suffolk: The Boydell Press, 1996.

Forey, Alan. *The Military Orders: From the Twelfth to the Early Fourteenth Centuries*. Toronto: University of Toronto Press, 1992.

France, John. *Victory in the East: A Military History of the First Crusade*. Cambridge: Cambridge University Press, 1994.

France, John. *Western Warfare in the Age of the Crusades, 1000–1300*. Ithaca: Cornell University Press, 1999.

Fulcher of Chartres. *A History of the Expedition to Jerusalem, 1095–1127* (translated by Frances R. Ryan and edited by Harold S. Fink). Knoxville: University of Tennessee Press, 1969.

Haldon, John. *Warfare, State and Society in the Byzantine World, 565–1204*. London: UCL Press, 1999.

Halecki, Oskar. *The Crusade of Varna*. New York: Polish Institute of Arts and Sciences, 1943.

Heath, Ian. *Armies of Feudal Europe 1066–1300*. Worthing, UK: Wargames Research Group, 1978.

Heath, Ian. *Armies of the Middle Ages* (volume 2). Worthing, UK: Wargames Research Group, 1984.

Houseley, Norman. *Crusading and Warfare in Medieval and Renaissance Europe*. Aldershot: Ashgate Variorum, 2001.

Housley, Norman (ed. and trans.). *Documents on the Later Crusades, 1274–1580*. New York: St. Martin's Press, 1996.

Housley, Norman. *The Later Crusades, 1274–1580*. New York: Oxford University Press, 1992.

John of Joinville [Jean de Joinville]. *The Life of St.Louis* (translated by M.R.B. Shaw). Baltimore: Penguin Books, 1967.

Jordan, William C. *Louis IX and the Challenge of the Crusades*. Princeton: Princeton University Press, 1979.

Keen, Maurice, ed. *Medieval Warfare: A History*. Oxford: Oxford University Press, 1999.

Imber, Colin (translator). *The Crusade of Varna, 1443–45*. Aldershot, UK: Ashgate, 2006.

Lilie, Ralph-Johannes. *Byzantium and the Crusader States, 1096–1204* (translated by J.C. Morris). Oxford: Clarendon, 1993.

Marshall, Christopher. *Warfare in the Latin East, 1192–1291*. Cambridge: Cambridge University Press, 1992.

Meyer, Hans E. *The Crusades* (translated by John Gillingham). Oxford: Oxford Univeristy Press, 1988.

Nicetas Choniates. *Oh City of Byzantium* (translated by Harry J.Margoulis). Detroit: Wayne State University Press, 1984.

Nicolle, David C. *Arms & Armour of the Crusading Era, 1050–1350*. London: Greenhill Books, 1998.

Nicolle, David. *The First Crusade, 1096–1099: Conquest of the Holy Land*. Westport, Connecticut: Praeger, 2005.

Nicolle, David. *Lake Peipus 1242: The Battle on the Ice*. London: Osprey, 1996.

Nicolle, David. *Nicopolis 1396: The Last Crusade*. Oxford: Osprey Publishing Ltd. 1999.

Nicolle, David C. *Medieval Warfare Source Book (Vol. 1): Warfare in Western Christendom*. London: Brockhampton Press, 1995.

Nicolle, David C. *Medieval Warfare Source Book (Vol. 2): Christian Europe and its Neighbours*. London: Brockhampton Press, 1996.

Nicholson, Helen, and David Nicolle. *God's Warriors: Crusaders, Saracens, and the Battle for Jerusalem*. Oxford: Osprey, 2005.

Queller, Donald E. and Thomas F. Madden. *The Fourth Crusade: The Conquest of Constantinople.* Philadelphia: University of Pennsylvania Press, 1997)

Richard, Jean. *Saint Louis: Crusader King of France* (translated by Jean Birrel). Cambridge, Cambridge University Press, 1992.

Rogers, R. *Latin Siege Warfare in the Twelfth Century.* Oxford: Clarendon Press, 1992.

Runciman, Steven. *A History of the Crusades.* Cambridge: Cambridge University Press, 1951–54.

Smail, R.C. *Crusading Warfare (1097–1193).* Cambridge: Cambridge University Press, 1956.

Stein, Paul. *Wargaming the Baltic Crusades.* Bournemouth, UK: Society of Ancients, 1984.

Stolarski, Piotr. '1410: White Eagle Ascendant' in *Miniature Wargames* magazine, No. 230. Bournemouth, UK: Pireme Publishing Ltd, 2002.

Strickland, Matthew. *War and Chivalry: The Conduct and Perception of War in England and Normandy, 1066–1217.* Cambridge: Cambridge University Press, 1996.

Turner, Steve. 'The Crusade of Nicopolis, 1396' in *Miniature Wargames* magazine, No 92. Bournemouth, UK: Pireme Publishing Ltd, 1991.

Urban, William. *The Teutonic Knights: A Military History.* London: Greenhill Books, 2003.

Vale, Malcolm. *War and Chivalry: Warfare and Aristocratic Culture in England, France and Burgundy at the End of the Middle Ages.* Athens, Georgia: University of Georgia Press, 1981.

Wieckowski, Andrzej. 'The Eagle and the Cross' in *Miniature Wargames* magazine, No 79. Bournemouth, UK: Pireme Publishing Ltd, 1989.

INDEX

Page numbers in *italics* refer to illustrations; those in **bold** type refer to map illustrations/text.
Abbreviations are as follows: (B) – battle; (S) – siege.

PICTURE AND ILLUSTRATION CREDITS